Shareholder Activism

Shareholder Activism

Corporate Governance Reforms in Korea

Han-Kyun Rho
BRESE Research Lecturer
Brunel Business School
Brunel University, UK

Foreword by
Robert A.G. Monks

© Han-Kyun Rho 2007
Foreword © Robert A.G. Monks 2007

All rights reserved. No reproduction, copy or transmission of this publication may be made without written permission.

No paragraph of this publication may be reproduced, copied or transmitted save with written permission or in accordance with the provisions of the Copyright, Designs and Patents Act 1988, or under the terms of any licence permitting limited copying issued by the Copyright Licensing Agency, 90 Tottenham Court Road, London W1T 4LP.

Any person who does any unauthorised act in relation to this publication may be liable to criminal prosecution and civil claims for damages.

The author has asserted his right to be identified as the author of this work in accordance with the Copyright, Designs and Patents Act 1988.

First published 2007 by
PALGRAVE MACMILLAN
Houndmills, Basingstoke, Hampshire RG21 6XS and
175 Fifth Avenue, New York, N.Y. 10010
Companies and representatives throughout the world

PALGRAVE MACMILLAN is the global academic imprint of the Palgrave Macmillan division of St. Martin's Press, LLC and of Palgrave Macmillan Ltd. Macmillan® is a registered trademark in the United States, United Kingdom and other countries. Palgrave is a registered trademark in the European Union and other countries.

ISBN-13: 978–1–4039–9160–7   hardback
ISBN-10: 1–4039–9160–X   hardback

This book is printed on paper suitable for recycling and made from fully managed and sustained forest sources.

A catalogue record for this book is available from the British Library.

Library of Congress Cataloging-in-Publication Data

Rho, Han-Kyun, 1965–
  Shareholder activism : corporate governance reforms in Korea / Han-Kyun Rho.
    p. cm.
  Includes bibliographical references and index.
  ISBN-13: 978–1–4039–9160–7 (cloth)
  ISBN-10: 1–4039–9160–X (cloth)
    1. Corporate governance—Korea (South) 2. Stockholders—Korea (South) I. Title.

HD2741.R48 2007
338.6095195—dc22   2006049097

10 9 8 7 6 5 4 3 2 1
16 15 14 13 12 11 10 09 08 07

Printed and bound in Great Britain by
Antony Rowe Ltd, Chippenham and Eastbourne

To my family and friends

Contents

List of Tables	ix
List of Figures	x
Acknowledgements	xi
List of Abbreviations	xii
Note on Korean Spelling	xiv
Foreword by Robert A.G. Monks	xv
Introduction: Shareholder Activism and Corporate Governance Reform	xvii

Part I A Review of Theories — 1

1 Defining the Object of Study — 3
　Previous definitions of shareholder activism — 4
　Three dimensions of shareholder activism — 5
　Meaning of emergence — 14

2 Explaining Activism (1): Existence of a Problem — 17
　Theoretical backgrounds — 17
　Investigation methods — 18
　Research results — 22
　Further thoughts — 24

3 Explaining Activism (2): Determinants of Choice — 26
　Theoretical backgrounds — 26
　Determinants of activism choice — 28
　Investigation results — 31
　Further thoughts — 34

4 Explaining Activism (3): Politics and Interpretations — 36
　Theoretical backgrounds: social movement theory — 36
　Investigation results — 41

Part II An Application: the Korean PSPD Case — 45

5 Political Opportunity — 47
Formal opportunity: government policy — 47
Informal opportunity: power relations — 58

6 Framing Process — 67
Three frames from the past — 67
Approaching shareholder rights — 69
Korea First Bank: the first attempt — 72
From a trial to regular use — 75
Frame alignment and a minimalist strategy — 80
Limitations of the PSPD activism — 83

7 Resource Mobilization — 86
Internal resources — 86
External resources — 95

8 Conclusion — 119
Findings on three emergences — 119
Implications — 126

Notes — 134

References — 141

Index — 155

List of Tables

1.1	Three dimensions of previous definitions	5
2.1	Results from single variable comparisons	23
2.2	Results from probability regressions	24
3.1	Percentages of the indexed equity portfolio, US	32
4.1	Two types of political opportunities	39
5.1	Shareholding requirements for minority shareholder rights	49
5.2	Internal ownership of the 30 biggest *chaebol*, 1983–1999	52
5.3	CCEJ activities related to the *chaebol*, 1990–1996	60
5.4	PSPD shareholder activism, 1997–1999	64
6.1	Reframing the *chaebol* problem	82
7.1	Composition of the PEC executive members, 1997–2000	86
7.2	Income of the PEC (won), 1998–2000	94
7.3	Shareholder supports for the PEC's legal actions	98
7.4	PSPD shareholding of the *chaebol*, as of 28 February 2001	99
7.5	Shareholder composition of the PSPD targets	101
7.6	Participants in the 10-Share Campaign, as of 8 Feb. 2000	103
7.7	Domestic institutional shareholdings, as of 31 Dec. 2000	105
7.8	Institutional shareholdings (%), 1986–1999	106
7.9	Institutions controlled by non-financial companies, as of 31 July 1999	107
7.10	Institutional investors' voting in the AGMs of all listed firms	108
7.11	Positions of institutional investors	108
7.12	Institutions' response to a PSPD proposal in Samsung Electronics	110
7.13	Comparing shareholder groups	118
8.1	Two models of corporate governance	130

List of Figures

0.1	Shareholder activism in corporate governance reform	xviii
0.2	Growth of shareholder resolutions, US, 1987–2005	xix
1.1	Monitoring and shareholder activism	11
1.2	Interactive model of shareholder activism	13
1.3	Number of resolutions per activists, US, 1995–2005	15
1.4	Three outstanding activists, US, 1995–2005	16
2.1	CAR for target companies	20
2.2	Inference in the first approach	20
5.1	Internal ownership of the 30 biggest *chaebol*, 1983–1999	52
5.2	Succession to the chairmanship in the four biggest *chaebol*	53
6.1	Three past frames	69
6.2	Press releases and news reports, 1997–2000	77
6.3	New framing from the old frames	82
7.1	Composition of the PEC income	94
7.2	Institutional shareholdings (%), 1986–1999	106
7.3	Growth of ESOAs, 1990–2000	111
8.1	Dynamics of collective action organization	125
8.2	Assumptions underlying corporate governance reforms	128
8.3	Shareholder activism as spinning cogwheels	129
8.4	Circular relation between the two models	131

Acknowledgements

My study at Cambridge University, the starting point of this long journey, would not have been possible without support from both the UK and Korean governments. The Foreign Commonwealth Office generously offered me the Chevening Scholarship and the Ministry of Commerce, Industry and Energy, my former employer, provided me with financial support including two years' paid leave. The research was also funded in part by the R.A.G. Monks Scholarship and Cambridge Political Economy Society Trust, for which I am very grateful.

This book is a result of the valuable time and experiences that the interviewees allowed me. Especially, I would like to thank the members of the People's Solidarity of Participatory Democracy (PSPD), including Hasung Jang and Seung-Hee Lee. In addition, Sang-Jo Kim, currently Chairman of the Participatory Economy Committee and Director of *Chaebol* Reform Monitoring Centre of the PSPD, reviewed the early drafts to give the book a lively and balanced description.

I am also indebted to the Korea Development Institute (KDI) that provided me an excellent research environment during the fieldwork in Seoul, Korea. I would like to express special gratitude to Seong Min Yoo for arranging my affiliation to the KDI. Kyong-koo Han, an anthropology professor now at Kookmin University, Korea, was a really comforting beacon to a novice fieldworker. I would like to thank John Hendry, Ha-Joon Chang, Ronald Dore and Peter Nolan whose incisive comments and constructive criticism have been an invaluable source of stimulation and encouragement.

I am grateful to the Von Hügel Institute, the European Business Ethics Network-UK, and European Group for Organizational Studies for having offered me an opportunity to share my research idea with colleagues. Alice Lam, my old colleague at Brunel and now at Royal Holloway, University of London, thankfully encouraged me to write this book. I would also like to thank Jacky Kippenberger of Palgrave Macmillan and Katie Jones of Judge Business School, Cambridge, for their help in the production of this book.

Finally, the research life made me understand why most scholars make acknowledgement of their families' patience. Like other fellow researchers, I also owe immeasurable thanks to my family – Hye-Sun, Jong-Youn, Curie, my parents, and my mother-in-law, to name a few nearest – for the loving support which they provided to me during my research.

Han-Kyun
Cambridge, UK

List of Abbreviations

ABI	Association of British Insurers
ACGA	Asian Corporate Governance Association
AFL-CIO	American Federation of Labor and Congress of Industrial Organizations
AGM	annual general meeting
APEC	Asia Pacific Economic Co-operation
AR	average abnormal return
ASA	Australian Shareholders Association
ASrIA	Association for Sustainable and Responsible Investment in Asia
BOK	Bank of Korea
BW	bond with warrant
CalPERS	California Public Employee Retirement System
Calstrs	California State Teachers Retirement System
CAR	cumulative average return
CB	convertible bond
CCEJ	Citizens' Coalition for Economic Justice (Korea)
CGCG	Center for Good Corporate Governance (Korea)
CII	Council of Institutional Investors (US)
Colpera	Colorado Public Employee Retirement System
CRSP	Center for Research in Security Prices
DSW	Deutsche Schutzvereinigung für Westpapierbesitz (Germany)
EGM	extraordinary general meeting
EIU	Economist Intelligence Unit
EPB	Economic Planning Board (Korea)
Eurosif	European Sustainable and Responsible Investment Forum
FIGHT	Freedom, Integration, God, Honor-Today (US)
FSBA	Florida State Board of Administration
FSC	Financial Supervisory Commission (Korea)
EIRIS	Ethical Investment Research and Information Service (UK)
ERISA	Employee Retirement Income Security Act (US)
ESOA	employee stock ownership association (Korea)
FKI	Federation of Korean Industries

FOE	Friends of the Earth
FSC	Financial Supervisory Commission (Korea)
FSS	Financial Supervisory Service (Korea)
FTC	Fair Trade Commission (Korea)
ICCR	Interfaith Center on Corporate Responsibility (US)
ICGN	International Corporate Governance Network
IFMA	Institutional Fund Mangers' Association (UK)
IMF	International Monetary Fund
IRAA	Investors Rights Association of America
IRRC	Investor Responsibility Research Center (US)
ISS	Institutional Shareholder Services (US)
KCCI	Korea Chamber of Commerce and Industry
KCTU	Korean Confederation of Trade Unions
KDI	Korea Development Institute
KFB	Korea First Bank
KIF	Korea Institute of Finance
KINDS	Korea Integrated News Database System
KLCA	Korea Listed Companies Association
KSE	Korea Stock Exchange
KSE-KIND	Korea Investor's Network for Disclosure System, KSE
LAPFF	Local Authority Pension Fund Forum (UK)
MOFE	Ministry of Finance and Economy (Korea)
MOTIE	Ministry of Trade, Industry and Energy (Korea)
NAPF	National Association of Pension Funds (UK)
NYSCR	New York State Common Retirement System
OECD	Organization for Economic Co-operation and Development
OSS	Office of Securities Supervision (Korea)
PEC	Participatory Economy Committee, PSPD
PIRC	Pensions & Investment Research Consultants Ltd (UK)
PSPD	People's Solidarity for Participatory Democracy (Korea)
S&P 500	Standard & Poor's 500 Common Stock Index
SEC	Securities and Exchange Commission (US)
SIC	Standard Industrial Classification
SMWIA	Sheet Metal Workers' International Association
SWIB	State of Wisconsin Investment Board
TIAA-CREF	Teachers Insurance and Annuity Association: College Retirement Equities Fund (US)
UBCJA	United Brotherhood of Carpenters and Joiners of America
UKSA	United Kingdom Shareholders Association
USA	United Shareholders Association (US)

Note on Korean Spelling

It is not easy to convey Korean pronunciation, with precision, via the English alphabet. The McCune–Reischauer System (or the Martin System for linguists) is the converting system that Western authors have usually resorted to. Notwithstanding, this book is based on a new guideline *How to Romanize Korean* prepared by the Korean government (Ministry of Culture and Tourism, Public Notice No. 2000-8).

I have tried to spell proper nouns as preferred by the individuals concerned. When it is difficult to identify their spelling, I followed the aforementioned guideline. With Korean names, the surname traditionally comes first. The given name then follows in the form of one word (whether hyphenated or not) or two words. To avoid Westerners' confusion, many Koreans, including myself, invert their names. This book has kept to the Korean way in its main body. Elsewhere, including the cover and acknowledgements, the name is inverted.

Foreword

There is a compelling neatness about the Korean iteration of shareholder activism. The syllogism is that national wealth is enhanced through corporate growth; the legitimate definition of wealth is political as well as economic; therefore, the process of monitoring corporate power is necessary – shareholder activists, thus, are performing a public good.

The asserted congruency of corporate and national interest colors shareholder involvement with purpose. It is a device through which the power of the *chaebol* can effectively be addressed without disturbing the delicate equilibrium of public and private power. "The virtuous cycle between corporate governance reform and shareholder activism" compels the conclusion that financial support for this institution should be forthcoming either from the corporation itself or from the government. Unhappily, the incapacity of societies to deal with the disabling conflicted interests of institutional investors – the largest global shareholders – deprives the movement of the breadth and depth of support necessary for full effectiveness.

The splendid tradition of courageous personal activism that has distinguished the last half century of Korean history is a unique and welcome addition to the global tapestry of corporate governance.

Robert A.G. Monks
Principal, Lens Governance Advisors
& Chairman,
Governance for Owners, LLP

Introduction: Shareholder Activism and Corporate Governance Reform

In recent years, there has been growing interest, both political and academic, in the operation and reform of international systems of corporate governance.[1] Of particular interest, in the wake of the 1997 Asian crisis, have been the use of shareholder rights and the encouragement of shareholder activism[2] in reforming corporate governance regimes (e.g., IMF staff, 1998).

Among policymakers, the general consensus has been that there exists a virtuous cycle between corporate governance reform and shareholder activism. With policy support, shareholders can monitor and thus assert their interest to corporate management more forcefully than before. This shareholders' self-assertion forces managers to adopt a more shareholder-interest-centered stance than before. Shareholder- or investor-centered management brings about more efficient operations, and thus the national economy as a whole can secure the foundation for sustainable growth. It is widely believed that the sustainable growth of the economy is one of the key policy goals a national government should achieve, and accordingly, corporate governance reform encouraging shareholder activism is regarded as desirable. Meanwhile, as a shareholder-centered view of firms becomes gradually more widespread, demands for the protection of shareholder interests will also increase, which will in turn reinforce shareholder-centered corporate governance reform.

The significance of shareholder activism within the overall process of corporate governance reform can be summarized as in Figure 0.1. For this reason, encouraging shareholder monitoring has been recommended as an important goal for corporate governance reform (e.g., Iskander, Meyerman, Gray and Hagan, 1999). International organizations such as the Organization for Economic Co-operation and Development (OECD) and the International Bank for Reconstruction and Development (World

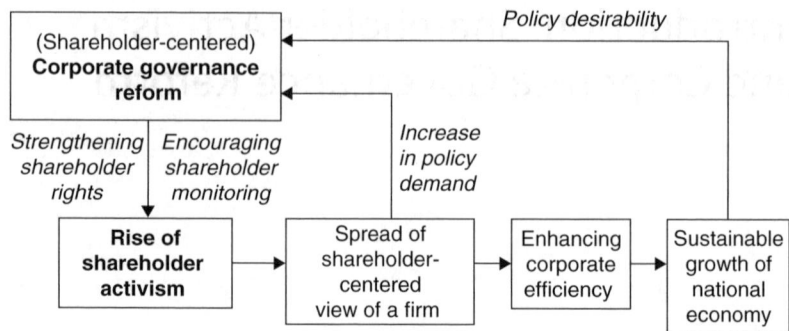

Figure 0.1 Shareholder activism in corporate governance reform

Bank) have helped developing and transition countries increasingly with the design and implementation of shareholder empowerment programs (World Bank, 1999). To take an example of a recent reform in an Asian developing country, the Malaysian government amended the Securities Commission Act in April 2000, allowing shareholders to pursue civil actions against companies, directors and their advisors[3] (World Bank, 2000). Similarly in European transition economies, recent legal reforms have concentrated on investor protection and empowerment (Pistor, 2000).

The growth of shareholder activism

Apart from the causal relationship between policy change and the growth of shareholder activism, which will be discussed in Chapters 3, 5 and 8, shareholder activism has increased quite dramatically in recent years. To take an example from the US experience, the number of shareholder resolutions on corporate governance issues (excluding those proposed by individual shareholders) has increased more than seven-fold over the last two decades (Figure 0.2). Although there have been some fluctuations, the trend line in Figure 0.2 clearly shows a steady growth during the period.

Observers maintain that shareholder power is now spreading on a global scale. In January 1999, for example, Phillips and Drew Fund Management, Hermes Lens Asset Management and other large shareholders ousted David Montgomery from the position of chief executive of the UK media firm Mirror Group (Sherer, 1999). Since the early 1990s, Deutsche Schutzvereinigung für Westpapierbesitz (DSW), Deutsche Bank's mutual-fund arm, has quietly prodded German companies to boost shareholder returns. The results of DSW's efforts were the restructuring of the three

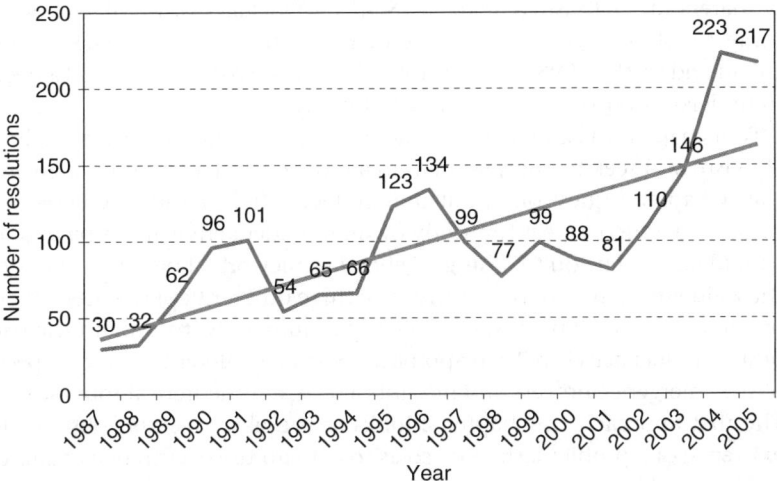

Figure 0.2 Growth of shareholder resolutions, US, 1987–2005
Sources: Gillan and Starks (2000), Georgeson Shareholder (various years). *Annual Corporate Governance Review.*

pillars of Germany Inc.: the conglomerate Siemens, the retailer Metro, and the chemical manufacturer Hoechst (Flynn, 1998). Shareholder activism can be observed in other corners of the world: to cite but a few, Hungary (*Central European*, 1999), Malaysia (Jayasankaran, 2000), China and Chile (Sherer, ibid.). Sherer (1999) concludes "[f]or years, agitating by stockholders was largely a US convention, held down overseas by long-held customs, practices or laws. . . . Now the picture is starting to change (n.p.)".

Studying the rise of shareholder activism

Considering the relatively long history of activism by other stakeholders such as employees and consumers, shareholder activism is a relatively recent form. Nevertheless, the current rapid growth of shareholder activism has attracted considerable academic attention and consequently a large body of research has accumulated over the last two decades. Two early channels for publication were law and financial economics journals, but recent research outlets include journals of general management, business and society, and business ethics. Current articles on shareholder activism appear not only in journals specializing in corporate governance, but also in those in labor (Chakrabarti, 2004) and the environment (Monks, Miller and Cook, 2004). Much work has been done to understand the rise of shareholder activism (Gillan and Starks, 1998; Karpoff, 1998). Although some scholars have reviewed the literature in this area (Black, 1998; Gillan and Starks, 1998; Karpoff, 1998; Romano, 2001), there is still a need to understand this in a more systematic way.

Four chapters in Part I review the achievements in the area of shareholder activism and seek to analyze them in a more critical and comprehensive way. Chapter 1 questions what shareholder activism and its emergence mean and which aspect the study of shareholder activism has paid, and should pay, attention to. Using a general framework of decision-making, the following three chapters introduce three different approaches which previous scholars have taken, explicitly or implicitly, to explain the rise of shareholder activism. Each approach looks at a different stage, or aspect, of the emergence process and presents a different theoretical foundation. The first approach in Chapter 2 looks at the objective and observable existence of a problematic state so as to explain the occurrence of shareholder activism. Chapter 3 introduces the second approach, exploring the conditions under which a dissenting shareholder finally chooses activism among many various alternatives to correct an unsatisfactory situation. The third approach in Chapter 4 criticizes the rational unitary actor model of the previous two approaches, whether explicitly or not, and suggests a political and symbolic approach based on social movement theory to understand the rise of shareholder activism.

The case of Korean shareholder activism

The emergence of shareholder activism and related corporate governance reforms in Korea have been warmly commended by Western economists. For example, John Plender (2000), former chairman of Pensions and Investment Research Consultants Ltd (PIRC) and a lead writer of the *Financial Times*, once dubbed them the most impressive gain in Asian corporate governance reform. Other observers also cite the Korean case as an outstanding example of the global spread of shareholder power (e.g., Sherer, 1999; Wright, 1999). The leading activists are described as a "classic activist group" (*Forbes*, 2001) and as the creator of a shareholder rights movement (EIU, 2001). Thanks to this remarkable success, Jang Hasung, a leader of Korean shareholder activism, was chosen as one of 50 Asian Stars by *Business Week* in 1998 and 1999, and as one of Asia's best Advocates of Shareholder's Rights by *Asia Week* in 2000. Along with Adrian Cadbury and Ira Millstein, he was selected to receive one of the first International Corporate Governance Network (ICGN) Annual Awards in 2001.

The prominent Korean shareholder activism was led by the People's Solidarity for Participatory Democracy (PSPD), a civil society organization. Originally it did not own shares of any target firms, nor was it concerned with enhancing shareholder rights. The PSPD's major concern is, as its name implies, participatory democracy, a political issue. Nevertheless, since its first shareholder activism against the Korea First Bank (KFB) in 1997, the PSPD has been leading Korean shareholder activism and has won international praise, as noted above. Despite its political nature, the PSPD is now piloting one of the most successful shareholder activism campaigns in developing countries.

What makes its success even more surprising is that the atmosphere in which the shareholder activism had emerged was not at first sight particularly favorable. Conventionally, Korea was thought to be a country where shareholders had been poorly protected, at least in practice, and almost inactive in corporate governance. It is a popular belief that, ever since the economy and the capital markets started developing in Korea since the 1960s, shareholder rights had usually existed only in legal textbooks and provisions. It has been believed that this poor corporate governance was one of the main causes of the 1997 financial crisis (e.g., IMF staff, 1998). Although the Korean government has continuously strengthened shareholder rights since 1998, even a survey of the public opinion on business reveals that most Koreans believe that business profits should be returned to the society rather than to the shareholders (*Maeil Business News*, 1999).

However, in December 1997, in the midst of the 1997 financial crisis, the PSPD launched its first shareholder activism; and its achievements since then have been highly praised. From this viewpoint, the PSPD exemplifies a unique case where an alternative activist group, a civil society organization, may complement or even encourage the monitoring role of more traditional activists such as institutional investors. Therefore, a question arising from the PSPD case is: "How could the shareholder activism led by the PSPD, a civil society organization, grow and thrive in the poor soil of Korea to become a success story of corporate governance reform in developing countries?"

The explosive development of shareholder activism in Korea might well become a matter of great concern for scholars (e.g., Kim and Kim, 2001; Choi and Cho, 2003; Milhaupt, 2004). Milhaupt (2004), for example, sees the dramatic rise of the PSPD and the series of remarkable victories achieved by PSPD-led shareholder activism as a real "puzzle". However, we have at least three challenges in applying the first and the second approaches reviewed in Part I to explain the PSPD case. First, an assumption that the PSPD tries to solve the problem of low stock returns through its shareholder activism is not plausible *prima facie*. Therefore, we need to examine what problems the PSPD is trying to solve and what meaning shareholder's financial interests, if any, bear in the PSPD shareholder activism. Second, we need to change the exit-voice alternatives that the existing theories of shareholder activism consider. If the PSPD, as a civil activist organization, tries to reform a current situation of a firm, it can regard neither exit nor takeover as appropriate alternatives. The alternative set of the PSPD as a civil society organization may contain traditional political voice options such as petitions, demonstrations, and boycotts. In this sense, it becomes important to examine how shareholder activism, an unusual voice tool, has entered into the PSPD's alternative set and why the PSPD has chosen it. Third, if the PSPD wants to take shareholder activism without having shares of the target firm, it will need to co-operate with shareholders of the firm to some extent. In this sense, we can apply the first or the second approaches to shareholder activism to the supportive shareholders rather than to the PSPD. However, this does not appear to be sufficient to explain the emergence of the PSPD activism fully.

For the reasons above, we think the third approach of social movement theory can address the three points above relatively well when we explore the rise of Korean shareholder activism.[4] The three chapters in Part II investigate the three elements of social movement theory (political opportunity, framing process and resource mobilization) respectively. Chapter 5 investigates the political relations between the government, the PSPD and other civil activists. Chapter 6 addresses the process in which the activists view a situation, decide to use shareholder activism to change it and legitimize their action. Chapter 7 identifies what resources the Korean activists required and how they mobilized them successfully. Chapter 8 concludes with the findings and their implications for policymakers, scholars and corporate managers interested in corporate governance reforms, especially those achieved through shareholder activism.

Part I
A Review of Theories

1
Defining the Object of Study

Shareholder activism is at the centre of this investigation and, as will be shown in Chapters 2 to 4, scholars generally try to relate it to other independent variables in order to explain its occurrence. It is, therefore, crucial for scholars of shareholder activism to clarify this key concept. No single study can cover the whole domain of shareholder activism completely. Nevertheless, a clear understanding of the boundary and features of the object of study will enable a researcher to position his/her study in a broader context. On an aggregate level, a clear boundary of shareholder activism also allows scholars to discover less explored areas in which they may be interested for future study.

How can we define shareholder activism? We have observed a wide range of actions so far. When corporate governance scholars talk about shareholder activism, their focus would be usually on names such as the California Public Employee Retirement System (CalPERS) (e.g., Nesbitt, 1994; English, Smythe and McNeil, 2004). On the other hand, when business ethics scholars mention the same term, they would recall action against Apartheid (e.g., Teoh, Welch and Wazzan, 1999; Graves, Waddock and Rehbein, 2001). How can a definition of shareholder activism encompass these various types of actions? Which aspects of shareholder activism should we consider when we define it? What does the 'emergence' of shareholder activism mean when we say that most studies have addressed it?

In order to answer these questions, this chapter first reviews definitions suggested by previous scholars. It will then introduce three dimensions of shareholder activism (target, actor and action) and seek more clarification on the suggested definitions of shareholder activism. Thirdly, we will consider various meanings of its 'emergence' which studies of shareholder activism can address.[1]

Previous definitions of shareholder activism

Some scholars have defined the term 'shareholder activism' in an explicit way. For Bernard Black, shareholder activism is seen as "any formal or informal effort to monitor corporate managers or to communicate a desire for change in a company's management or policies" (1990, p. 522, fn.3). Later he views it as "*proactive* effort to change firm behavior or governance rules" (emphasis in original, 1998, p. 459). Here Black does not include any 'reactive' action such as voting on an issue presented by someone else in his definition of shareholder activism.

Hernández-López (2003) defines shareholder activism as "any action a shareholder may take, based on his [sic] rights as a shareholder, with the objective of influencing the management of the corporation" (p. 128, fn.2). In this definition, he makes it clear that shareholder activism is waged on the basis of shareholder rights.

Gillan and Starks (1998) maintain that an investor who is taking shareholder activism tries to change the *status quo* through 'voice' without a change in corporate control. They conceive shareholder activism as an intermediate action in a continuum of responses to corporate performance, which has two extreme types of responses (that is, selling shares and taking over control of the firm). Gillan and Starks' idea raises an interesting point regarding the definition of shareholder activism. A definition normally consists of two elements: (1) the wider class to which the concept belongs (*genus*); and (2) features by which the concept can be distinguished from other concepts in the wider class (*differentia*) (Worlfram, 2005). Gillan and Starks suggest that the wider class to which shareholder activism belongs is the various ways in which shareholders express their dissatisfaction with the current state of a firm. According to Hirschman (1970), dissatisfaction can be expressed in two forms – exit and voice. When dissatisfied shareholders take an exit option by selling their stocks, the consequent declining stock price should warn the company that some shareholders are unhappy with a certain aspect of its policy. In a voice option, on the other hand, shareholders express their dissatisfaction directly to management to change corporate policy or behavior. The main difference between the two is that the exit option, when taken, terminates the existing relationship between the dissenting shareholders and the firm while the voice option allows the shareholders to maintain their status. Takeovers are an extreme way of expressing dissatisfaction. Since a successful takeover attempt will render the dissenting shareholders control over the company, it will also change the nature of the shareholders' original relationship with the company. Therefore, a feature distinguishing shareholder activism from other responses is, as Gillan and Starks (1998) suggest, no fundamental change in the initial relationship between the activist shareholders and their target firm.

Three dimensions of shareholder activism

The definitions reviewed above shed light on some important aspects of shareholder activism. However, we can examine the definitions in a clearer way by introducing three dimensions of shareholder activism – target, actor and action. Table 1.1 breaks down the previous definitions according to the three dimensions.

Target

The previous definitions all suggest that the target of shareholder activism is a company-specific *status quo*. In terms of activism target, we can consider three questions: (1) Does shareholder activism encompass an attempt to change the regulations that affect shareholder rights generally?; (2) Can we include the current situation that activist shareholders endeavor to change in the definition of shareholder activism?; and (3) Can we also include the ultimate motive of activist shareholders in the definition of shareholder activism?

Table 1.1 Three dimensions of previous definitions

	Target	Actor	Action
Black (1990)	a company's management or policies	—	any formal or informal effort to monitor corporate managers or to communicate a desire for change
Black (1998)	firm behavior or governance rules	shareholder	proactive effort to change
Hernández-López (2003)	the management of the corporation	shareholder	any action based on rights as a shareholder with the objective of influencing
Gillan and Starks (1998)	the *status quo* (of a corporation)	investor	change through 'voice' without a change in corporate control

Source: Rho (2006).

Firm level? Or regulatory level?

Hirschman (1970) proposes that the voice option includes not only direct appeal to management but also 'indirect' appeal to management through other authority to which management is subordinate or attentive. Such authority may exist either in an internal body such as a board of directors or an external entity such as a regulatory body or the media. If a definition of shareholder activism incorporates Hirschman's voice as a distinguishing feature, does this mean that it should embrace shareholders' attempt to change social, not company, rules in their favor?

Davis and Thompson (1994) appear to imply that it should. Although they measure shareholder activism in terms of a company-specific action (that is, shareholder resolutions submitted to individual firms), they also mention activist investors' success in changing the regulatory rules by which they may influence corporate governance in general.

However, as the previous definitions endorse, shareholder activism is concerned mainly with a company-specific situation. Although regulatory changes are an important determinant of the rise, and success, of shareholder activism as illustrated in Chapter 2, they are not a primary concern of activist shareholders. For example, the Medical Committee for Human Rights filed a legal action against the US Securities and Exchange Commission (SEC) and as a consequence the US Court of Appeals for the District of Columbia Circuit allowed the use of shareholder proposals on business matters with a social impact in July 1970 (Talner, 1983). This is praised as a memorable achievement in the history of US shareholder activism, but the primary target of the Medical Committee was to prevent Dow Chemical from manufacturing napalm, an inhumane weapon. The historic court decision was a spinoff obtained from the fact that the SEC endorsed Dow's omission of the Medical Committee's proposal from its proxy statement and obstructed the action against Dow.

Although Davis and Thompson (1994) mention activists' attempt to change regulatory environments, they frequently use more general terms such as "politics of corporate control" or "shareholder-rights movement" instead of "shareholder activism" when they mention both company-specific and regulatory targets of activist shareholders (see also Thompson and Davis, 1997).

Objects of change

If shareholder activism seeks to change the current situation of a company, what is the nature of this situation? Activist shareholders have raised a wide range of issues. Recent US shareholder resolutions show the main concerns of activist shareholders range from executive compensation to board-related issues and poison pill rescission in the 2005 proxy season (Georgeson Shareholder, 2005). Another survey of 2004/2005 resolutions in the US reveals that shareholders are also concerned about discrimination (for example, sexual orientation and board diversity) and social and environmental reporting (for example, emissions reduction, genetically modified organisms, HIV and sustainability) (ICCR, 2005).

Can a definition of shareholder activism delimit the firm's situation? The previous definitions do not include any issue-related elements. A reason for this is that it is difficult and also risky to use specific issues in a definition of shareholder activism. Shareholders have the right to raise any issues they wish within the remit of the law. The inclusion of an issue may risk precluding any other issues which may arise in the future from the boundary of shareholder activism.

We now consider the taxonomy of shareholder activism. Scholars and practitioners frequently divide shareholder activism into two broad categories: (1) corporate governance activism; and (2) social issue activism. The two surveys cited above exemplify this dichotomy well. Since 1987, Georgeson Shareholder has investigated shareholder resolutions centered on corporate governance issues, while the Interfaith Center on Corporate Responsibility (ICCR) compiles information about social issue resolutions.

This dichotomy must, however, be used with care, since a single issue may be interpreted from different perspectives. For example, both the Georgeson Shareholder and ICCR surveys contain shareholder resolutions on executive compensation. From the perspective of corporate governance, mainly influenced by agency theory, which Chapter 2 will elaborate on, this issue can be understood as an instrument for aligning managers' incentives with shareholders'. On the other hand, from the social point of view, executive compensation can be viewed as an issue of distributive justice – an unfairly excessive income gap between the top executives and the lowest-level employees.

Strict use of the dichotomy may also lead to highly segregated or imbalanced research on shareholder activism. Gillan and Starks (1998), for example, acknowledge that shareholder activists are often social activists, but they maintain that nevertheless it is corporate governance issues that are critical from the economic perspective. Although some scholars have studied shareholder activism focusing on social issues (e.g., Teoh, Welch and Wazzan, 1999; Graves, Waddock and Rehbein, 2001), most have centered on the narrowly financially defined corporate governance issues. Today we can witness that the term 'shareholder activism' tends to be monopolized by purely economic, corporate governance activism and that social issue activism is renamed 'socially responsible investment' or 'ethical investment'.[2] As discussed above, however, the definition of shareholder activism cannot be limited by means of its issues and the concept of shareholder activism encompasses social issue activism. To conclude, the study of shareholder activism as a whole should keep its balance across various issues.

Immediate or ultimate goal?

In the previous section, we discussed objects of change. These are the immediate results of successful shareholder activism. To borrow some Karpoff's (1998) six definitions of the 'success' of shareholder activism, these immediate goals include high vote support for a shareholder proposal, actions sought by the activist and adopted by the target firm, other corporate actions taken as a result of shareholder pressure, and changes in operations or management. However, they may be a means by which shareholder activists try to achieve longer-term goals. For example, the remaining definitions of success in Karpoff (1998), such as increase in share values and in accounting measures of performance, are the goals that activist shareholders seek in the long term but cannot materialize in the short term. A question here is whether we can include an activist's ultimate motive in the definition of shareholder activism.

Attempts have been made to include the activist's motive in the definition of shareholder activism. A recent example is a suggestion made by Jamie Allen, Secretary General of Asian Corporate Governance Association (ACGA), defining shareholder activism as any "action ... to ... raise company value over time" (ACGA, 2005, n.p.).

Here we need to distinguish the use of definition from the normative and from the descriptive perspective. The definition including the activist's motive has a normative aspect. This view comes mainly from the regulators, who argue that if a shareholder's voice against a firm is to be recognized as shareholder activism and duly protected by the regulatory authority, it should aim to increase certain economic value. The US SEC's attitude towards the Medical Committee's proposal in our previous example illustrates this view. The SEC allowed Dow Chemical to omit the Medical Committee's proposal in its proxy statement because the proposal was concerned with social rather than economic aspects. On the other hand, the purpose of this chapter is to clarify the descriptive definition of shareholder activism. The main question is how a definition of shareholder activism can encompass the various types of actions which have already happened. To this end, for the same reasons discussed above in relation to the immediate objects of change, it is not only difficult but also harmful to include the *ex ante* motive in the definition. Furthermore, it should be noted that even though we allow a normative definition of shareholder activism to include a certain motive, the boundary of legitimate motives can change depending on the wider socio-political environment. Again, the Medical Committee case succinctly demonstrates this point with the US Court of Appeals finally expanding the scope of legitimacy. As in the previous discussion on the objects of change, therefore, the study of shareholder activism as a whole, which looks at existing shareholder activism, should pay balanced attention to activism with various motives.

Actor

The previous definitions reviewed in the first section indicate, almost unanimously, that the actor of shareholder activism is a shareholder. It is true that there can be no shareholder activism without a shareholder. Hernández-López (2003) points out that the power base of shareholder activism is shareholder rights. Two more points that need clarification here are: (1) whether a shareholder is always a 'leading' actor in shareholder activism; and (2) whether the definition of shareholder activism should contain the shareholder proactivity, as Black's (1998) account proposes.

In relation to this point, recent developments focus our attention on the burgeoning role of mediating groups in the field of shareholder activism. There are various types of mediating groups operating in this area. In the UK, for example, trade associations of financial institutions such as the Association of British Insurers (ABI) and the National Association of Pension Funds (NAPF) serve as a communication channel for their members' collection action. Organizations such as Pensions and Investment Research Consultants Ltd (PIRC) and Ethical Investment Research and Information Service (EIRIS) offer independent services to their clients. US examples of mediating groups are the Council of Institutional Investors (CII), Institutional Shareholder Services (ISS), Investor Responsibility Research Center (IRRC), ICCR, and Wilshire Associates. In Europe, the European Sustainable and Responsible Investment Forum (Eurosif) covers ethical investment issues and the Association for Sustainable and Responsible Investment in Asia (ASrIA) is working in the region. Although less prominent, there are also some collective vehicles for individual shareholders – for example, the now extinct United Shareholders Association (USA) in the US, the United Kingdom Shareholders Association (UKSA), the Australian Shareholders Association (ASA) and the Association of Minority and Smaller Investors in India.

Traditional rating agencies such as Standard & Poor's and Moody's have expanded their services to corporate governance areas. Some of the corporate governance service organizations outlined above produce their own corporate rating indices (for example, ISS's *Corporate Governance Quotient*). New rating agencies specializing in corporate governance or ethical aspects are also growing rapidly. Board Analysts, CoreRatings, Deminor Rating, GovernanceMetrics International, and the Open Compliance Ethics Group are such examples. There are also rating agencies focusing on the emerging markets – CRISIL Ltd and ICRA Ltd in India, for example.

These developments pose a challenge to our job of defining shareholder activism and the scope of activism studies. How can we embrace the growing importance of mediating groups in our definition and research of shareholder activism? Which group is usually leading shareholder activism, shareholders or mediating groups? How can we distinguish between proactive, leading actors and passive, supporting actors in particular activism? These questions should be answered in relation to action, the third dimension of shareholder activism.

Action

The previous definitions raise two points in terms of the actions shareholder activists can take. The first point is concerned with sub-activities of shareholder activism such as monitoring and voice (Gillan and Starks, 1998). The second point is about possible methods of implementing the sub-activities, especially with regard to voice. Black (1990) and Hernández-López (2003) do not restrict voice options in their definitions. They take the view that shareholder activism can take any form of voice, whether formal or informal. This section examines these two points and Black's (1998) shareholder proactivity thesis.

Monitoring and voice

Previous definitions of shareholder activism suggest two distinct sub-activities – monitoring and voice.[3] What relationship can we find between monitoring, voice and shareholder activism? Black (1990) explains that shareholder activism comprises two activities: (1) monitoring corporate managers; or (2) communicating a desire for change with them. His definition implies that both monitoring and voice are distinct elements of shareholder activism. In contrast to this view, Rho (2004) suggests that shareholder activism is a part of shareholder monitoring, "a logical extension of shareholder monitoring" (p. 3). Which view depicts the relationship between shareholder activism and shareholder monitoring more accurately?

The interpretative gap comes from two different notions of both shareholder activism and monitoring. Figure 1.1 illustrates this conceptual difference. A simple model of human action has two elements.

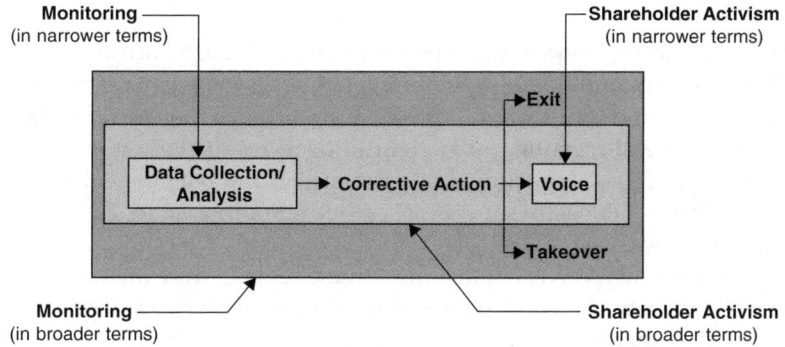

Figure 1.1 Monitoring and shareholder activism
Source: Rho (2006).

First, a decision-maker will collect data that he/she may be interested in from the outside world and analyze them. Second, if the decision-maker finds a gap between the reality established from the data and his/her ideal state, he/she will try to fill the gap. This stage can be termed as 'corrective action'. To this model, previous definitions of shareholder activism add three possible means of corrective action – exit, voice and takeover. These elements are shown in Figure 1.1.

In this framework, a narrower notion of 'monitoring' means collection and analysis of company data and it does not include any subsequent corrective action. This is the meaning of 'monitoring' employed by Black (1990). On the other hand, a broader concept of 'monitoring' implies both data collection/analysis and subsequent corrective action. Rho (2004) uses the term 'monitoring' in this way when he says "Shareholder monitoring comprises two essential activities: (1) collection and analysis of corporate data; and (2) corrective action when these data reveal an unsatisfactory level of corporate performance" (p. 3). In this usage, monitoring involves any type of corrective action including exit, takeover and voice. Likewise, the term 'shareholder activism' has two different meanings. In narrower terms, shareholder activism refers to a 'voice' option of corrective action only (Rho, 2004). In broader terms, it contains data collection/analysis as well as a voice option as a corrective action (Black, 1990).[4] Since Black (1990) combines a narrower notion of 'monitoring' with a broader one of 'shareholder activism', monitoring is a part of shareholder activism in his definition. For Rho (2004), shareholder activism is a part of monitoring because he employs a broader concept of 'monitoring' and a narrower one of 'shareholder activism' (see Figure 1.1).[5]

Methods of voice

There are various ways of implementing a voice strategy: private negotiation (sometimes termed 'jawboning'), public announcements of target firms, shareholder resolutions, questioning corporate policies at a shareholders' general meeting, proxy fights, litigations (including derivative suits[6]), appeals to a regulatory body, the media, and public opinion, and so on. Shareholder activism comprises, but is not limited to, all of these voice methods.

A point to mention here is that most studies use the voice methods as an operational definition of shareholder activism. In other words, researchers can observe shareholder activism when one of the voice methods is visibly active. Two operational definitions most frequently used in previous studies are: (1) a shareholder proposal (Daily, Johnson, Ellstrand and Dalton, 1996; Gillan and Starks, 1996; Karpoff, Malatesta, Walkling, 1996; Johnson and Shackell, 1997; Bizjak and Marquette, 1998; Carleton, Nelson, and Weisbach, 1998; Del Guercia and Hawkins, 1999; Prevost and Rao, 2000); and (2) an announcement of target firms (Opler and Sokobin, 1995; Smith, 1996; Strickland, Wiles and Zenner, 1996; Huson, 1997; Carleton, Nelson, and Weisbach, 1998).

Operational definitions in previous studies concentrate on a limited number of methods. A reason for this concentration is that observation of these two methods is easier than for other methods and so scholars can easily obtain large sample data. Although a limited number of academic attempts have been made in other areas (for private negotiation, Black and Coffee, 1994; Carleton, Nelson and Weisbach, 1998; Chidambaran and Woidtke, 1999; for litigation, Romano, 1991; Grundfest and Perino, 1996; Beck and Bhagat, 1998), the other voice methods are still awaiting more academic attention. Considering the fact that the most popular voice method varies from country to country, this imbalance may result in relatively limited understanding of a certain economy's shareholder activism. For example, unlike the high-profile activism by US investors, the activism by UK investors has long remained behind the scenes (Black and Coffee, 1994). Therefore, with the two popular operational definitions, we can only draw a very limited picture of the UK landscape.

Who does what? – On shareholder proactivity

In the previous discussion on the 'actor', noting the growing importance of mediating groups, we raised two questions: whether a shareholder is always 'leading' shareholder activism and whether shareholder proactivity should be included in the definition of shareholder activism. The following case can give us some insight into the dynamic relationships between activist shareholders and mediating groups.

The Local Authority Pension Fund Forum (LAPFF) is a group of pension funds which operate under the Local Government Pension Scheme in the UK. It is a kind of mediating group functioning as a communication channel for its members. In its meeting in September 1995, LAPFF noted the changes Royal Dutch Shell had had to make regarding Brent Spar. It also expressed concern over certain aspects of the company's operations in Nigeria (PIRC, 1996). It considered that these situations exposed a potential weakness within the company's social and environmental policy. Following its client's concern, PIRC, investment adviser to LAPFF and another type of mediating group, carried out research and dialogue with Shell on behalf of LAPFF. PIRC presented a shareholder resolution containing five recommendations to the company's 1997 annual general meeting (AGM). After a series of actions, PIRC felt that Shell had made significant progress in the company's social and environmental policy (PIRC, 1998).

Who led the activism in this case? It is very difficult to determine for sure which group – a local authority pension fund, LAPFF, or PIRC – had a leading role in the shareholder activism against Shell. The individual groups involved in this activism each played a role throughout. Identifying a leading figure would require an in-depth investigation of the whole process. There is no reason to believe *a priori* that a particular shareholder presided over the activism throughout. Therefore, we can suggest a more realistic picture of the interactions between shareholders and mediating groups as shown in Figure 1.2.

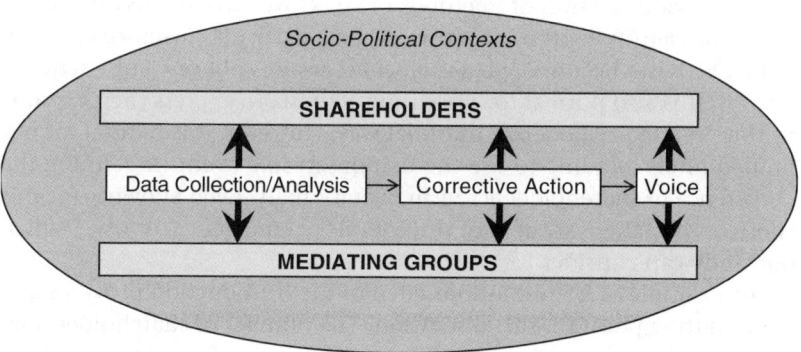

Figure 1.2 Interactive model of shareholder activism
Source: Rho (2006).

Taking into account the varying degrees of intervention from mediating groups, we can say that in most cases, throughout the course of shareholder activism, shareholders and mediating groups are constantly interacting. For example, a rating agency provides the most updated company data and relevant analysis to shareholders. Shareholders select companies they think should be under closer scrutiny and ask another mediating group (like PIRC in the previous case) to investigate these firms further. After investigation, the mediating group reports back to the shareholders with some recommendations on possible actions the shareholders can take. Shareholders decide a course of action on the basis of the recommendations and other available information and ask the mediating group (or another mediating group) to carry out their decision. These interactions between shareholders and mediating groups are also influenced by a broader socio-political context. For example, when LAPFF noticed the issues of Brent Spar and the Nigerian operations, these issues had already appeared in the public domain.

From this discussion, we cannot say firmly that shareholders are always proactively leading shareholder activism. It is certain that they have authority to make a key decision in the process of shareholder activism. At the same time, it is possible that mediating groups, and frequently the media, can exert the power of gate-keeping and agenda-setting (McCombs and Shaw, 1972) over the shareholders. Shareholders obtain some, if not all, critical information from mediating groups, who have already filtered and reconstructed the raw data to produce such information.

Meaning of emergence

In the previous section of 'methods of voice' we have discussed the difficulty of identifying the exact time when a particular instance of shareholder activism occurred. Shareholder activism is not one but a series of actions. It is also normal for dissenting activists to express their dissatisfaction in a more moderate informal way. However, it is natural for our limited understanding to use the first observable event in defining the occurrence of shareholder activism operationally. Even allowing for this shortcoming, there are at least three levels of emergence, or rise,[7] which our study can consider.

The example of US resolutions cited in the Introduction provides us a good starting point for this discussion. The number of shareholder resolutions on corporate governance issues has increased steadily more than seven-fold over the last two decades (Figure 0.2). In this case, the rise of shareholder activism denotes its steady increase on an aggregate level.

The overall increase of shareholder activism can be caused by the increase of activists, or the increase of activism per activist, or both.

To discover the driver of the steady growth of US resolutions, the average numbers of resolutions per activists are calculated between 1995 and 2005. On average US shareholder activists presented 4.6 resolutions to the target firms over the last decades. Figure 1.3 illustrates that there were two periods when activists tendered more resolutions than the average (1995–97 and 2003–05). The number of activists has increased during the whole period and the relatively higher number of resolutions during the two sub-periods caused the higher averages.

We investigate further which activist group proposed the most resolutions. Interestingly the three sub-periods witnessed that different groups were the most active. Between 1995 and 1997, the Investors Rights Association of America (IRAA), an association of individual investors, presented the largest number of shareholder resolutions (e.g., 65 resolutions in 1996). Between 1997 and 2000, ICCR, a group of religious organizations, was the most active. However, their activism was quite moderate (18 resolutions in 1997 and 2000), and other groups maintained an average level of activism. This kept the overall number of resolutions relatively low during the period. The most active groups since 2003 are trade unions.

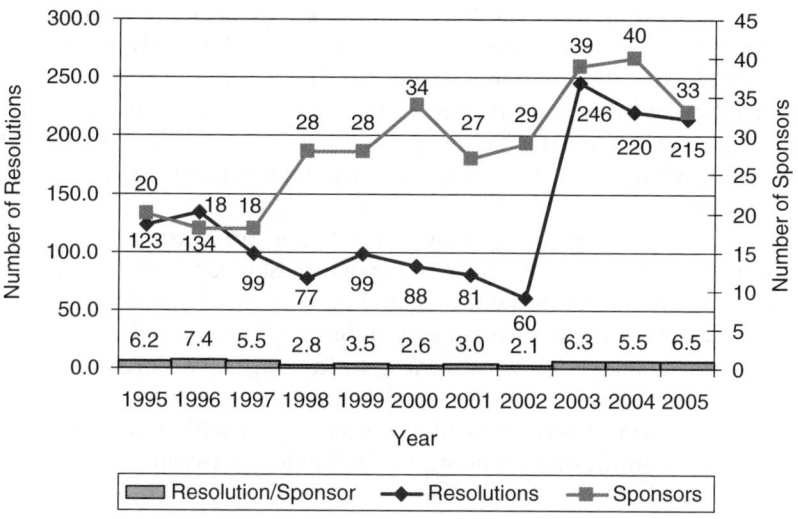

Figure 1.3 Number of resolutions per activists, US, 1995–2005
Source: Georgeson Shareholder (various years). *Annual Corporate Governance Review*.

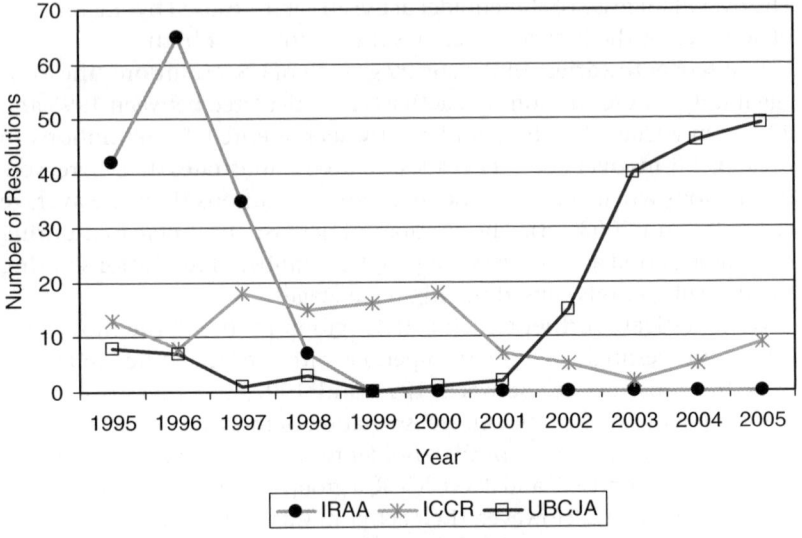

Figure 1.4 Three outstanding activists, US, 1995–2005
Source: Georgeson shareholders (various years). *Annual Corporate Governance Review.*

In Figure 1.4, we show one of the most forceful examples, the United Brotherhood of Carpenters and Joiners of America (UBCJA). UBCJA's activism (49 resolutions in 2005) is relatively moderate in comparison with that of IRAA, but this time other fellow trade unions such as the Sheet Metal Workers' International Association (SMWIA) and the American Federation of Labor and Congress of Industrial Organizations (AFL-CIO) are also jumping on the bandwagon (28 resolutions from SMWIA and 20 from AFL-CIO in 2005). This sent the total number of resolutions skyrocketing.

The results suggest that although there has been a constant increase in the number of activists, a small number of activist groups could contribute greatly to the overall growth of shareholder activism. In this sense, in order to understand the overall growth of shareholder activism, the first meaning of emergence, we also need to investigate two organizational levels of emergence: (1) how a potential activist group which has not previously used shareholder activism gets to grips with it, and (2) what makes it continue, or even boost, its shareholder activism.

2
Explaining Activism (1): Existence of a Problem

The first approach explains the occurrence of shareholder activism in terms of the existence of an unsatisfactory situation before the activism. A large number of studies, and almost all in corporate finance, have taken this approach, which investigates whether relatively underperforming companies have been more likely to experience shareholder activism. Although it is not always expressed explicitly, the two major theoretical grounds of this approach are equity theory of human motivation and agency theory.

Theoretical backgrounds

Equity theory

Equity theory, formulated by George Caspar Homans (1951; 1961) and popularized by the work of J. Stacy Adams (1965), proposes that perceived inequality is an ultimate motivational force. According to this theory, when they believe that they are treated less favorably than comparable others, shareholders, like other human beings, will take an action to eliminate the inequity (Adams, 1965 cited in Donnelly, Gibson and Ivancevich, 1995). In the theories of human motivation, there are two distinct groups: (1) content theories and (2) process theories. Equity theory is a part of process theories, which try to explain and describe the process of how human behavior is energized, directed, sustained, and stopped (Donnelly, Gibson and Ivancevich, 1995). Therefore, equity theory does not say much about what specific things motivate people, which is a major concern of content theories. The first approach to the rise of shareholder activism compensates for the lack of motivation content by borrowing from agency theory.

Agency theory

In agency theory, a firm is viewed as a nexus of contracts (Fama and Jensen, 1983), in which shareholders are principals and managers are agents taking actions on the principals' behalf. In this principal–agent contract, managers agree that they will provide their resources (including their time and managerial talents) in exchange for the pre-determined payoff so that shareholders can use the managers to satisfy the interests of shareholders. At the same time, shareholders bear both the residual risk (which means "the risk of the difference between stochastic inflows of resources and promised payments to agents" (Fama and Jensen, 1983: p. 302)) and the rights to net cash flows. In this sense the shareholders are the residual claimants and residual risk bearers. Being residual claimants and risk bearers, shareholders are sensitive to managerial decisions which may affect current and future net cash flows. Based on these behavioral assumptions, the first approach seeks to demonstrate whether unsatisfactory levels of financial performance causes shareholder activism.

Investigation methods

Studies taking the first approach may be divided on their approach to three methodological questions: (1) what indicator should be used to gauge managerial impacts on net cash flows? (2) what is the comparable (or reference) group? and (3) how we can test the impacts of the indicators on the rise of shareholder activism?

Indicators of financial performance

The most frequently used indicator in the first approach is an 'abnormal return'. Finance theory says that a company's stock prices encapsulate implications of managerial decisions on net cash flows quite visibly (Fama and Jensen, 1983). Stock prices are determined by two forces: (1) overall market conditions and (2) events particular to the firm (Fabozzi, Modigliani and Ferri, 1994). If a firm's shareholders beat the market and earn a certain amount of stock returns, the earnings are not due to market-wide influences (which yield 'normal' returns) but company-specific 'events' (and thus 'abnormal') (Fama, Jensen and Roll, 1969; Brown and Warner, 1980). In the same context, the first approach assumes that a company must have exhibited negative abnormal returns for a certain period before shareholders of the company realized that their managers had performed less well than those in other comparable firms.

Using financial market data, an event study measures the impact of a firm-specific event on the value of the firm.[1] While there is no universally accepted procedure, there is a general flow of analysis. The first step of an event study is to define the event of interest (e.g., proposing a shareholder resolution to a target firm) and to identify the period over which the security prices of the firms involved in this event will be examined (the 'event window'). It is customary to define the event window to be longer than the specific period of interest. Longer periods will ensure that all the effects are captured, but, on the other hand, the estimate is subject to more noise in the data. The next step is to calculate a predicted (or normal) return for each day in the event period for each firm. The normal return represents "the return that would be expected if no event took place" (Weston, Chung and Siu, 1998: p. 93). There are many models of calculating the normal return. The market-adjusted return method is one of the simplest. In this method, the normal return for a firm for a day in the event period is simply the return on the market index for that day. For most cases, other methods yield similar results. Given the selection of a normal performance model, the estimation window needs to be defined. Next the residual, or abnormal return, is calculated for each day for each firm. The abnormal return is the actual return for that day for the firm minus the predicted normal return. This is the part of the return which is not predicted and is therefore an estimate of the change in firm value on that day, which is caused by the firm-specific event. For each day in the event window the abnormal returns are averaged across the firms to produce the average abnormal return (AR) for that day. The reason for calculating AR is that stock returns are noisy, but the noise tends to cancel out when averaged across a large number of firms. The final step is to cumulate the AR for each day over the entire event period to produce the cumulative average return (CAR). The CAR represents the average total effect of the event across all firms over a specified time interval. Figure 2.1 shows Weston, Chung and Siu's (1998) graphical presentation of how the CAR of the target companies changed in the events of three major mergers in the US oil industry in the 1980s with the $[-40, 40]$ event window.

One may wonder how an event study could explain the rise of shareholder activism, given that its major aim is to measure the 'impact' of a firm-specific event (e.g., a shareholder resolution to the firm) on the value of the firm. The first approach has consisted of two major strands: studies of 'motivation' and of 'effect' (Gillan and Starks, 1998; Karpoff, 1998). Although an event study better fits the second research concern, the inference process of the first approach follows a more or less symmetric scheme as illustrated in Figure 2.2.

To give a causal explanation is usually to specify some prior event, condition, or state of affairs without which the event in question would not

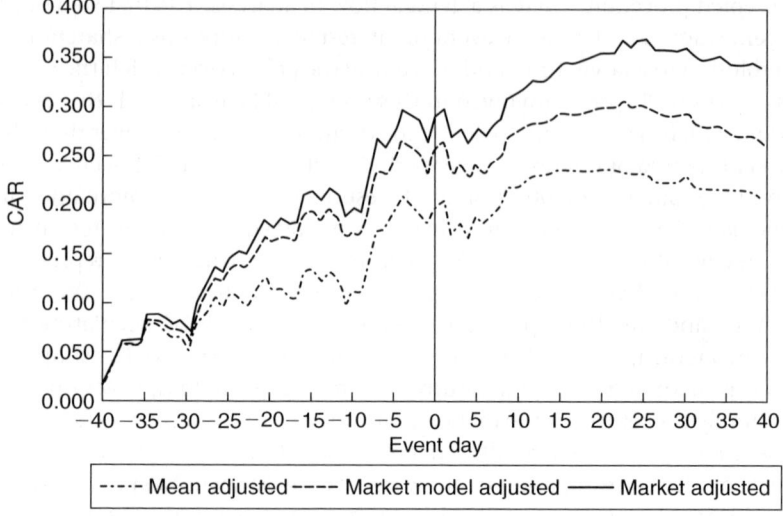

Figure 2.1 CAR for target companies
Source: Weston, Chung and Siu (1998), p. 100.

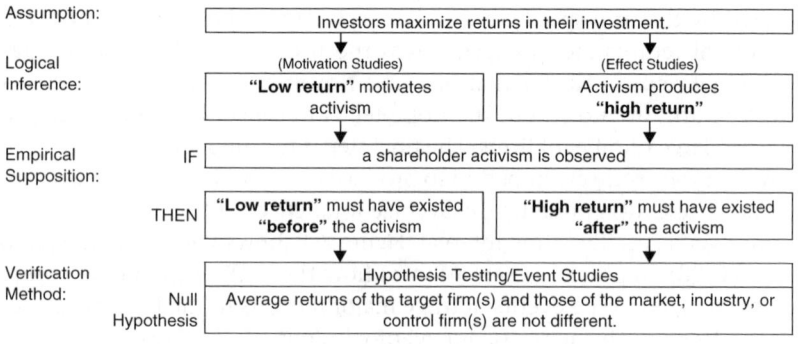

Figure 2.2 Inference in the first approach

have occurred (Marshall, 1994). If we can usually observe a significantly lower level of firm-specific abnormal returns before the occurrence of shareholder activism, then we can infer that financial underperformance causes shareholder activism.

Other financial performance indicators which the first approach studies employ vary from market-to-book ratio (Karpoff, Malatesta, and Walkling, 1996; Smith, 1996; Strickland, Wiles and Zenner, 1996; Johnson and

Shackell, 1997) to operating income (Johnson and Shackell, 1997; Bizjak and Marquette, 1998), sales (Karpoff, Malatesta, and Walkling, 1996; Johnson and Shackell, 1997), return on assets (Strickland, Wiles and Zenner, 1996) and return on equity (Strickland, Wiles and Zenner, 1996).

Comparable groups

To which group should the target firms be compared? Previous studies use three groups: (1) the stock market, (2) the industry to which the target firms belong and (3) control firms which the researchers deem to be comparable to target firms.

The use of abnormal returns is directly linked to the choice of a comparable group. The abnormal return for a given stock in a time period is defined as the difference between its actual *ex post* return and that which is predicted *ex ante* under a model generating 'normal' returns (Brown and Warner, 1980). Shareholder activism studies use three models to calculate the expected *ex ante* returns. In the market-adjusted return method, the predicted return for a firm for a day is simply the return on the market index for that day (Weston, Chung and Siu, 1998). For this purpose, Smith (1996) and Strickland, Wiles and Zenner (1996) use the value-weighted index of the Center for Research in Security Prices (CRSP). To obtain the industry-adjusted returns, Strickland, Wiles and Zenner (1996) define them as the target firm's holding period return minus the equally weighted average return of all firms on CRSP with the same three-digit code of Standard Industrial Classification (SIC) as the target firm. In the control-firm-adjusted return method, firm size measured variously is a major point of comparison. Karpoff, Malatesta, and Walkling (1996) choose a control firm with market capitalization closest to that of the target firm from among firms which receive no shareholder proposals during the sample period. Johnson and Shackell (1997) select firms for comparison which received no proposals during the sample period, but had a market value of common equity closest to that of targeted firms and were within the same four-digit SIC code as the target firms. Bizjak and Marquette (1998) identify a set of control firms matched by size and industry and with shareholder rights plans.

The first approach uses similar comparison groups when it compares other financial indicators, as will be discussed below.

Testing methods

Previous studies rely on two methods to test the impacts of performance indicators on the rise of shareholder activism.

The first method is univariate comparison, which looks at differences in a single performance indicator (for example, abnormal returns) between the two groups – the target firms and a comparable group which has not experienced shareholder activism. In the case of abnormal returns, this comparison involves a statistical testing to infer, with a certain level of confidence, that the abnormal returns calculated according to the abovementioned methods (that is, market-, industry-, and control-adjusted) are significantly different from zero. For other indicators, this comparison implies a statistical testing of a null hypothesis that the differences between the two groups' indicators are equal to zero.

The second method is to estimate regressions to uncover the effects of firm performance indicators on the probability of the firm's undergoing shareholder activism. The dependent variable in these regressions has a value of one for the targeted firms and zero for the other comparable firms (Karpoff, Malatesta and Walkling, 1996). This method can be either univariate or multivariate (which estimates the effects of various performance indicators at the same time). The sign, magnitude, and statistical significance of the coefficients of independent variables tell us how individual variables influence the probability of receiving shareholder activism.

Research results

Univariate comparisons

Smith (1996) measures five-year market-adjusted abnormal returns of 51 firms targeted by the CalPERS from 1987 to 93. He uncovers that the median abnormal returns of the target firms are significantly negative. Strickland, Wiles and Zenner (1996) study the market performance of 85 firms targeted between 1990 and 1993 by the USA, a US organization primarily composed of small individual investors. They conclude that USA targeted firms underperformed the market "by about 8% in each of the two years preceding their listing on the *Target 50*" (Strickland, Wiles and Zenner, 1996: p. 326).

Unlike the results from the market-adjusted returns, Strickland, Wiles and Zenner (1996) find that the USA targets performed about as well as the industry. However, they also argue that USA targets underperformed the industry "by about 8% over the two years prior to listing" (Strickland, Wiles and Zenner, 1996: p. 326) if cumulative industry-adjusted returns are considered.

Bizjak and Marquette (1998) find that 116 companies receiving shareholder proposals between 1987 and 1993 tend to have slightly abnormal market performance prior to the shareholder proposal compared to matched firms. In their study of 269 companies receiving shareholder proposals during the 1987–1990 proxy seasons, Karpoff, Malatesta and Walkling (1996) observe that the target firms have relatively low prior cumulative abnormal stock returns compared to control firms.

Univariate comparisons of other financial performance indicators were less conclusive. Wahal (1996) reports that firms targeted by pension funds underperformed their industries from two years before targeting in terms of the ratio of operating income to total assets and the net income divided by total assets. Karpoff, Malatesta and Walkling (1996) also describe that, compared to control firms, the target firms have relatively low market-to-book ratios, operating returns on sales and recent sales growth rate. Contrarily, Strickland, Wiles and Zenner (1996) conclude that return on equity and return on assets for USA targets do not differ from industry averages. They stated that the mean market-to-book value of equity ratio of the *Target 50* firms is smaller than the industry mean, but not significantly so. Johnson and Shackell (1997) find that there is no difference in the market-to-book ratios of the two groups of firms. Bizjak and Marquette (1998) report that growth rate in operating income is substantially lower for target firms but that the level of operating income scaled by total assets for the three years prior to the shareholder proposal is similar between the two groups. Table 2.1 summarizes the results from the univariate comparisons.

Table 2.1 Results from single variable comparisons

Indicator	Stock returns			Others		
Reference groups	Market	Industry	Control firm	Market	Industry	Control firm
Smith (1996)	●					
Strickland, Wiles and Zenner (1996)	●	●/○			○	
Wahal (1996)					●	
Bizjak and Marquette (1998)		●				●/○
Karpoff, Malatesta and Walking (1996)		●				●
Johnson and Shackell (1997)						○

Note: ● The targets' performance was significantly lower than that of comparable firms.
○ The targets' performance was not significantly lower than that of comparable firms.

Probability model

Results from probability regressions are mostly unconvincing. Karpoff, Malatesta and Walkling (1996) say "The market-to-book ratio, operating return on sales, and recent sales growth all are negatively and significantly related to the likelihood of receiving a proposal. The coefficient for the prior three years' cumulative abnormal stock return, however, is not statistically significant" (p. 375). Johnson and Shackell (1997) report that the sales growth variable has negative sign but that neither of the two measures of profitability (return on sales and abnormal returns) is associated with the proposal filing decision. Smith (1996) finds the coefficient for abnormal return statistically insignificant and suggests that prior performance is not a significant factor in target selection. He also concludes that the market-to-book ratio is negatively related to the probability of being targeted but is not significant. Bizjak and Marquette (1998) report that neither abnormal return nor operating income is a significant factor in the targeting decision. Table 2.2 summarizes the results from probability regressions.

Table 2.2 Results from probability regressions

Indicator	Stock returns			Others
Reference groups	Market	Industry	Control firm	
Smith (1996)	☐			☐
Bizjak and Marquette (1998)		☐		☐
Karpoff, Malatesta and Walking (1996)		☐		■
Johnson and Shackell (1997)		☐		■/☐

Note: ■ The performance indicator was significantly and negatively associated with the probability of activism.
☐ The performance indicator was not significantly associated with the probability of activism.

Further thoughts

The causal explanation sought by the first approach is understood as an attempt to achieve scientific analytical rigor. However, instead of addressing the 'perceived' inequality as suggested by equity theory, this approach focuses on the inequality of 'objective measurable' conditions such as abnormal returns. This raises two questions as to whether the methods used in the first approach are valid to understand the perceived inequality, especially when the findings are mixed as reviewed above.

First, opinions diverge regarding shareholders' time horizon. How long should low returns persist before shareholders refuse to accept them? The differences in the researchers' interpretations taking the first approach are reflected in the differences in what they regard as the appropriate event period in their motivation studies. The periods chosen ranged from six months to five years.

Second, there is an issue of the comparison or referent group. It is usually assumed that shareholders evaluate returns in relative rather than in absolute terms. Do shareholders really look at the three reference groups to decide that their investment returns are unfairly low? Although many authors have preferred market average, some have presumed that shareholders would consider performance in the particular industry to which the target firm belongs or that of control firms as a yardstick.

Some scholars argue that the inconclusiveness of the first approach may not be due to the problem of its research design but to its behavioral assumption of value maximization. Romano (1993) and Murphy and Van Nuys (1994), for example, observe that public institutional investors ultimately are subject to political control and sometimes pursue objectives other than value maximization. Romano (1993) argues that public pension funds are subject to pressures to take politically popular actions that may harm the funds' investment performance. Murphy and Van Nuys (1994) maintain that public pension funds are run by individuals who do not have the proper incentives to maximize fund value. Moreover, if we are to take seriously the recent upsurge of activism by non-institutional investors such as trade unions and to expand the scope of the study to this area as discussed in Chapter 1, it would be much more difficult to base the first approach on the value-maximization assumption of agency theory.

Lastly, the first approach fails to provide specific methods for restoring equity. Even if shareholders perceive the inequality measured in the first approach exactly and their goal is to maximize stock returns, a significantly low level of company-specific financial performance is simply "the first [but not the final] link in the chain of events" (Donnelly, Gibson and Ivancevich, 1995: p. 315) leading to shareholder activism. The existence of an unsatisfactory condition does not always lead to a particular type of corrective action (in our case, shareholder activism). Shareholder activism occurs only when shareholders undergo a unsatisfactory situation (the main concern of the first approach) and, at the same time, they try to improve the situation by means of activism. The second approach to the occurrence of shareholder activism starts with this criticism.

3
Explaining Activism (2): Determinants of Choice

Apart from a situation shareholders may regard as being unsatisfactory or unfair, the second approach addresses why activists finally choose the option of activism to ameliorate the problematic situation. A question, therefore, would be under what conditions activism prevails over other corrective actions (Hirschman, 1970). Based on collective action theory and expected utility theory, the second approach investigates factors which make dissident shareholders favor activism.

Theoretical backgrounds

Hirschman's exit and voice

According to Hirschman (1970), shareholder dissatisfaction can be expressed in two forms. Firstly, some shareholders may sell their stocks in the firm and terminate their relationship with the firm as shareholder. This is the exit option. Alternatively, the firm's shareholders may express their dissatisfaction directly to management or to another authority to which management is subordinate or attentive. This is the voice option. Here takeovers can be seen as an extreme type of the voice option. A successful takeover attempt gives the dissenting shareholders complete control over the company and thus, unlike activism, it changes the nature of the shareholders' relationship with the company (Gillan and Starks, 1998; Rho, 2006; see also Chapter 1).

Traditionally, it is believed that shareholder activism is less economical than other disciplinary measures (Milgrom and Roberts, 1992). When waging shareholder activism, a shareholder has to rely on costly legal, accounting, and consulting services. An activist shareholder also has to search for sympathetic fellow shareholders and persuade them into activism. For many theorists, therefore, more efficient disciplinary mechanisms are: (1) the capital markets (Rozeff, 1982; Easterbrook, 1984); and (2) the external market for corporate control or takeovers (Manne, 1965; Shleifer and Vishny, 1986). In explaining the rise of shareholder activism, theorists must address the question of how and why a dissenting shareholder should prefer activism to other disciplinary measures that seem to be more efficient or effective.

Collective action theory

Collective action theory (Olson, 1965) points out that, for two reasons, a rational individual would not engage in a collective action such as shareholder activism which furthers the overall interest of the group to which he/she belongs. First, it is extremely unlikely that a small number of individuals' action would change the current situation to improve the group's welfare as a whole. Second, if individuals in the group really do share their common interest as a public good, the resulting furtherance of the interest will automatically benefit all individuals in the group, regardless of whether they bear the costs of collective action or not. Therefore, a rational individual will tend to 'free-ride' on someone else's efforts rather than lead a collective action. Hirschman (1970) also maintains that the presence of the exit option can sharply reduce the probability that the voice option will be taken up widely and effectively and thus voice is likely to play an important role in organizations where exit is virtually ruled out. He presents two reasons why the exit option is usually preferred, as will be explained in relation with expected utility theory below.

Expected utility theory

Scholars taking the second approach draw on expected utility theory to explain why a shareholder chooses the less preferable option of activism. Expected utility theory (von Neumann and Morgenstern, 1953) says that in an uncertain situation, a rational actor will take an action which maximizes his/her expected utility. Expected utility has three components: (1) benefits that an actor can obtain if the action succeeds; (2) probability of such success; and (3) costs of action. It equals the probability of success times the benefits from success minus the costs of action. Expected utility theory explains why an actor generally prefers the exit option. Hirschman (1970) argues that the results of the exit option are more foreseeable than those of the voice option and that this fact positively affects the expected utility of the exit option. Therefore, we can infer that dissenting shareholders, if they are rational, will choose activism only when the expected utility of activism exceeds that of other alternatives (including the exit and other voice options such as takeover) (Black, 1990; Admati, Pfleiderer and Zechner, 1994; Smith, 1996).

Determinants of activism choice

Scholars have outlined several factors which may change the expected utility structure of possible actions, mostly based on institutional investors' activism. These factors can be divided into two groups: 'push factors' and 'pull factors'. Push factors make other measures less feasible than direct voice and thus 'push' dissenting shareholders into activism. As will be explained below, the increasing tendency towards indexing investment and large shareholdings makes the exit option difficult. Anti-takeover measures, at both the corporate and state level, make it hard for dissenting shareholders to select the takeover option. Pull factors are those making shareholder activism more workable than other alternatives. Here we will introduce three pull factors: (1) activists' large shareholdings; (2) large shareholdings of other institutional investors; and (3) regulatory changes which encourage the shareholders to take activism.

Push factors

Indexing investment

It is widely believed that an indexing investment strategy by public pension funds imposes a severe constraint on their exit option – selling shares in underperforming firms (Monks and Minow, 1991; Wahal, 1996; Carleton, Nelson, and Weisbach, 1998; Gillan and Starks, 1998, 2000; Karpoff, 1998; Del Guercio and Hawkins, 1999).

Modern portfolio theory states that, in a price-efficient market, the 'market portfolio', which refers to a portfolio of financial assets with characteristics similar to those of a portfolio consisting of the entire market, offers the highest level of return per unit of risk (Fabozzi, Modigliani and Ferri, 1994). According to this theory, investors should hold shares mimicking the composition of a market index such as Standard & Poor's 500 Common Stock Index (S&P 500) in order to generate the level of returns achieved by the index. This passive investment strategy is called 'indexing'.

In the 1980s, US entities which had established and sponsored pension plans became increasingly aware that their money managers were unable to outperform the stock market. As a consequence, the amount of funds managed by means of an 'indexing investment strategy' has grown substantially. Greenwich Associates estimates that about 30 percent of institutionally managed assets in the US were indexed throughout the 1990s (Malkiel and Radisich, 2001). An indexing policy, however, precludes institutional portfolio managers from following the traditional 'Wall Street Rule', which advises investors to vote for the management or to sell their shares. Since the market portfolio prohibits pension fund managers from selling shares of underperforming firms, fund managers must either accept the corporate governance systems of such firms as they are or attempt to change them somehow (Carleton, Nelson and Weisbach, 1998). As a result, activist efforts to prod firms into better performance have become an important way of challenging underperforming firms (Monks and Minow, 1991).

Activists' large shareholdings

Even for pension funds which do not take an indexing investment strategy, it is not easy to sell shares in underperforming firms.

The shareholdings of institutional investors have become larger in US equity markets. These holdings grew from 24.2 percent in 1980 to just under 50 percent in 1994 (Sias and Starks, 1998 cited in Gillan and Starks, 2000). Given their increasing dominance in the equity markets, it is perhaps not surprising that institutions have become more active in their role as shareholders.

Institutional investors' block holdings may be so large that they cannot sell their shares without driving the price down and suffering further losses (Gillan and Starks, 2000). Empirical studies suggest that large block trades by institutional investors affect stock value greatly (Kraus and Stoll, 1972; Holthausen, Leftwich and Mayers, 1987, 1990; Brown and Brooke, 1993; Chan and Lakonishok, 1993, 1995; Keim and Madhavan, 1996). For example, Kraus and Stoll (1972) and Holthausen, Leftwich and Mayers (1987) document that large block trades have a substantial price impact relative to the prior day's closing price in excess of one percent.

Anti-takeover measures

In the United States of the 1980s, firm- and state-level anti-takeover provisions were widely adopted. Various corporate practices were spawned as boards and the managers sought to defend their firms and themselves against attempted hostile takeovers. To take a representative example of such anti-takeover measures, 'poison pills' are designed to give the existing shareholders a right to acquire shares at a greatly reduced price in the event of a control change. In effect, this dilutes the shares held by the acquirers (Milgrom and Roberts, 1992). From the government's side,

40 states in the United States passed anti-takeover laws in the late 1980s and early 1990s, almost all at the behest of managers of local businesses seeking protection from hostile takeovers (Roe, 1994).

Leaving aside the question as to whether these measures have in fact suppressed takeover activities, it is true that takeovers actually decreased in the United States of the late 1980s and that the growth of shareholder activism coincided with the demise of the 1980s hostile takeover market. From this observation, it is argued that the demise of the takeover market turns the 'market-based model' of corporate governance (i.e., takeovers) into a 'politics-based model' (i.e., shareholder activism) (Pound, 1992a; 1992b).

Pull factors

Activists' large shareholdings

It is understood that activists' large shareholdings work both as a push and as a pull factor. A pull-factor explanation is that the presence of a large minority shareholder provides a partial solution to the free-rider problem. A large enough stake and thus a large enough return on a large shareholder's own shares suffice to cover high monitoring costs (Shleifer and Vishny, 1986). As a shareholder's stake increases, the shareholder is willing to take independent monitoring and research and to pay for a higher probability of finding an improvement. Therefore, Shleifer and Vishny (1986) continue, when a method of influencing the incumbent management (such as jawboning or takeover) is available, the market value of a firm rises with the firm's shares initially held by a single risk-neutral large shareholder, unaffiliated with management.

On top of this, large shareholdings reduce monitoring costs (such as proposal preparation and communication cost) since some monitoring issues cut across a number of firms in which institutional shareholders hold shares (Black, 1990). By offering the same proposal at these firms simultaneously, an activist shareholder can reduce costs per firm. Furthermore, if we take into account the widespread indexing investment among institutional investors, other institutions' shareholdings are most likely to overlap with those of the activist, which also reduces the activist's costs of communications per firm. In other words, economies of scale and scope lead a large shareholder to become more active and to make more proposals than an individual who owns the same amount of shares in a single firm.

Other institutions' shareholdings

Shleifer and Vishny (1986) ague that like an individual large shareholder, a group of several large shareholders acting together have an increased incentive to monitor and influence the firm. As the group's stake increases, they are willing to pay for a higher probability of finding an improvement and the market value of a firm rises with the sum of the firm's shares held by the group. They also argue that the presence of a large shareholder is also likely to provide an incentive for outsiders to monitor and evaluate the performance of the incumbent management.

Regulatory changes

It is argued that the institutional shareholder activism of the 1990s was related to relaxed regulations (Hawthorne, 1993). For example, until 1992 in the United States, shareholders were required to file and distribute a proxy statement with the SEC when they were communicating in writing or orally with ten or more shareholders. The 1992 abolishment of this policy allowed shareholders to communicate and coordinate their activities with less laborious regulatory oversight. The SEC also eliminated its provision that it should review materials distributed to shareholders by activist shareholders (such as advertisements and letters) in advance.

Sometimes regulatory changes directly forced shareholders or their trustees to become more active. For example, the US Department of Labor demands that 'fiduciaries' as defined by the Employee Retirement Income Security Act (ERISA) should treat voting rights as a plan asset (Gillan and Starks, 1998). This requires that the pension plan vote its shares, instead of abstaining, and does so for the exclusive benefits of plan beneficiaries. On 29 July 1994, the Department of Labor reaffirmed this position in its *Interpretative Bulletin* (IB 94-2), which calls for proxy vote decisions to enhance the value of the shares and active monitoring and communication with corporate management. The *Bulletin* states that ". . . active monitoring and communication with corporate management is consistent with a fiduciary's obligations under ERISA where the responsible fiduciary concludes that there is a reasonable chance that such activities . . . are likely to enhance the value of the plan's involvement, after taking into account the costs involved" (cited in Gillan and Starkes, 1998).

To cite a UK example, the Cadbury Report called upon institutional investors to make positive use of their voting rights and to disclose voting policies (Lannoo, 1999).

Investigation results

Indexing investment

A challenge regarding indexing investment is that we do not have a generally accepted measurement method or data of the extent to which an investor adopts an indexing strategy. Wahal (1996) estimates the percentages of the indexed equity portfolio in seven major activist institutional investors and concludes that, with the exception of the State of Wisconsin Investment Board (SWIB), the total equity holdings of the six pension funds are heavily indexed (Table 3.1).

In this study, however, Wahal does not explain how the percentages were obtained. Gillan and Starks (2000) argues that equity turnover reflects the level of indexing. They claim that the New York Retirement funds and CalPERS, heavily indexed pension funds, have annual turnover in their equity holdings of approximately 7 percent and 10 percent respectively. Johnson and Shackell (1998) measure the presence of indexed investors in a firm with the firm's membership in S&P 500 because an indexed fund tends to have a higher proportion of stock in S&P 500 firms.

Another question is the level to which we can say that a fund is heavily indexed and shows behavior that is expected from an indexed fund. Carleton, Nelson and Weisbach (1998) say that the Teachers Insurance and Annuity Association: College Retirement Equities Fund (TIAA-CREF) is one of the leading index funds with approximately 80 percent of its stock account's domestic portfolio indexed. This figure is much higher than Wahal's estimates of New York and California pension funds. Nevertheless, Del Guercio and Hawkins (1999) doubt whether TIAA-CREF behaves more like the indexed funds or more like SWIB, given that the fund is largely indexed but also devotes a significant dollar amount (16 percent of its portfolio) to active management. However, Del Guercio and Hawkins (1999) report that the New York and California pension funds, with a much lower level of indexing than TIAA-CREF, show typical index fund behavior (less changes in target holdings for example).

The relationships between indexing investment and a propensity for activism are as yet empirically inconclusive. In a survey of the 40 largest pension funds, 40 largest investment managers, and 20 largest charitable

Table 3.1 Percentages of the indexed equity portfolio, US

Institutional investors	Percentages
New York State Common Retirement System (NYSCR)	67
California State Teachers Retirement System (Calstrs)	66
Florida State Board of Administration (FSBA)	60
California Public Employee Retirement System (CalPERS)	53
Colorado Public Employee Retirement System (Colpera)	33
State of Wisconsin Investment Board (SWIB)	8

Source: Wahal (1996).

foundations, Useem, Bowman, Myatt and Irvine (1993) find that some index fund managers are highly active while others engaged in no activism (cited in Gillan and Starks, 1998). Johnson and Shackell (1998) argue that indexed institutions are less willing to vote against management and prefer quieter forms of activism ('behind closed doors' dialogue with management) than public antagonism such as the proposal mechanism. Del Guercio and Hawkins (1999) show that a major difference between indexed and non-indexed funds is not the 'level' of activism but the 'issue' of activism and that this difference results from the fact that an indexed fund cannot bear the high costs of company-specific activism. According to them, a heavily indexed fund pursues activism tactics aimed at 'spill-over effects' that boost the performance of the stock market overall rather than that of specific stocks. In contrast, proposals sponsored by TIAA-CREF and SWIB are not associated with general governance-related issues but company-specific changes. In their interviews, Kurt Schacht at SWIB states that "SWIB has always had a focus on anti-takeover issues" (Del Guercio and Hawkins, 1999: p. 306) while John Lukomnik of NYC fund replies that they do not sponsor poison-pill proposals because they "require too much company-specific knowledge" (ibid.: pp. 305–6).

Large shareholdings

In order to investigate an impact of the level of TIAA-CREF's shareholdings on their targeting decision, Carleton, Nelson and Weisbach (1998) estimate logistic regressions which compare the differences between firms targeted by TIAA-CREF and a sample matched by the market value of equity and the two-digit SIC code. The effect of the fractional ownership of TIAA-CREF is positive, but statistically insignificant. They explain that the lack of significance might be due to TIAA-CREF's indexing investment policy. Since the majority of TIAA-CREF's portfolio is indexed, there is likely to be very little variability in the ownership of TIAA-CREF and hence lower explanatory power.

Most studies (Karpoff, Malatesta and Walkling, 1996; Smith, 1996; Strickland, Wiles and Zenner, 1996; Bizjak and Marquette, 1998) find a positive relationship between the aggregate level of institutional ownership and the probability of activism. Johnson and Shackell (1998), on the other hand, report a negative association between the probability of receiving a shareholder proposal and the percentage of shares held by institutions.

Carleton, Nelson and Weisbach (1998) test a hypothesis that the specific distribution of institutional ownership is more relevant in target selection than the overall level of institutional ownership. To this end, they include the fractional ownership of TIAA-CREF, the fractional ownership of other 'activist' institutions, as defined by Wahal (1996), the fractional ownership of 'non-activist' institutions and insider ownership. Their analysis shows that TIAA-CREF is more likely to target larger firms with high levels of institutional ownership. However, once overall institutional ownership is controlled, TIAA-CREF's own holdings and those of other 'activist' institutions do not affect the targeting decision. Therefore, they fail to support the view that the distribution of institutional ownership is more important than the level of institutional ownership.

Further thoughts

In the two approaches to shareholder activism in Chapters 2 and 3 it has been generally assumed that decision-makers are rational and can match means and ends to bring about the best decision for their interests. Furthermore, these two approaches think of groups or organizations as though they were monolithic homogeneous rational entities which can be understood in terms of individual rationality. The main questions in this 'rational unitary actor model (Allison, 1971)' are: What is the main problem? What are the alternatives? What are their costs and benefits? What are the underlying values and beliefs? (Kleindorfer, Kunreuther and Schoemaker, 1993). As we have seen, the two approaches center on some of these questions. The first, considering the existence of a problematic situation, is concerned with the main problem and the underlying values and beliefs, while the second, considering on the determinants of action choice, is concerned with the alternatives and their costs and benefits.

However, as Simon (1997) points out, even an individual decision-maker who is regarded as maintaining a fully rational facility for decision-making as envisaged in the unitary rational actor model has a limited information-processing ability. This 'bounded rationality' has a fundamental impact on how an individual makes a choice. Because of information overload it would be difficult for a decision-maker to specify a comprehensive meaningful set of goals and objectives. Individuals often examine alternatives sequentially and locally until an acceptable 'satisficing' alternative is found rather than making complete global comparisons between them.

The decision-making process in a group or an organization is also understood as rather simplistic, reactive and local (Cyert and March,

1963). For example, only after a problem has clearly been viewed as serious by key people in an organization might solutions be sought. The 'political model' of group decision-making (Allison, 1971) emphasizes the divergence between individual and group goals. It especially highlights that, in addition to their formal positions, people are part of informal networks and coalitions, and that organizational rationality may not always prevail because of hidden agendas. Actions are part of a portfolio of decisions and their outcomes, and are influenced by the relative power positions of the group participants. In this sense, the main questions of the political decision-making model are: Who are the key players? What are their aims? What pressures exist on the decision-makers? What are the constraints? What coalitions exist? Where do individual and organizational goals diverge? (Kleindorfer, Kunreuther and Schoemaker, 1993). Based on social movement theory, the third approach to shareholder activism focuses on this political aspect of decision-making.

4
Explaining Activism (3): Politics and Interpretations

Since social movement theory is concerned with the origin and development of various types of collective action, it can provide a useful analytical tool for exploring the emergence of shareholder activism. Why collective action arises is the "*sine qua non* of the study of social movement" (Jenkins 1983a: p. 530). Furthermore, compared to the short history of shareholder activism studies, social movement theory has evolved over more than forty years into a well-developed body of knowledge, both theoretical and empirical.

In the corporate governance literature, attention has already been paid to the usefulness of social movement theory for explaining the emergence of shareholder activism. Noting that "[rationality-based] efficiency-oriented approaches [of the existing studies of shareholder activism] . . . are limited in their ability to explain . . . the rise of shareholder activism" (p. 141), Davis and Thompson (1994) suggest that the study of shareholder activism considers the framework developed in social movement theory. Rowley and Moldoveanu (2003) use social movement and social identity theories to construct a more general model of stakeholder group action and challenge the current notion that interests drive stakeholder group action.

Theoretical backgrounds: social movement theory

Social movement theory is not a single consistent theory. It comprises a set of various theories such as grievance theory (Gusfield, 1968; Tilly, 1978; Opp, 1988), resource mobilization theory (Jenkins and Perrow, 1977; Jenkins, 1983a; Zald and McCarthy, 1987), political process theory (Eisinger, 1973; McAdam, 1982; Tarrow, 1989) and symbolic theory (Snow, Rochford, Worden and Benford, 1986; Snow and Benford, 1988). Even these sub-theories have variants. However, McAdam, McCarthy and Zald (1996a) observe that recent developments in social movement theory have converged around three concepts: (1) political opportunity; (2) mobilizing structure; and (3) framing process. According to this view, most social movements are set in motion by social changes which render the established order more vulnerable or receptive to challenge. These political opportunities, however, are only a prerequisite of social movements. In the absence of adequate mobilizing structures, whether formal or informal, such opportunities are not likely to be seized. Finally, framing process, the emergent meanings and definitions shared by the movement adherents, mediates between the structural requirements of political opportunity and organization and makes a real action happen. It is activists or movement entrepreneurs which facilitate framing and structural mediation.

Therefore this chapter discusses four points of social movement theory which can be usefully employed for studies of shareholder activism. These are: (1) key actors; (2) political opportunities; (3) resource mobilization; and (4) the framing process.

Key actors

As discussed above, collective action theory (Olson, 1965) says that since a rational actor would not become involved in a collective action, the occurrence of a collective action could be irrational. This theory states that if we are to find any rationality in a collective action, it would be a 'selective incentive', which is not directly related to the enhancement of the common good. According to Olson (1965), the enhancement of the common good is a 'by-product' of groups organized for some other purpose.

In the same vein, social movement theory has examined the role of 'movement entrepreneurs' (Anheier, 2003). The level of participation in a collective action varies among participants: from the professional full-time officers through the hard-core activists to the rank-and-file members and fellow sympathizers from the public (Gusfield, 1970). The presence of activists or movement entrepreneurs is the 'active component' which facilitates the other three elements of social movements. In order to maximize the number of members, and the movement's influence and success, movement entrepreneurs take a leading role in mobilizing resources, connecting groups, forging cognitive cultural understanding, and capitalizing on political opportunities within and outside the movement (Gerhards and Rucht, 1992 cited in Anheier, 2003).

This implies that more weight should be placed in the small group of core actors instead of the whole group when we choose a unit of analysis in studying shareholder activism. This does not suggest an elitist approach to shareholder activism, but for a fuller understanding of why certain issues do or do not achieve political salience, we need to study the activities and influence of agenda setters.

Political opportunity

Scholars have long recognized the importance of socio-political context in shaping the emergence, development and ultimate impact of collective action. Peter Eisinger (1973) used the concept of 'political opportunity structure' to explain the likeliness of riots in US cities. According to him, "such factors as the nature of the chief executive, the mode of aldermanic election, the distribution of social skills and status and the degree of social disintegration, taken individually or collectively, serve in various ways to obstruct or facilitate citizen activity in pursuit of political goals" (p. 11).

In the US it was the work of theorists such as Charles Tilly (1978), Doug McAdam (1982) and Sidney Tarrow (1989) which firmly established the link between institutionalized politics and social movements (McAdam, McCarthy and Zald 1996a). In his work on black insurgency, Doug McAdam (1982) explains that "any event or broad social process that serves to undermine the calculations on which the political establishment is structured occasions a shift in political opportunities" (p. 41). Meyer and Staggenborg (1996), therefore, argue that "[o]f critical importance here is the recognition that movement development, tactics and impact are profoundly affected by a shifting constellation of factors exogenous to the movement itself" (p. 1633). Drawing on these works, a number of European scholars (e.g., Kriesi, 1989) brought to the study of collective action a comparative contextual dimension which explains the differential outcomes of social movements across nations.

In an attempt to bring more analytic clarity to the concept, various authors have sought to specify what they see as the relevant dimensions of a given system's 'structure of political opportunities' (McAdam, 1996). As shown in Table 4.1, we can distinguish two types of political opportunities: (1) the 'formal' institutional or legal structure of a given political system; and (2) the more 'informal' structure of power relations which characterize the system at a given point in time.

Resource mobilization

It is argued that interest intensity by itself is insufficient because resources are required to organize group members for collective action (McCarthy and Zald, 1977). Recognizing the importance of various resources in collective action, social movement theory investigates the range of necessary resources and the ways in which such resources are deployed.

Table 4.1 Two types of political opportunities

	Formal structure	Informal structure
Brockett (1991)	• Meaningful access points	• Presence of allies • Elite fragmentation and conflict
Kriesi et al. (1992)	• Formal institutional structure	• Informal procedures in relation to a given challenge • The configuration of power as regards a given challenger
Tarrow (1994)	• Openness or closure of the polity	• Stability of political alignments • Presence/absence of elite allies • Divisions within the elite
Rucht (1996)	• Access to the party system	• The alliance structure as regards a given challenger • The conflict structure as regards a given challenger

Source: Adopted from McAdam (1996), p. 27.

Mobilization is a process by which a group secures collective control over the resources needed for collective action (Jenkins 1983a). Here the term 'resource' takes on a wide array of meanings, including economic resources, ideologies, rhetoric and symbols. Little agreement has been reached on what types of resources are significant. Instead of identifying significant resources, some scholars have offered useful classificatory schemes of social movement resources. In order to maintain itself, the leading group of collective action requires 'internal resources'. The leading group also needs 'external resources' if it is to have its desired influence on a target group. Rogers (1974) has named the former as 'infra-resources' and the latter as 'instrumental resources'. Similarly, Jenkins (1983a) has distinguished 'mobilizing resources' from 'power resources'.

In broader terms, social movement scholars suggest three levels of mobilization: macro-, meso- and micro-mobilization. Here our discussion will focus on 'meso-mobilization', a structural channel through which leading groups, supporting groups and the society at large communicate. ('Macro-mobilization' refers to changes in power relationships and political opportunity structures which facilitate collective action. 'Micro-mobilization' is a cultural interaction between potential resource providers and the leading group. These two types of mobilization are related to the notions of political opportunity and symbolic interactions, which are discussed in other parts of this chapter).

Meso-mobilization takes various types of structure. At one end of the spectrum are informal relationships such as families and networks of friends. There is a structure that is more organized than the informal relationships but still have other primary goals than social movement *per se* (e.g., prayer groups, study groups and sports teams). Another common form is a free-standing protest campaign committee which links networks and organizations together in order to coordinate events and efforts. There are formally organized dedicated mobilizing structures which can be termed social movement organizations (SMOs).

Framing process

Among the recent developments in social movement theory, one of the most important concerns is the cultural aspect of collective action. While the range of analytical perspectives applied is wide, the so-called 'framing' perspective is dominating current research (Johnston and Klandermans, 1995; McAdam, McCarthy and Zald, 1996b; McAdam, Tarrow and Tilly, 1997).

David Snow and his colleagues (Snow et al., 1986; Snow and Benford, 1988) applied Erving Goffman's concept of framing to their study of social movements. According to Goffman (1974), the frame denotes the 'schemata of interpretation' which enable individuals to locate, perceive, identify and label occurrences within their life space and the world at large. Frames build up events or occurrences in accordance with the principles of organization which govern social events and our subjective involvement in them, and enable us to legitimize our action, whether individual or collective. Like other socialized actors, movement supporters act on the basis of internalized values and sentiments as well as calculations of self-interest.

A major task in micro-mobilization between the social movement leaders and participants, then, is to generate solidarity and moral commitment to the broad collectivities in whose name movements act. Snow et al. (1986) argue that 'frame alignment' is a necessary condition for movement participation. According to them, frame alignment refers to the linkage of interpretative orientations between individual participants and the aim of collective action, such that some set of individual interests, values and beliefs and collective activities, goals and ideologies are congruent and complementary.

Successful framing in mobilizing collective action was said to have three elements: diagnostic, prognostic and motivational framing (Wilson, 1973; Snow and Benford, 1988). 'Diagnostic' framing involves the identification of a problem and the attribution of blame and causality. 'Prognostic' framing involves a proposed solution to the diagnosed problem. 'Motivational' framing involves a call to arms for engaging in ameliorative or corrective action.

In social movement theory, it has been argued that frames, the emergent meanings and definitions shared by the movement adherents, play a crucial role in movement breakout. In this sense, McAdam, McCarthy and Zald (1996a) argued that "the impetus to [collective] action is as much a cultural construction as it is a function of structural vulnerability" (p. 8). Although traditional explanations of social movements emphasize sudden increases in short-term grievances (Gusfield, 1968), contemporary scholars counter-argue that grievances are secondary to the emergence of collective action and can be 'manufactured' by the mobilizing efforts of movement entrepreneurs (Jenkins, 1983b).

Investigation results

Key actors

Taking for granted that shareholders are key participants and decision makers in shareholder activism, the existing studies have paid little attention to the question of who is involved in shareholder activism and to what extent (Rho, 2006). The framework of the existing studies has only two components: (1) the problem the shareholders face, and (2) possible remedies they can use to solve it.

A very limited number of studies address the 'actor' aspect of shareholder activism. Marens (2002) criticizes accounts of the history of shareholder activism for giving the early 'gadflies', individual shareholder activists, less attention than they deserve. He demonstrates entrepreneurial roles of early gadflies such as careful strategizing in the media, networking with like-minded investors, and arguing for and defending shareholder rights at the SEC and in court. In another study of union financial activism, Marens (2004) argues that some unionists followed the examples of previous social movement entrepreneurs who had expanded the law and practices of shareholder activism.

Political opportunity

In some aspects, the second approach reviewed in Chapter 3 has similarities with the explanation of political opportunity structure. According to the second approach, factors external to shareholder activism (i.e., indexing investment strategy, anti-takeover measures, large shareholdings and regulatory changes) encourage shareholder activism. However, the discussion of socio-political context in social movement theory points out that the political opportunity structure goes beyond the discussions made by the second approach and varies according to the action under study. Political opportunities may relate to government structure, public policy, general social settings, or power relations between organized allies and opponents, but they do not have any predetermined set which can be applied to all types of collective action universally. We should, therefore, identify what types of political opportunities have worked for the emergence of particular cases of shareholder activism, case by case. The factors suggested by the second approach do not have general applicability to all shareholder activism. Furthermore, although the second approach considers certain outcomes of power relations in terms of regulatory change, it does not explicitly address power relations between shareholder activists and others, which are an important element of political opportunity structure.

Ryan and Schneider (2003) recognize three conditions that affect the relationship between institutional investors and their portfolio firms, which are (1) the institutions' market power; (2) the complex role of financial intermediaries; and (3) possible involvement in simultaneous and opposing agency contracts. Based on these findings, they propose a new agency relationship.

Davis and Kim (forthcoming) report that the magnitude of mutual funds' business ties with their portfolio firms affects funds' proxy votes at specific firms and overall voting practices. They argue that funds' business ties and their propensity to vote with management have a positive relationship because the votes take place when the funds know their votes will be publicly scrutinized.

Davis and Thompson (1994) and Thompson and Davis (1997) show how activist shareholders increased their influence in corporate governance in the early 1990s through the changing capacities of shareholders and managers to act on their interests in control at the firm, state and federal level. These two studies also argue that pro-market and pro-shareholder attitudes of the Reagan administration fostered the group identity of shareholders.

Resource mobilization

One of the most important mobilizing structures in shareholder activism is various mediating groups such as the USA (Rho, 2006). In most cases shareholders and various mediating groups interact constantly throughout the course of shareholder activism. Although shareholders have authority to make a key decision, mediating groups filter and reconstruct the raw data to produce information critical to shareholder activism.

Opler and Sokobin (1995) study the CII representing pension funds. Beginning in 1991, CII has provided a list of poorly performing firms to its members and some of the members have often targeted the listed firms. Strickland, Wiles and Zenner (1996) describe the USA as a conduit through which small shareholders unite and attempt to influence the governance of large US corporations. They suggest that USA-sponsored shareholder activism enhanced shareholder value. Black and Coffee (1994) describe the role of UK trade associations such as the ABI and the NAPF as a communication channel for their members' collection action.

In a more general study of stakeholder activism, Rowley and Moldoveanu (2003) propose that overlapping memberships across multiple stakeholder groups affect stakeholder group action.

Framing process

We do not have many studies which look at the framing process of shareholder activism directly. Rho (2002) shows how the PSPD, now a well-known Korean pioneer and leader in shareholder activism, combined the two different frames which had developed separately in the past to legitimize their shareholder activism.

Some management scholars focus on the level of shared meanings as significant elements in how organizations function (e.g., Alvesson, 1998; Strati, 1998). Although sparse, a few studies have showed how important culture is in the corporate governance area. Hirsch (1986) examine the process of the normative framing of hostile takeovers. According to him, this framing facilitates the diffusion and legitimization of hostile takeovers and helps to recreate or sustain order despite the disruptions engendered by takeovers. Zajac and Westphal (1995) argue that CEO compensation is driven by symbolic as well as substantive considerations. On a more general level, Rowley and Moldoveanu (2003) argue that mobilization can be motivated by a desire to express a social identity as well as protect interests.

Part II
An Application: the Korean PSPD Case

5
Political Opportunity

In Chapter 4, we have distinguished two types of political opportunities: (1) the 'formal' institutional or legal structure; and (2) the more 'informal' structure of power relations. We will look at these two types of political opportunities for the PSPD shareholder activism.

Formal opportunity: government policy

Until the mid-1990s, the Korean government had not challenged the corporate governance structure of the *chaebol*.[1] Indeed, the government had protected the current management by suppressing potential activism by stakeholders such as employees, consumers and shareholders against the *chaebol*. It had mostly been concerned with the economic results attained by the *chaebol* (e.g., exports and foreign currency earnings) no matter what governance structure they might have had. In January 1997, however, as a part of the so-called 'New *Chaebol* Policy', the Korean government amended the Securities and Exchange Act (hereinafter called "the Securities Act") for the first time since its enactment in 1962, to lower the requirements for minority shareholder rights. This regulatory change influenced the emergence of PSPD shareholder activism in various ways. This section describes how this change happened.

Corporate governance reforms in Korea

The corporate governance structure of the *chaebol* was first discussed from the perspective of competitiveness. In November 1994, on his way back from the 1994 Asia Pacific Economic Co-operation (APEC) Summit, President Kim Young Sam (1993–1998) declared *Segehwa* as the nation's goal (*Segehwa* roughly means complying with international standards and being a first-class nation in the world). It was a big task for the Korean policymakers to transform this vague idea into concrete policies. For this task, a committee was formed under the auspices of the Prime Minister in January 1995 and many scholars were invited to produce reports for *Segehwa* strategy in their own fields.

In economic terms, *Segehwa* was understood as acquiring global competitiveness. The committee asked Chung Kwang Sun,[2] a finance professor at Chung-Ang University, to write a report on how to achieve *Segehwa* by way of corporate governance reform. Chung's unpublished *Segehwa* report contained many suggestions, including introducing outside directors, allowing institutional investors to vote on behalf of their trustees and lowering the legal requirements of minority shareholder rights.

On hearing these suggestions, business organizations such as the Federation of Korean Industries (FKI), the Korea Chamber of Commerce and Industry (KCCI), and the Korea Listed Companies Association (KLCA) started presenting a very negative view of them (Kim, H., 1995), and in the end their opposition thwarted even the less sensitive issues such as minority shareholder rights from being put on the public policy agenda.

However, in January 1995 the Office of Securities Supervision (OSS), the then regulatory body of the securities market, highlighted the possibility of checking controlling shareholders by using minority shareholder rights. Its amended regulations obliged a corporation to obtain approval from a shareholders' general meeting when disposing of or donating cash or equities worth more than 10 percent of the paid-in capital. This amendment aimed to prevent the arbitrary use of corporate assets by dominant shareholders for their selfish purposes. In their press release, the OSS cited, as an example of dominant shareholders' selfishness, Dong Ah Engineering and Construction's decision to donate a replacement bridge following a scandal involving a collapse of a bridge it had constructed (Yim, K.-J., 1995).[3]

In November 1995, an event occurred that overcame the business opposition to corporate governance reform and moved the hesitant government into action. A rumor that former president Roh Tae Woo (1988–1993) had accumulated a secret fund up to 400 billion won (US$ 333 million) turned out to be true. He was tried and jailed for bribery. Although corruption had been believed to be prevalent in Korea, this was still shocking, for the former head of the government and several top businessmen (e.g., Lee Kun Hee of Samsung) were prosecuted or even jailed. It was said that the day of Roh's jailing was the day that the establishment collapsed (Kim, Y.-B., 1995). For this event, the FKI, an association of the *chaebol*, publicly apologized to the nation and the Prime Minister promised to prepare a fundamental policy to uproot corruption and illegitimate government–business collusion.

Responding to growing social demands for corporate governance reform, the government finally publicized its new position, the so-called 'New *Chaebol* Policy', in May 1996. The government announced a strengthening of disclosure, auditing and minority shareholder rights. As a result, in January 1997, the Securities Act was amended to lower the requirements for minority shareholder rights. It was the first time since the enactment of 1962 that the government had loosened the requirements. In contrast to their previous attitude, the Korean government has lowered the requirements further a few times since then, as illustrated in Table 5.1.

Chaebol policy before corporate governance reforms

Since the government's view on the *chaebol* had a great influence on that of Korea society as a whole, including civil activists such as the PSPD, it needs to be examined in great detail. Citing the oldest issue first, *chaebol* policy has been concerned with four major issues: (1) ownership concentration (and succession); (2) diversification; (3) inter-affiliate supports that enable

Table 5.1 Shareholding requirements for minority shareholder rights

Rights	Date of Effectuation			
		1.4.1998	25.5.1998	28.3.2001
• To call an extraordinary general meeting (EGM) (§191–13④)	3% (1.5%)	Not changed	Not changed	Not changed
• To demand a cumulative voting[4] (§191–18)	—	—	—	1%
• To review accounting books (§191–13③)	3% (1.5%)	1% (0.5%)	Not changed	0.1% (0.05%)
• To propose dismissal of directors or internal auditors (§191–13②)	1% (0.5%)	0.5% (0.25%)	Not changed	Not changed
• To file an injunction against directors' allegedly illegal action (§191–13②)	1% (0.5%)	0.5% (0.25%)	Not changed	0.05% (0.025%)
• To bring a derivative suit (§191–13①)	1% (0.5%)	0.05%	0.01%	Not changed

Source: Securities Act (amended on 28 March 2001).
Note: The requirements in the parentheses apply to the shareholders of a corporation with capital of 100 billion won (US$ 83 million) and above.

the *chaebol* to maintain their structure; and (4) corporate management swayed by the *chongsu* and his family. This section addresses the first three issues, for the previous section has covered the last issue already.

Ownership concentration and succession

It was in the early 1960s that the government first raised the issue of ownership concentration. Since the funds for industrialization were in chronic shortage at that time, the government pressed the founding families of the *chaebol* to sell their shares and to finance their businesses in the domestic capital market. For example, the First Five-Year Economic Development Plan (1962–66) tried to procure about 25 percent of the total funds for the industrialization plan from domestic savings (KDI, 1995). The stock market was thought of as an important channel for this fund-raising (O, 1996). For this purpose, the government prepared relevant legal statutes such as the Securities Act of 1962 (BOK, 1993).

For fear that outsiders might meddle in their businesses, however, the founding families tended to hold on to their shares. The government believed that this tendency prevented the businesses from procuring funds in the stock market and made the financial structures of the businesses too highly leveraged. This financial fragility, in turn, was perceived as a burden on the whole national economy.

The first measures for dispersing ownership were legal coercion and financial sanctions. The Capital Market Furtherance Act of 1968 provided preferential treatment to public corporations in taxation. In 1972, right after the 8.3 Measure,[5] the Public Corporation Inducement Act was enacted to enable more drastic measures than before. According to this Act, corporations that had benefited from 100 million won or more from publicly raised funds were designated as to-be-public corporations. Examples of publicly raised funds were foreign debts, write-offs by the 8.3 Measure, and bank loans. Failure to go public cost the target corporations disadvantages in tax and bank loans (BOK, 1993).

In the 1980s, it was argued that "only by popularizing going public among the *chaebol* companies, can ownership concentration be lessened" (Lee and Lee, 1990: p. 114). The solution was to lead as many people as possible, including employees, to the stock market (Lee and Lee, 1985). Accordingly, the government tried to boost demand for stocks. In 1987, in order to revitalize the Employee Stock Ownership Associations (ESOAs), the government amended the Capital Market Furtherance Act and provided them with more detailed legal status.[6]

In the 1990s, the government drew attention to another problem of ownership concentration. According to this view, concentrated ownership and owner-dominated management suppress the rise of professional managers (EPB, 1993). Some in policy circles believed that the professionally managed firm represented a more evolved management system than the owner-managed firm (e.g., MOTIE, 1997). For enhanced corporate competitiveness, therefore, ownership dispersion was seen as important because it allowed salaried professional managers more managerial power (FTC, 1994).

It was difficult, however, for the governments of the 1990s, which, unlike their authoritarian predecessors, were more democratically accountable, to 'induce' the *chaebol* families to concede their shares to others. The best that governments could do was to exempt the *chaebol* companies with more dispersed ownership from existing regulations. For example, the 1994 amendment of the Monopoly Regulation and Fair Trade Act (hereinafter called "the Monopoly Act") excluded companies with more dispersed ownership from the 40 percent ceiling of total equity investments in other companies. A further detail of this regulation will be discussed in relation to 'intra-group support' below.

The Korean government evaluates the degree of ownership concentration in the *chaebol* in terms of 'internal ownership'. The internal ownership is measured by the shareholdings owned by the founding family and relatives and those owned by other affiliates in the group. Generally speaking, the internal ownership of the 30 biggest *chaebol* has gradually decreased. To be specific, family ownership has constantly decreased, while the shares owned by affiliates remained relatively constant throughout the 1990s. After the 1997 crisis, however, affiliates of the *chaebol* increased share ownership in the process of restructuring the *chaebol* groups, which in turn increased the total internal ownership (See Table 5.2 and Figure 5.1).

Compared to concentration of ownership, ownership succession had not been a central concern of the government. This issue was, however, addressed in the 1990s from two perspectives: (1) facilitating ownership dispersion; and (2) establishing just taxation.

Although the government in the 1990s could not directly intervene in the ownership transfer, they believed that strict application of the Inheritance Tax and Gift Tax Act would make it more difficult to transfer concentrated ownership from the *chongsu* of the present generation to that of the next. Some policy advisors argued that stricter tax administration was the most essential and fundamental measure for ownership dispersion (Lee and Lee, 1985; Lee and Lee, 1990). The government also predicted that, when inheritance and gift taxes were implemented as appropriate, the *chongsu* family's shareholdings would naturally diminish because of the growing demand for external funds (EPB, 1993).

Table 5.2 Internal ownership of the 30 biggest *chaebol*, 1983–1999

	1983	1987	1989	1990	1991	1992	1993	1994	1995	1996	1997	1998	1999
Total	57.2	56.2	47.2	45.4	46.9	46.1	43.4	42.7	43.3	44.1	43.0	44.5	50.6
Family	17.2	15.8	14.7	13.7	13.9	12.6	10.3	9.7	10.5	10.3	8.5	7.9	5.4
Affiliates	40.0	40.4	32.5	31.7	33.0	33.5	33.1	33.0	32.8	33.8	34.5	36.6	45.2

Sources: MOFE and KDI (1997); OECD (1998a); FTC (1999).

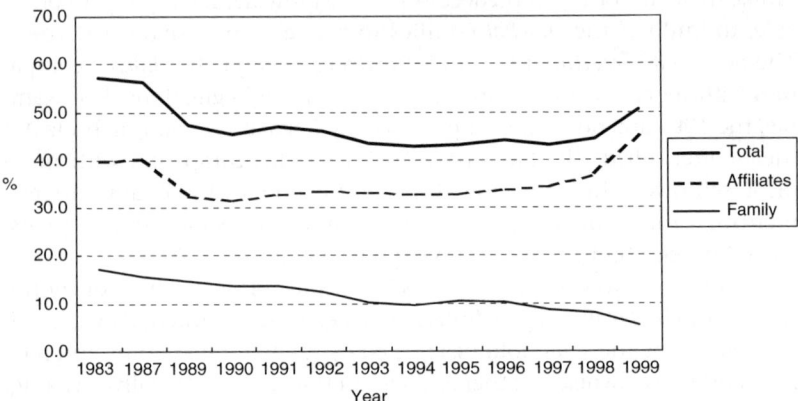

Figure 5.1 Internal ownership of the 30 biggest *chaebol*, 1983–1999
Sources: MOFE and KDI (1997); OECD (1998a); FTC (1999).

Strict implementation of the Inheritance Tax and Gift Tax Act was also consistent with the public sentiment of justice because it regulated "inheritance of wealth without taxation" (Korean Government, 1993). It was pointed out that the relative ineffectiveness of the existing tax system in dispersing *chaebol* ownership did not lie in the tax system itself but in its administration, with key problems being the inaccurate identification of tax sources and the lack of administrative will to levy taxes (Yoo, 1992).

Figure 5.2 shows the chairmanship succession in the four biggest *chaebol*. Notably the 1990s witnessed many changes in chairmanship, compared to previous periods. Whatever the reason, these frequent changes in chairmanship were certainly remarkable enough to intensify public attention to the issue of *chaebol* succession.

Diversification

At the early stage, the problem of diversification, like that of ownership concentration, was linked with the financial fragility of the corporation.

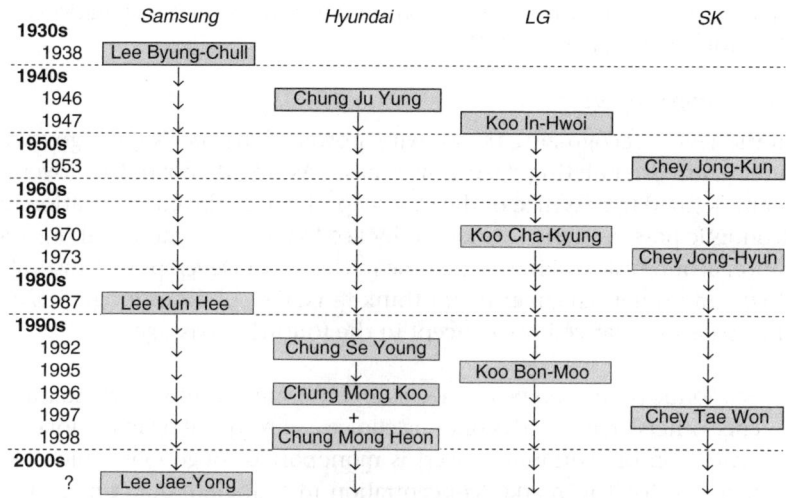

Figure 5.2 Succession to the chairmanship in the four biggest *chaebol*

In 1974, for example, the government announced a policy suppressing diversification, arguing that diversification without appropriate financial capability would make the national economy unstable (KDI, 1995). The *chaebol*'s growth in the 1970s was quite explosive in terms of the number of affiliates. The number of affiliates of the 30 largest *chaebol* increased from 126 in 1970 to 429 in 1979 (Yoo, 1997).

Like other responses in the 1970s, the early response of the government to diversification was coercive. The government required the *chaebol* with shaky financial structures to submit plans to dispose of inessential affiliates. The government also prohibited the *chaebol* from establishing or acquiring new businesses (KDI, 1995). In the 1980s, partly as a measure of reducing concentration of economic power and partly of discouraging diversification, the government designated certain industries as being allowable only to small- and medium-sized enterprises and forbade the *chaebol* from entering such industries.

In the 1990s, diversification was linked with competitiveness. It was believed that scarce resources should be concentrated on businesses with competitive advantage. The so-called 'specialization policy' was introduced in 1991 to induce the *chaebol* to refrain from excessive diversification and concentrate their investment resources into their core businesses. The basic policy measures were exemptions from the existing *chaebol* regulations such as the credit control system and equity investment regulations in the Monopoly Act (Yoo, 1997).

Intra-group support

In the 1980s, recognizing the growing power of the *chaebol*, the government started regulating their power base. As noted above, the government defined the essence of the *chaebol* problem as the concentration of economic power, a term introduced by Lee Kyu Uck, an industrial organization economist working at the time in the Korea Development Institute (KDI), an influential government think-tank. One of his monographs on this issue summarized the concept in the following passage:

> Economic power can be defined as an economic agent's power to influence others' free-willed economic choice. . . . A typical structure [of concentration of economic power] is monopoly or oligopoly, which can manifest itself in market concentration in a single product market or industrial concentration in a single industry. Occasionally, however, concentration of economic power can be general concentration, which means that a few top companies hold great importance in the whole economy or other larger sector [than an industry] (e.g., the manufacturing sector). . . . In Korea, there have emerged business groups . . . called the *chaebol* as a kernel of concentrated economic power and they not only comprise but also transcend the three types of concentration [that the authors have mentioned above]. (Lee and Lee 1990: p. 17)

Anti-*chaebol* scholars have generally accepted this idea (e.g., Kang, Choi and Chang 1991). In Korea, raising concerns about concentration of economic power has been frequently used as a way of attacking the *chaebol* without mentioning them.

The government identified three methods by which the *chaebol* maintained and multiplied its concentrated economic power. These were: (1) equity investment, (2) mutual loan guarantees, and (3) in-group transaction. To regulate these behaviors, the Monopoly Act was first amended in 1986.

Recognizing that cross equity investment between the *chaebol* affiliates was a major way of maintaining the founding family's control over the *chaebol* group, as reported by Lee and Lee (1985), the government decided to regulate four investment-related behaviors of the *chaebol*.[7] First, the Monopoly Act prohibited direct cross-shareholdings between any affiliates of the *chaebol*. This ban was, however, lifted in February 1998 because it was thought to cause reverse discrimination against domestic firms. It was pointed out that, with hostile takeovers fully allowed in the same year, it would be unfair to deprive the *chaebol* of the opportunity to defend themselves. A surge of cross-shareholdings afterwards, however, forced the government to restore the prohibition immediately in 1999. Second, an affiliate of a *chaebol* was not allowed to hold equities worth more than 40 percent of its net assets. The 1994 amendment lowered the ceiling to 25 percent, which became effective in March 1995. Third, a pure holding company was not permitted. However, the 1997 crisis demanded the facilitation of sales of loss-making affiliates, and as a result, this regulation was abolished in 1999. Lastly, the *chaebol*-owned financial institutions such as insurance companies were not allowed to exercise voting rights in relation to affiliate companies.

Mutual loan guarantees refers to the practice of one affiliate's underwriting another's liabilities to financial institutions. This was a widespread practice among Korean firms, and the financial institutions had even demanded this as a condition for loans (Yoo, 1997). It was pointed out that loan guarantees enabled the *chaebol* to grow beyond their capability through excessive debt financing. It was also argued that this practice hindered non-viable affiliates from exiting in a timely manner, and that once the exit happened, chain bankruptcy was more likely, which is obviously a more negative consequence than the bankruptcy of a weak affiliate alone. In 1992, the Monopoly Act was amended to set a ceiling of mutual loan guarantees equivalent to 200 percent of the equity capital of each *chaebol* affiliate. The ceiling was lowered to 100 percent in 1996. Finally, in 1998, the Monopoly Act barred new guarantees and required all existing ones to be settled by March 2000.

In general, any transactions with discriminatory nature have been one of the main concerns of the Monopoly Act since it was enacted in 1980. On top of this, the 1986 amendment provided that preferential transactions within the *chaebol* affiliates should be treated separately in order to suppress the concentration of economic power. Compared to equity investment and loan guarantees, however, the government had paid less practical attention to this practice until it set guidelines for the investigation of in-group preferential transactions in 1992. It was only in 1993 that the Fair Trade Commission (FTC) started investigating in-group transactions as a form of unfair trading. At that time the Monopoly Act covered in-group transactions only in goods and services. In response to the *chaebol*'s intricate practices, the 1996 amendment included transactions in funds, assets and personnel. A new guideline was established in 1997, on the basis of which the FTC launched more comprehensive investigations. In December 1999, the FTC amended the Monopoly Act, which now stipulates that some types of in-group transactions are subject to disclosure and resolution of the board of directors.

Expected roles of the *chaebol*

Underlying the four main issues of *chaebol* policy were three roles that the *chaebol* were expected to assume. First, the government viewed the *chaebol* as an instrument of a social goal, that is, of national prosperity. Second, the government often emphasized that the *chaebol* had an obligation as a beneficiary of national support. Third, especially because their growth owed much to state intervention, the *chaebol* were expected not to exercise their economic power against the interest of social justice. Policies suppressing corporate despotism in the 1990s placed similar restrictions on economic power, but on that of the *chongsu* families that time. Together, these three views produced a socio-political image of the *chaebol*.

Engine of national prosperity

Since the 1960s, the state has assumed the *chaebol* would contribute to industrialization and economic development. In developing countries like Korea, economic development through industrialization *per se* is a public affair in the sense that it is a concern for the whole nation and that the whole nation is often forced to make sacrifices for it. In his book *The Country, the Revolution, and I*, Park Chung Hee, who presided over Korean industrialization from 1961 until 1979, emphasized the importance of utilizing big businesses to achieve national capitalism (Amsden, 1989). In this view, the performance of the *chaebol* was one of the foremost public concerns, but stock return was not the most important measure of their performance. In Korea, exports, foreign currency earnings, and national competitiveness were more important than stock returns.

This view of a corporation as an engine of national prosperity is not unique to Korea. It is also a prominent feature of the corporate governance systems of France and Japan (Charkham, 1994). Generally, corporations have been considered to have two social functions of wealth creation and distribution (Ackoff, 1990), and current corporate governance discussions also emphasize these social roles. For example, the Business Sector Advisory Group on Corporate Governance (1998) reported to the OECD that national economies rely on the corporation to raise capital, create jobs, earn profits and divide the value added among those contributing to its success. The view of the corporation as an engine of national prosperity is, however, much more established in Korea than in countries such as the US or UK.

Prudential trustee of national assets

This view sees the corporation as responsible for repaying society what it owes in return for the social support for its existence and operation. According to this view, a corporation comes into being and continues as a legal entity only with governmental concurrence. It is the legal institutions which grant a corporation its juridical personality, limited liability and perpetual life, and such legal institutions are justified by the state's interest in promoting general welfare (Monks and Minow, 1995).

This view is also ubiquitous in many economies, but Korean society gave more concrete support to the *chaebol* than the above-mentioned institutional support. In effect, the whole nation toiled for the *chaebol*'s prosperity, although the sacrifice was not voluntary but enforced by the authoritarian regimes. In the nation's early development attempts, all available national resources, including the nation's nearly nonexistent financial resources, were effectively bet on a handful of the *chaebol*'s prosperity. The state forced workers to put up with subsistence wages and servile working conditions. If businesses were financially distressed, their losses were made up through indirect taxation such as the inflationary refinancing of non-performing loans or through direct taxation such as expansion of the state equity share of the banks (Woo, 1991).

Right after the 8.3 Measure, the government stated the measure's major beneficiary corporations should go public. It argued that while the 8.3 Measure was intended to ensure stability and growth of the corporations at the sacrifice of national wealth, especially that of many private creditors who had lent in good faith, the corporations who had benefited should repay this sacrifice by going public (KDI, 1995).

In fact the *chaebol* were never nationalized, but the government frequently regarded them as national firms. The Capital Market Furtherance Act of 1968, which provided for the ESOAs, reflected such a tendency. Even in the 1990s, the government would say that the *chaebol* would become national firms in the long run because of a growing demand for external funds and resulting decrease in the *chongsu* family's shareholdings (EPB, 1993).

Restrained exerciser of economic power

This view of the corporate role is related mostly to large corporations, while the previous roles apply to all corporations regardless of size. The view is based on the ideal of democracy. It argues that, as is the case with political power, those who are subject to economic power should be entitled to have a say in the exercise of that power. In this view, the far-reaching decision making powers of a corporation should remain in the public arena (Parkinson, 1993).

This view developed in response to the concentration of economic power. Drawing on Russell (1938) and Galbraith (1984), Lee Kyu Uck first introduced the term "concentration of economic power" to the Korean public policy debates in 1985. Although it was acknowledged that they had made some positive contributions to national welfare, the *chaebol*'s growth was widely thought of as somewhat undesirable from the viewpoint of democracy and social justice as well as from that of efficiency. As Lee explained:

> [Concentration of economic power] may hamper efficiency in resource allocation by inhibiting free competition in a market. Neither does it conform to the democratic principle founded on the holding of power by the many. Resulting in concentration of wealth, it also impairs fairness in distribution. (Lee and Lee, 1985: p. 12)

In the 1990s, this view of the *chaebol*'s responsibility to society was extended to the *chongsu* families who controlled the *chaebol*. Like the *chaebol* group in relation to the economy and society, the *chongsu* families were required not to exercise their economic power over the *chaebol* groups arbitrarily.

Government policy on the *chaebol* has influenced the PSPD's shareholder activism in various ways. For example, it reduced mobilization costs, legitimized PSPD activism and affected PSPD's diagnostic and prognostic framing. We will discuss its influences in relevant parts below.

Informal opportunity: power relations

We can examine the informal political opportunities of power relations with at least three groups – activists, target firms and governments. In the previous section, we have reviewed the government's view on corporate governance and shareholder activism. In relation to this point, we have also introduced the initial opposition from businesses to government policy on shareholder activism and the scandals which have damaged the legitimacy of the businesses' resistance (such as the collapse of Seongsu Bridge and the bribery of the president). This section will, therefore, concentrate on the nature of the civil society organization challenging the *chaebol*.

CCEJ

Until the "Spring of Democratization" in 1987,[8] the Korean government had effectively suppressed social activism against the *chaebol*. Moreover, activism occurring up to that time, if any, had focused on specific interests such as labor conditions or consumer protection and had not addressed the *chaebol* problem *per se*. The first civil society organization to address the *chaebol* problem directly was the Citizens' Coalition for Economic Justice (CCEJ).

Fundamentalist reformists, a leading faction of social activists before the CCEJ, understood the basic problem of Korean society as a class conflict between the people (such as labor and farmers) and monopoly capital and its guardian, the government. Based on this understanding, their immediate task was to establish the government by the people. For them, the primary target of reform was the government, and the *chaebol* issue was secondary. Since monopoly capital exercised its controlling power over the people by way of state power, a people's government which would nationalize the *chaebol* was also thought of as a solution to the problem of *chaebol* power (Lee, S.-H., 1999). As a consequence, in the 1992 presidential campaign, Paik Ki-Wan, who represented these fundamentalist groups, raised dismantling the *chaebol* as an election pledge, but did not present any specific plan for it (*Hankyoreh*, 1992).

In contrast with the previous movements which propagated radical systemic reform in opposition to state power, the CCEJ addressed more down-to-earth issues and sought concrete and tangible reforms. After political power was legitimately transferred through the direct presidential election of 1988, the Korean social movement sector had to abandon its previous attitude of a head-on opposition to the government. In the pre-1988 period, a slogan, 'overthrow the military dictatorship' was the main rallying cry for Korean social movements. However, once political power had gained legitimacy, at least formally, in 1988, this approach was no longer feasible. Participation by the people in the process of government's exercising political power became a more realistic and persuasive cause for democracy.

The CCEJ was a pioneer of Korean social movements in the economic area and adapted itself well to the changed political environment after 1988. Founded in 1989, it had already developed into a unique civil organization covering extensive economic issues, by the time of the PSPD's birth. By and large, the CCEJ accepted the *chaebol* problem which the government had defined. For example, in a book published by the CCEJ to inform the public of its position on the *chaebol*, three CCEJ economists (Kang, Choi and Chang 1991) accepted Lee Kyu Uck's notion with little modification.

Table 5.3 CCEJ activities related to the *chaebol*, 1990–1996

Date			Issues	Statement	Public debate	Petition	Survey	Training	Public rally	Boycott
			General Issues							
90	11	9	*Chaebol* policy in general		✓					
91	2	7	Credit control	✓						
91	3	7	Credit control	✓						
91	5	29	*Chaebol* policy in general		✓					
91	10	18	Inheritance and gift		✓					
92	8	11	Monopoly Act amendment	✓						
92	10	31	Monopoly Act amendment				✓			
93	9	24	Labor's participation					✓		
94	5	2	*Chaebol* policy in general		✓					
94	6	30	*Chaebol* and privatization	✓						
94	8	25	Monopoly Act amendment	✓						
95	11	22	Government–*chaebol* collusion		✓					
96	5	17	*Chaebol* policy in general		✓					
96	8	26	Monopoly Act amendment			✓				
96	9	1	*Chaebol* policy in general	✓						

			Issue						
	10	15	Monopoly Act amendment					✓	
	10	28	Monopoly Act amendment		✓				
			Subtotal	6	7	2	1	0	0
			Specific Issues						
91	3	29	Doosan Group(Pollution)	✓					
91	4	27	Doosan Group(Pollution)	✓					
91	6	1	Sunkyung Group (Unfair trade)		✓				
91	7	8	Hanbo Group (Preferential loans)	✓					
91	10	26	Hankook Explosive Group (Government preference)					✓	
92	7	6	Samsung Group (Diversification)	✓					
92	7	14	Samsung Group (Diversification)		✓				
93	8	20	Sunkyung Group (Diversification)	✓					
93	4	21	Hankook Explosive Group (Diversion)	✓					
	12	7	Samsung Group (Diversification)	✓					
			Subtotal	7	2	0	0	1	1
			Total	13	9	2	1	1	1

Source: CCEJ (www.ccej.or.kr).

A study of the CCEJ's activities regarding the *chaebol* from 1990 to 1996 reveals three characteristics (Table 5.3). First, as mentioned before, the CCEJ activities were mostly focused on problems which the government had raised. Second, the CCEJ's major response to the *chaebol* issues was to demand that the government thoroughly enforce the existing *chaebol* policy. Its concern was mostly with the general policy, not with the specific actions of a particular *chaebol*. Sometimes, the CCEJ attacked the behavior of an individual *chaebol* group, but it was rather exceptional. Third, the measures on which the CCEJ relied against both the government and the *chaebol* were traditional social movement measures such as public statements, debates and petitions.

PSPD

Founded on 10 September 1994, the PSPD is dedicated to promoting participatory democracy and human rights. The PSPD had three founding groups:[9] (1) practicing lawyers; (2) leftwing social theorists; and (3) young social activists (Cho, H.-Y., 1999). Despite their experiences in different social movements prior to the formation of the PSPD, a common need for a pragmatic approach united these groups to establish the PSPD.

Before the PSPD, Park Won-Soon, a lawyer and the current General Secretary of the PSPD, and many other lawyers in the PSPD had been involved in public-interest juridical movements such as Lawyers for a Democratic Society (also known as 'Minbyun'). In establishing the PSPD, these lawyers' basic motive was to expand the scope of their legal activism from defense of the victims of human rights violation to comprehensive social reform (Cho, H.-Y., 1999). At his talk to the PSPD and the public members on 6 November 1999, Park Won-Soon responded to the criticism that the PSPD could not change society fundamentally by saying: "Do we [social activists] have any other [practical] measures [than legal ones in checking the power of the government and large corporations]? I would like to ask them [those who criticize the PSPD for being only moderate reformists] what they have achieved so far."

Leftwing social theorist groups also realized that "no further good was going to come out of the orthodox [Marxist] theory [that they had stuck to]" (PSPD academic *G*, interview on 2 January 2001).[10] For example, Cho Hee-Yeon, a representative figure of this group, organized the Allied Policy Group in 1992 to produce a realistic policy alternative instead of engagement in a hollow theoretical debate (Lee, G.-S., 1992). This group believed they must turn the law from "a tool for dictatorship" into "an instrument for promoting the rights of citizen, labor and the people" in order to make its fight against the establishment more effective (Cho, H.-Y., 1999).

The third group, young social activists, was also inclined to be practical. Having participated in the student movement before joining the PSPD, many members in this group were involved in various forms of social activism, such as the labor movement. Through these experiences, this group became conscious that an unsophisticated demand such as a pay raise did nothing to change the established order. In order to find a way of countering the structural forces of society, they associated, before the PSPD, with groups such as the League of Members of Society for Participatory Democracy. A wish of Kim Ki-Sik, an organizer of the League and current Director of the Policy Office in the PSPD, was "to see a winning civil movement" (Suh Y.-A., 1997).

We can observe that this pragmatic attitude has manifested itself both in terms of the economic issues raised by the PSPD and in terms of the PSPD's actions directed at them. Like the CCEJ, the PSPD adopted the *chaebol* problem as its foremost concern in economic affairs. Rather than a fundamentalist focus on class conflict or systemic revolution, the PSPD preferred to focus on the more practical, *chaebol* problem. The PSPD was sympathetic to the established state view of the *chaebol* problem from the beginning. Six months after its foundation, the PSPD formed a Committee on Concentration of Economic Power, the Participatory Economy Committee (PEC)'s antecedent,[11] to take charge of economic issues. As "concentration of economic power" in the committee's name implies, the PSPD attempted to challenge the *chaebol* as the foremost problem in the Korean economic system. Kim Ki-Won,[12] an economics professor at Korea National Open University and executive member of the PEC, identified four aspects of the *chaebol* problem as follows: (1) ownership concentration and succession; (2) corporate despotism; (3) "octopus-tentacle-like" diversification; and (4) "convoy-style" intra-group supports (Kim, K.-W., 1999). As we have seen, this frame is quite similar to that of the state and of the CCEJ. As a result, the PSPD's activities from 1997 to 1999 were mainly concerned with the four traditional issues of the *chaebol* problem (Table 5.4).

However, the PSPD went further. In addition to focusing on the *chaebol* problem, the PSPD concentrated on specific actions of the *chaebol*, rather than the *chaebol* problem in an abstract sense. Lee Seung-Hee, a full-time PEC officer, evaluated the CCEJ activities as follows:

> The CCEJ should have not only raised the overall problem of the *chaebol* system but also disputed concrete cases in which the *chaebol* problem is manifested in the actions of individual companies. (Lee, S.-H., 1999: p. 412)

Table 5.4 PSPD shareholder activism, 1997–1999

	Date of first action	Company (Companies)	Action in question	Ownership	Diversification	In-group support	Despotism
1	97-06-24	Samsung Electronics	Private offer of CBs (Lee Jae-yong)	✓			
2	97-12-26	SK Telecom	In-group transactions (Daehan Telecom, etc.)	✓		✓	✓
3	98-02-10	Samsung Electronics	In-group transactions (Joong-Ang Ilbo)			✓	✓
4	98-02-11	SK Telecom	In-group transactions (SK Engineering and Construction)			✓	✓
5	98-02-11	SK Telecom	Investment (SK Securities)			✓	✓
6	98-02-11	Samsung Electronics	Gratuitous supports (The Group Secretariat Office)			✓	✓
7	98-02-11	Samsung Electronics	Investment (Samsung Motors)		✓	✓	✓
8	98-03-27	Samsung Electronics Samsung SDI Samsung Electro-Mechanics	Investment/Loan guarantee (Samsung Motors)		✓	✓	✓
9	98-06-03	Samsung Electronics	In-group transactions (Samsung Corporation)			✓	✓
10	98-07-20	SK Group	Investment (SK Telecom)		✓		✓
11	98-08-05	Samsung Electronics	Investment (AST Research)			✓	✓
12	98-08-05	Samsung Electronics	Capital increase		✓	✓	✓
13	98-08-15	Samsung Electronics	Gratuitous supports (Samsung Motors)		✓	✓	✓
14	98-10-20	Samsung Electronics	Investment/Loan guarantee (Lee Chun Electric)			✓	✓
15	98-10-20	Samsung Electronics	In-group transactions (Samsung General Chemicals)			✓	✓

No.	Date	Company	Transaction				
16	98-10-20	Samsung Electronics	In-group transactions (Samsung Corporation, etc.)			✓	✓
17	99-01-14	Hyundai Heavy Industries	Investment (Kia Motors)		✓	✓	✓
18	99-01-14	LG Semiconductor	Investment (Zenith)			✓	✓
19	99-04-09	Hyundai Securities	Investment (Hyundai Electronics)	✓		✓	✓
		Hyundai Heavy Industries					
		Hyundai Merchant Marine					
20	99-05-08	LG Group	Investment (Dacom)		✓		✓
21	99-05-21	Samsung Life Insurance	Capital increase		✓	✓	✓
22	99-06-11	Samsung Life Insurance	Credit loan (Samsung Motors)		✓	✓	✓
23	99-06-22	Samsung SDS	Private offer of BWs (Lee Jae-yong)	✓		✓	✓
24	99-06-24	SK Telecom	Capital increase	✓			✓
25	99-06-30	Samsung Life Insurance	Listing		✓		✓
26	99-08-17	Samsung Electronics	Undertaking of liabilities (Samsung Motors)		✓	✓	✓
27	99-08-23	SK Group	Investment (SK Telecom)	✓			✓
28	99-10-27	Cheil Communications	Investment (Samsung Life Insurance)		✓	✓	✓
		Samsung Fine Chemicals					

The PSPD's actions against specific problematic behaviors of the *chaebol* were also realistic. They opted for a forcible remedy that could bring about a substantial change. To this end, the PSPD utilized the binding force of a juridical decision from the start. For this reason the PSPD movement was viewed as "basically attempts to reform the society through the court" (PSPD academic *G*, interview on 2 January 2001).

A good early example illustrating the PSPD's propensity for legally binding measures was a petition for the Constitutional Court's ruling on the constitutionality of a provision in the Monopoly Act. This petition was filed just a week after the PSPD's foundation. In this petition, the PSPD argued that the provision, which allowed only the FTC to make a complaint against offending companies, unduly restricted the citizens' right to make a complaint against unfair trade.

We can understand that the objectives of this petition were two-pronged. By means of the binding force of the Constitutional Court's ruling, the PSPD tried to force the Executive to abolish the provision of the Monopoly Act. At the same time, the petition also aimed at allowing any interested party such as consumers to make a complaint to the prosecution office, thus facilitating citizens' legal actions against the business. In this way many citizens could have become involved in challenging the unfair practices of the business.

This inborn inclination towards legalistic pragmatism was of great influence when the PSPD conceived and selected their measures for *chaebol* reform. In order to wage legal activism against the *chaebol*, the PSPD searched for a legally interested party to the *chaebol*. PEC officer *E* recalled:

> We looked for a way of dealing with real-life companies. The answer was to become an [legally] interested party to the company, like shareholders, consumers and employees. (Interview on 11 October 1999)

As we will see in Chapter 6, the pragmatic attitude of the PSPD functioned as a magnet throughout the process of its noticing and selecting shareholder activism.

6
Framing Process

In Chapter 4, we have said that framing mobilizing collective action successfully has three elements: (1) identification of a problem and the attribution of blame and causality (diagnostic framing); (2) a proposed solution to the diagnosed problem (prognostic framing); and (3) a call to arms for engaging in corrective action (motivational framing). We will first investigate the pre-existing frames which might be supposed to have impacted on the PSPD's frame. By looking into the past frames, we infer what corporate behavior is expected within each frame and by what remedies each frame force the firm concerned to change its behavior.

Three frames from the past

The past frames can be divided into two different views of the firm: the 'private property' view and the 'social entity' view.[1] As seen in Chapter 5, the social entity view has been dominant for the government and civil activists. They have required the *chaebol* to contribute to national prosperity, to exercise their concentrated economic power in a restrained manner, and to manage prudentially the corporate assets that they saw, given state channeling of subsidized funds into them, as having accumulated at the cost of society as a whole.

To this end, the Korean government has used two main policy measures: (1) credit control and (2) regulation under the Monopoly Act. At an early stage, credit control dominated. In 1961, the government of Park Chung Hee nationalized commercial banks which the previous government of Rhee Syngman (1948–1960) had denationalized some years earlier (Amsden, 1989). This nationalization gave the government tight control over corporate financing. However, progressive deregulation and liberalization of markets which had begun in the 1980s made it difficult for the government to rely on credit control to the extent which it had previously. In 1981, the government introduced the Monopoly Act as a new strong measure of regulating the *chaebol* from the perspective of free competition and anti-trust. Since then, the provisions of the Monopoly Act have been at the centre of the *chaebol* regulation. In the 1990s, the major tools for inducing the *chaebol* to comply with government policy were exemptions from the remaining credit control and the Monopoly Act regulations.

On the other hand, as shown in Chapter 5, civil activists such as the CCEJ have relied on public statements, debates, petitions, and similar remedies.

The third group from whom we can find the past frame is shareholders who have taken to activism in the past. Contrary to the conventional understanding that Korean shareholders were inactive before the PSPD, dissenting minority shareholders have argued, albeit sparsely, since the 1950s that the corporations in which they invested should enhance their financial interests. Their major complaints centered on breaches of the current conventional principles of corporate governance such as the *OECD Principles of Corporate Governance*. For example, arguments made by previous shareholders included such propositions as "[s]hareholders have the right to participate in, and to be sufficiently informed on, decisions concerning fundamental corporate changes" (OECD, 1999: p. 5) or "[a]ll shareholders of the same class should be treated equally" (ibid.: p. 6).

The measures these dissenting shareholders have relied on are: (1) to challenge the validity of the "procedural irregularities" (Boros, 1995) of the corporation concerned; (2) to complain of the corporate insiders' breach of trust or misappropriation to the prosecution office or the court; (3) to demand that the corporation concerned purchase their shares; (4) to claim damages; and (5) to call an extraordinary general meeting to challenge the management.[2]

Figure 6.1 summarizes the assumptions and remedies of the three past frames. How is the PSPD's frame linked to the three frames? Chapter 5 shows that the PSPD shares a concern of the *chaebol* problem from the beginning with the government and the CCEJ. The countermeasures to the *chaebol* problem that the PSPD came up with in those early days were also similar to those considered by the state and the CCEJ. In launching the Committee on Concentration of Economic Power, the PSPD argued that ownership dispersion, employees' participation in management, and the strengthened Monopoly Act regulations were possible countermeasures (PSPD, 1995). In particular, the Monopoly Act was thought to be the most effective measure for limiting the concentration of economic power. PEC academic *A* recollects: "a PEC member [who was influential in the group's opinion] used to say, 'if only the Monopoly Act could be

Framing Process 69

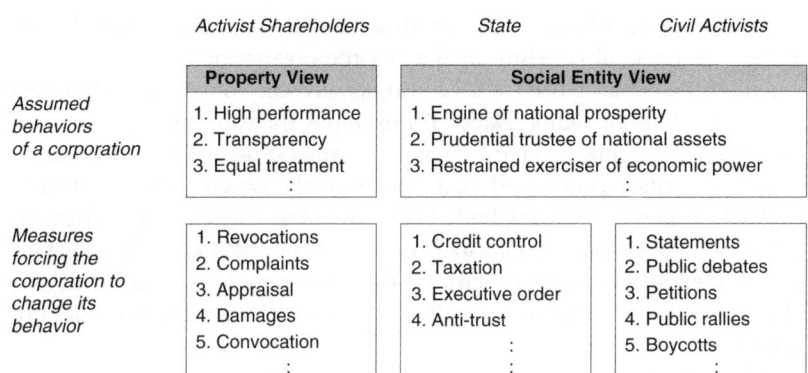

	Activist Shareholders	State	Civil Activists
Assumed behaviors of a corporation	**Property View** 1. High performance 2. Transparency 3. Equal treatment :	**Social Entity View** 1. Engine of national prosperity 2. Prudential trustee of national assets 3. Restrained exerciser of economic power :	
Measures forcing the corporation to change its behavior	1. Revocations 2. Complaints 3. Appraisal 4. Damages 5. Convocation :	1. Credit control 2. Taxation 3. Executive order 4. Anti-trust :	1. Statements 2. Public debates 3. Petitions 4. Public rallies 5. Boycotts :

Figure 6.1 Three past frames

abided by, most *chaebol* problems would be solved'" (Interview on 6 February 2001).

On the other hand, PSPD shareholder activism developed independently of past activist shareholders. The PSPD argues that their activism is different from any previous shareholder activism. They argue that financial self-interest, which is the main motive of previous shareholder activism in Korea, is not the major concern of the PSPD (PEC lawyer C, interview on 11 January 1999; PEC academic D, interview on 23 February 2001). In other words, the PSPD states that purely self-interested return maximization, which the existing studies of shareholder activism envisage, is not their aim. How did the PSPD, sympathetic to the social entity view, cross over to embrace shareholder activism, a remedy developed in the private property view?

Approaching shareholder rights

When prompted to action, people tend to examine only options close to the current solution because this is an easy way of reducing the costs of data collection (Simon, 1997). Several studies (e.g., Kaufman, 1991) illustrate how human decision-makers often get locked in by their experiences to perceiving and/or solving new problems the way they have solved previous problems (Simon, 1997). Seen from this perspective, shareholder activism might not have been an appropriate local solution for the PSPD because it had never been utilized before by any civil society organization in Korea.

We can find at least three sources from which the PSPD became familiar with shareholder activism to some degree.

The first source of the PSPD's attention to shareholders was related to its inclination for legal activism. In shaping the organization, the PSPD drew much on the Public Citizen, a US consumer advocacy organization founded in 1971 by a lawyer, Ralph Nader. For example, the early PSPD bore resemblance to Public Citizen in terms of organizational structure. Both had watchdogs (e.g., Justice Watch and National Assembly Watch in the PSPD and Congress Watch and Global Trade Watch in Public Citizen) and a litigation group (the Public Interest Litigation Center in the PSPD and the Litigation Group in Public Citizen). Furthermore, right after their foundation, the PSPD planned to invite Nader to Korea (PSPD, 1995), although this plan did not materialize.

Although they paid most attention to other parts of the legal activism of Public Citizen (e.g., consumer campaigns), the PSPD also became aware that Ralph Nader, its model leader, was himself a shareholder activist. PSPD academic G, who had greatly contributed to the PSPD's early notion of shareholder activism, recalled a conversation:

> A lawyer [who is leading the PSPD] favored Public Citizen. [So I asked him] "Do you know who Ralph Nader is? He is the one who has risen in the world with Campaign GM in the mid and late 1960s." [He asked me] "What was that?" [I answered] "It was a prototype shareholder activism." . . . [I told him] "Up to now the *chaebol* has been tackled by the National Assembly or the Executive. From now on, tackle them from within, in the shareholders' general meeting." . . . [He responded] "That makes sense!" (Interview on 2 January 2001)

Therefore, through the earlier experience of this organization on which they modeled their activity, some early PSPD members realized that shareholder activism was an important tool for legal activism.

Secondly, the most urgent issue the PSPD needed to address in the early days concerned the *chongsu's* arbitrary decisions on the disposal of corporate assets. As an early member of the PSPD recollected:

> [In early 1995] we [The PSPD] needed to question the perpetrators of the Seongsu Bridge accident [i.e., Dong Ah Engineering and Construction] and Chung Ju Yung [the *de facto chongsu* of Hyundai Group at that time]. [In order to attack the morality of the then ruling party] Chung abruptly disclosed that he had offered a regular bribe to Roh Tae Woo every Chuseok [i.e., Korean Thanksgiving Day] and at the end of every year. (PSPD academic G, interview on 2 January 2001)

As sketched in Chapter 5, it had already been suggested by many events that such arbitrary decisions could be mitigated by shareholder monitoring. For example, the local press viewed Chung Kwang Sun's report *Corporate Competitiveness and Corporate Governance* from this vantage point. *Dong-A Ilbo* (1994)[3] reported that Korean corporations had few mechanisms to block corporate despotism and pointed out that the existing policies, such as ownership dispersion, were of limited use in preventing this. Introducing Chung's report, the newspaper suggested that corporate governance should be reformed to give minority shareholders more power and to block corporate despotism. And the amendment of the OSS regulation in January 1995 showed the possibility of checking corporate despotism with minority shareholder rights.

When the PSPD started focusing in on the *chongsu's* abuse of power, therefore, it was natural that shareholder monitoring should come into their frame.[4] PSPD academic G once proposed to other colleagues as follows:

> Buy some shares of a listed company of Hyundai Group. Then charge them with political donation: "Are you [the management] aware of the responsibilities of big business is in obeying the law?" Right after Seongsu Bridge had collapsed, Dong Ah Engineering and Construction announced that it would rebuild the bridge without delay and donate it to the state. It would cost 16 billion won [US$ 13 million]. [In the shareholders' general meeting, we may press the company with questions such as] "Are you [the management] ransoming Choi Won-suk for 16 billion won [which are corporate assets, not Choi's personal ones]?" (Interview on 2 January 2001)

From this, we can infer that the PSPD conceived several trial frames in which the *chongsu's* arbitrariness such as bribery could be tackled through shareholder activism, although the framing did not lead to actual action. Through these trials, the PSPD could pay more formal attention to shareholder rights right after the Roh's secret funding was revealed. In February 1996, Kim Ki-Won first presented a paper on "Corporate Governance in the *Chaebol* and Participatory Economy" as a part of a PSPD's symposium on participatory democracy (PSPD, 1996).

A third source of the PSPD's increasing attention to shareholder activism was the so-called "New *Chaebol* Policy" announced by the government in May 1996. This policy shifted the *chaebol* policy's focus from mitigating concentration of economic power to reforming corporate governance and empowering minority shareholders. This change implied that the situation was becoming more favorable to shareholder activism. PEC officer *E* described that time as follows:

> Noticing the suggestion for strengthening minority shareholder rights in the KDI's report *Enhancing the Transparency of Corporate Management*, a key document which informed the New *Chaebol* Policy, we formed a team to commence examining what minority shareholder rights are and what sorts of legal precedents have been established in that area. (Interview on 11 October 1999)

Even before this policy was implemented, it reinforced the framing process in the sense that the government authorized the newly emerging frame as above and assured the public that this frame was legitimate. Accordingly, the PSPD's response to this new political opportunity became more positive and formalized than before. They included shareholder rights in their alternative set and started exploring how to use them.

From these observations, we conclude that socio-political contexts provided the PSPD with a clue to utilizing shareholder activism. These contexts include domestic debates on corporate governance reform and resulting government policy. From the PSPD's side, their pragmatic approach made them relatively adaptable to shareholder rights which had been neglected, and avoided, by other social organizations. This approach also made the PSPD more sensitive than other social movement organizations to a series of changes in socio-political contexts which legitimated shareholder activism. We will now investigate how the PSPD finally selected shareholder rights from their newly expanded set of alternative.

Korea First Bank: the first attempt

On 28 January 1997, Hanbo Iron and Steel, an affiliate of the then 14th-largest *chaebol*, went bankrupt. To build a steel complex, Hanbo had borrowed an extravagant five trillion won (US$ 4.2 billion), which was 16 times its own capital. The sheer magnitude of the money involved immediately made the nation associate the case with political corruption: How did the company get banks to lend it so much? Speculation was that Chung Tae Soo, Hanbo Group *chongsu*, bribed bankers and politicians with part of the loans to help him arrange them (Lee, C.S., 1997).

Reflecting this social sentiment, the PSPD described the Hanbo case as "a super-colossal scandal in which the political, business and financial worlds have all been involved" (PSPD's letter to the prosecution office, 13 February 1997: n.p.). Needless to say, corruption was already a major concern of the

PSPD even before the Hanbo case. In 1996, for example, in response to the Roh Tae Woo's secret funding, the PSPD advocated the enactment of what the PSPD called an 'Anti-Corruption Act'. Given this background, it was only natural that the PSPD reacted strongly to the Hanbo case.

The PSPD pondered how to approach this case in their own 'pragmatic' way. PEC lawyer *B* recalled a suggestion of a member who had then just joined the PSPD as follows:

> Hanbo is a typical case of business–politics collusion, but even the punishment of those who are implicated in this particular case, such as members of the National Assembly, ministers, high-ranking officials and businessmen, would not change the situation fundamentally. Judging from past experiences, the bankers will remain unscathed as usual. But it is the bank which mediates between the two [i.e., business and politicians]. How about questioning the bankers about a decision based on political considerations? (Interview on 2 November 1999)

From this statement, we can see that the PSPD's pragmatic approach led to a reinterpretation of the existing frame of business–politics collusion. The PSPD shifted its focus from the big players behind the scandal, whom the past anti-corruption measures had targeted, to those who actually put the collusive relationship into action. This shift was in harmony with the PSPD's legalistic approach. After all corporate misbehaviours are committed following managerial decisions and, in that sense, it is the managers who are legally responsible for the misdemeanors. It was believed that charging them on the basis of their legal responsibility, which was the PSPD's basic stance, would reduce corporate misdemeanors. This interpretation was expressed explicitly in a PSPD's letter to the prosecution office. This letter reads:

> From the legal perspective, it is the presidents of the banks, not the 'black politicians' behind them who should shoulder responsibility [for the excessive loans]. (Emphasis in original. 13 February 1997)

What then would be an appropriate prognostic frame for this new diagnosis? As we discussed earlier, the influence of the *chaebol* over society is so extensive that there exist many interested parties the PSPD can mobilize for their pragmatic approach. Aside from the employees and consumers, many people regarded even the entire nation as a party with a legitimate financial interest in the *chaebol*.

In fact, the measure by which the PSPD first attacked the bankers was not through the rights of shareholders but rather traditional, civil rights such as those of taxpayers. "On behalf of the nation" the PSPD members lodged a charge of breach of trust at the prosecution office against the presidents of the banks which lent money to Hanbo. This action was justified by the fact that, in the end, the whole nation would pay for the burden of the misallocated loans. The PSPD argued as follows:

> The entire nation will sustain ultimate damage [from the Hanbo scandal] because taxes paid by the sweat of an average citizen's brow will be predictably spent on the bankrupt firm [Hanbo Iron and Steel] and related banks via tax benefit and financial aid. (PSPD, 1997)

In order to prove the legal legitimacy of their intervention in the Hanbo case, the PSPD argued that these loans were not only a matter of social justice but also a matter of money in citizens' pockets.

In parallel with general civil rights, minority shareholder rights were also utilized as one of the possible options for punishing corruption. On 7 March 1997, the PSPD took its first shareholder action by attending the annual general meeting of the KFB in order to rebuke the management for irresponsibility. However, we do not find any definite evidence that, when first deciding on shareholder activism, the PSPD fully appreciated the effects which might be caused by this activism. On the contrary, our impression is that the PSPD did not grasp the effectiveness of shareholder activism until they made use of it. A doubt as to whether minority shareholder rights would work well for checking corporate misdemeanors seems to have persisted even after the PSPD decided to use shareholder rights in the KFB case (PEC lawyer B, 2 November 1999; PEC academic D, 23 February 2001; PEC academic H, 10 November 1999). PSPD member G recalled that during the discussion of using shareholder rights he predicted that "It [shareholder activism] will not be so effective, though. It will only draw media attention at best" (interview on 2 January 2001).

Thus seen, the first emergence of the PSPD shareholder activism is explained better by the garbage can model (Cohen, March and Olsen, 1972) than by the rational model on which the existing studies of shareholder activism are premised. The garbage can model highlights the fact that organizational decisions are the results of timely combinations of situation, problem, actor and alternative. However, the application of the garbage can model to the PSPD case does not necessarily lead to a conclusion that we can say only that PSPD shareholder activism emerged purely by accident. What we are emphasizing here is that the actor's pragmatic disposition, the solution's relative advantages and favorable social contexts threw a new element of shareholder activism into the garbage can and rendered a greater cohesive power to the PSPD than to other potential activists who also shared the same problem and socio-political contexts (e.g., the CCEJ).

From a trial to regular use

This section investigates how PSPD shareholder activism transformed itself from a one-off trial to a regular instrument for their movement. Even after a problem-solving action is taken, there is always a possibility of terminating the action once and for all. This termination will happen either when the actor obtains what he/she wants or when the actor realizes that the action is not useful for achieving his/her intended goals.

It would be unlikely for the PSPD to stop using shareholder activism, because it does achieve its goal. If its goal is to uproot the *chaebol* problem, it cannot materialize with a single event of shareholder activism (even though it is very successful as is the case with the KFB). If the *chaebol* problem persists and the PSPD continues to use shareholder activism to tackle it, then we can focus our discussion on the usefulness of shareholder activism to deal with the *chaebol* problem.

The PSPD people witnessed diminishing doubt about the effectiveness of shareholder activism when they actually exercised minority shareholder rights. The trial at the KFB AGM convinced the PSPD members of the power of minority shareholder rights in challenging corporate wrongdoing:

> It was after we attended the 1997 annual general meeting of the KFB that we realized, "Ah! This [minority shareholder rights] has some potential [for pressure on a corporation]". And then, if my memory serves me, we made up our mind to keep it up. (PEC academic *H*, interview on 10 November 1999)

What was the "potential" which the PSPD members noticed? We can identify three levels of advantages that the PSPD may have when it uses shareholder activism: (1) advantages in comparison to other stakeholder action; (2) advantages inherent in shareholder rights; and (3) advantages applicable to the *chaebol* problem.

Advantages over other stakeholder action

From our observations, we can identify four advantages, in comparison to the activism of other legally interested groups such as consumers and employees, which shareholder activism might have had.

First, the PSPD realized that, through shareholder activism, their direct intervention in corporate management could be legitimized legally and socially (PSPD academic G, interview on 2 January 2001). Since the *Segehwa* Committee in 1995, a series of events had popularized the idea that shareholders have, and should have, a say in the company in which they invest. Once this perspective was accepted, it was natural that the PSPD could legitimately intervene in the KFB in its capacity as an agent of some KFB shareholders.[5]

Second, shareholders were more clearly defined and were smaller in size than other interested parties such as consumers or the general public. As PEC officer *E* expressed, "we [the PSPD] knew that a consumer campaign [like that of Public Citizen] was a fundamental approach to affect a company, but consumers were too scattered to mobilize" (interview on 11 October 1999). For the PSPD, with limited physical and human resources, having a definite target group was an important consideration.

Third, a consumer campaign, the obvious alternative to shareholder activism, would inevitably have a limited influence on the *chaebol*, because "a few *chaebol* monopolize the whole national market" (PEC officer *E*, interview on 12 November 1999). This problem was well expressed by Saul Alinsky long ago:

> An economic boycott was rejected because of Kodak's overwhelming domination of the film-negative market. Thus a call for an economic boycott would be asking the American people to stop taking pictures, which obviously would not work as long as babies were being born, children were graduating, having birthday parties, getting married, going on picnics and so forth. (Alinsky, 1971: p. 172)

Lastly, the PSPD had tried not to encroach into the territory of existing social movements. They thought that policy-related activities were the CCEJ's field, on which they abhorred trespassing "on grounds of division of labor among civil organizations" (PEC officer *E*, interview on 11 October 1999). And "[among the candidates for legally interested parties to a company] [e]mployees already had a long tradition of labor movement and relevant organizations" (PEC officer *E*, 11 October 1999). In this sense, the shareholder was seen as a niche for the PSPD.

Advantages inherent to shareholder rights

The PSPD became aware of the great ability of shareholder activism to affect company practices. The potential of shareholder rights to change company policies and practices is the results of four factors.

First, shareholder rights allowed the PSPD to gain access to the inner core of the corporation in question. Shareholder activism was already seen by previous social activists as "a way to gain entrance to the annual stockholders' meeting" (Alinsky, 1971: p. 172). With other traditional methods of pressing the business (such as demonstrations and public statement), the activists were not likely to see the top management of the company concerned face-to-face. On the other hand, a close encounter, based on shareholder rights, with the top management in a general meeting or an informal negotiation gave the activists a better chance to negotiate and to deliberate over necessary actions to move the head of the corporation. Furthermore, shareholders are given the legitimate legal power to access detailed information not accessible to others, such as the shareholder register and accounting books.

Second, shareholder activism was effective in attracting the public attention necessary to amplify the activists' demands.[6] It was through the KFB case that the press first gave attention to the PSPD's activities. Although treated as a passing episode at that time, it was reported that "by way of attending a shareholders' general meeting in its capacity as an agent of some minority shareholders, a civil organization embarked upon a new movement not only to protect minority shareholders' rights and interests but also to improve the transparency of the corporate management" (Suh, S.-B., 1997).

Since then, as Figure 6.2 shows, the PSPD has tried to attract media attention by producing press releases continuously. At the same time, the media has responded to several specific events such as confrontations in

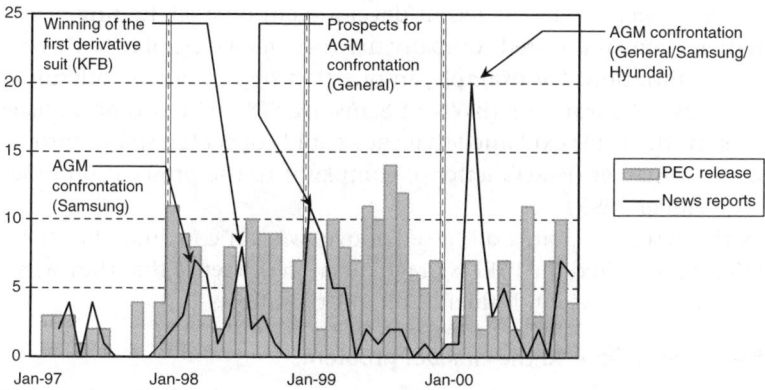

Figure 6.2 Press releases and news reports, 1997–2000

annual general meetings and the first winning of a derivative suit, and the intensity of such media responses has been increasing.

Third, the status of a shareholder as a residual claimant makes it easy to prove the effect of corporate behavior on his/her financial interest. This is a persuasive argument in mobilizing the shareholders, attacking corporate policy and resorting to legal action. The issues which activists raise can be converted from a matter of abstract justice to a matter of money in their own, and other fellow shareholders', pockets. In the KFB case in which the PSPD represented two interested parties, that is, the shareholders and the general public, it was much easier for the PSPD to prove substantial loss to a shareholder than to a citizen. The use of shareholder rights thus facilitated the use of the judicial system and its binding force, which was a main instrument of the PSPD movement.

Fourth, most advantages of shareholder rights can be obtained by holding only one share. In this sense, shareholder rights are also an economic way of challenging the business. We should note here that the stock market does not only function as a market for corporate control, which previous scholars have emphasized, but also, we might say, as a market for 'corporate infiltration'. In the former case, the corporation may impede a hostile party's bid for corporate control by holding, or at least gaining support from, the majority of the issued shares. In the latter case, on the other hand, the corporation cannot completely defend itself against the infiltration unless it maintains a closed company. Once a share is issued and listed on the stock market, it is transferred through a highly standardized contract in the stock exchange, which is obviously outside the control of the issuing corporation. A corporation cannot screen out completely share purchasers with non-economic motives.

Furthermore, due to the recent development of stock trading via the Internet, even an unlisted company may become vulnerable to this corporate infiltration. For example, in questioning the private offering of the bonds with warrants (BWs) of Samsung SDS, which is an unlisted company, the PSPD explained that they could collect ten shares through this cyber-market (PSPD's letter of complaint to the prosecution office, 17 November 1999).

With these four points discussed above, we can conclude that shareholder rights suited the PSPD's pragmatism in the sense that they were a powerful, and efficient, influence on a corporation.

Advantages unique to the *chaebol* problem

While the above advantages were general to any shareholder activism, there was one specific to the PSPD case which attacked the *chaebol*, a business group. Since the Commercial Act, a basic law for shareholder rights in Korea, was premised on the companies being freestanding, shareholder rights could be instrumental in blocking the maintenance of the *chaebol* structure. In fact, Korean company law in general assumes an isolated, individual company so that claiming a shareholder right in an individual *chaebol* affiliate may be a way of running against the management of the *chaebol* as a business group. Some PSPD members clearly comprehended this merit of claiming shareholder rights. As PEC lawyer *B* argued:

> The way of maintaining the *chaebol* is in breach of the principle of corporate management envisaged in the Commercial Act. The Commercial Act stipulates an individual company. . . . Although the Monopoly Act acknowledges the existence of the *chaebol*, the Commercial Act does not. The *chaebol* is not a corporation that the Commercial Act premises. (Interview on 2 November 1999)

A major argument of the PSPD was that all *chaebol* problems, as described in Chapter 5, impaired the interest of the shareholders in an individual company which provided supports to other affiliates. The transfer of assets and profits out of firms for the benefit of their controlling shareholders has recently been termed "tunneling" (Johnson, La Porta, Lopez-de-Silanes and Shleifer, 2000). Many of the *chaebol* problems previously defined by the state could be described as tunneling, which clearly conflicted with the interests of shareholders other than the *chongsu* family.

Based on the effectiveness of shareholder activism explained above, the PSPD won several consecutive victories against the KFB. In December 1997, in support of the PSPD claim alleging that their right to speak at the annual general meeting was unduly restricted, the court nullified the KFB's 1997 general meeting. In July 1998, the PSPD won a derivative suit against four former KFB executives, which was the first brought, and naturally the first won, in Korean history. It was decreed that the four executives should jointly pay 40 billion won (US$33.3 million) to cover damages on the KFB's loss resulting from the Hanbo insolvency.

These successes reinforced the PSPD's incentive to keep on using minority shareholder rights. Moreover, with the exception of the confrontations at annual general meetings, the winning of the KFB derivative suit brought about their strongest press response yet. Winning this suit, counted as "the greatest success of the PSPD shareholder activism" (PEC academic *D*, interview on 23 February 2001), positively affected the reformation of the PSPD shareholder activism in September 1998.

"Popular responses encouraged us to enlarge the scope of the PSPD shareholder activism to the big five *chaebol* [by adding Hyundai, Daewoo and LG to the already targeted Samsung and SK]" (PEC lawyer B, interview on 2 November 1999).[7]

Frame alignment and a minimalist strategy

The view of the *chaebol* as a social entity and the use of shareholder rights as a measure to influence them had not been naturally linked to each other in real action before the PSPD shareholder activism. Ever since the first trial, the PSPD has tried to align these two different views in order to mobilize positive resources and to prevent negative challenges. This has been done in two ways, that is, alignment of the prognostic and of the diagnostic frame.

With regard to the prognostic frame, the PSPD viewed shareholder rights through the window of a civil movement. In order to collect the support of the shareholders in the first shareholder activism campaign, an early PSPD pamphlet argued:

> The PSPD, which has led in protecting civil rights and interests, . . . is now launching the movement to help minority shareholders claim their just rights. (5 February 1997)

The PSPD legitimized shareholder activism as a measure for a noble cause and not as an end in itself. They also emphasized that, in the end, shareholders were a part of the citizenry which the PSPD represented. Therefore, there was no problem for the PSPD in representing the shareholders, as far as they were seen only as part of civil society.

With regard to the diagnostic frame, the PSPD viewed the *chaebol* problem through the window of shareholder rights. From the first trial, some PSPD members called their shareholder activism "a movement faithful to selected measures [that is, shareholder rights]" (PEC lawyer C, interview on 11 October 1999). This frame alignment is evident when we look at Table 5.4. Three traditional *chaebol* problems, that is, ownership concentration, diversification and in-group support, were all reinterpreted as problems of corporate despotism. Obviously, the latter is a more immediate concern of shareholder activism than the former.[8]

Furthermore, in order to defend itself from external criticism, including that from colleagues in other PSPD bodies, who still had doubts about the compatibility problem,[9] the PSPD adopted a 'minimalist approach'. In selecting issues and relevant arguments, they extracted elements common to the social entity and property perspectives, and sought arguments which could be defended on either ground. They never went into an area specific to one view, and refrained from expressing a position on such areas, saying that they were not their immediate concern.

Examples of this minimalist interpretation of the *chaebol* problem were: (1) insistence on the fair operation of a public company; and (2) insistence on observance of the law. These requests were so simple and uncontentious that some PSPD members referred to them as "principles".

A basic argument of the PSPD was that corporate assets should not be managed only for a specific group of the shareholders, in particular for the *chongsu* family. This is a basic principle of shareholder-centered corporate governance. A central concern of corporate governance theorists has been the expropriation of minority, or outsider, shareholders by majority, or insider, shareholders (e.g., Black, 1999; Claessens, Djankov, Fan and Lang, 1999; Johnson, et al. 2000).

In addition, this basic argument is also consistent with the social entity view. Jang Hasung's explanation of the term "public company" is a good example of how the PSPD tried to accommodate the earlier idea of the *chaebol* as a trustee of national assets. Jang argued:

> This [the term "public company"] does not mean a state-owned enterprise but a company that procures capital from the public, from an unspecified number of investors, that is, from average citizens. The institution guarantees that everyone can be a shareholder of a listed company and that the owner of the joint stock company is the shareholder, which everyone is entitled to be. In other words, the joint stock company premises the ownership of many average citizens. (Private letter to Cho Hee-Yeon, reproduced on Cho's personal homepage, social-movements.skhu.ac.kr, accessed on 10 May 2001)[10]

Another example was the argument that a corporation should abide by the law. Law observance is one of the basic concepts of corporate social responsibility (Donnelly, Gibson and Ivancevich, 1995), and the PSPD emphasized that the *chaebol* had avoided even this basic responsibility. "The *chaebol* ignores current law and order as well as general practices established in the market" (PEC member *B*, interview on 2 November 1999). "It is ridiculous and deceptive for the *chaebol* to mention its social responsibility while they do not obey the existing law" (PEC lawyer *C*, interview on 11 October 1999). This plain statement also contained the previous argument made by the state and the CCEJ. As pointed out before, claiming minority shareholder rights could effectively suppress the *chaebol* structure, given

82 Shareholder Activism

the premise of an isolated individual company in the company law. Therefore, it could be argued, strict observance of the law requires the *chaebol* to give up maintaining their structure.

The minimalist strategy of the PSPD helped transform the long-term and abstract nature of the *chaebol* issue into an immediate and pecuniary problem, but within the scope of the traditional *chaebol* problem.[11] Table 6.1 compares the differences between the previous frame and the PSPD frame of the *chaebol* problems.

Along with the potentials of shareholder activism as an effective influence on a corporation, this frame shift has one further political advantage. In a Korean society with experience of authoritarian regimes, the PSPD shareholder activism was politically more appealing than the previous controls over the *chaebol*. It entailed ordinary citizens, not the

Table 6.1   Reframing the *chaebol* problem

	Previous frame	PSPD frame
Problem	Harm to efficiency, justice and democracy	Expropriation of minority shareholders
Key monitor	Public sector (e.g., FTC)	Private sector (e.g., minority shareholders *via* the PEC)
Law	Monopoly Act	Commercial Act Securities Act
Keyword	Concentration of economic power	Corporate governance (a shareholder model) Legalism

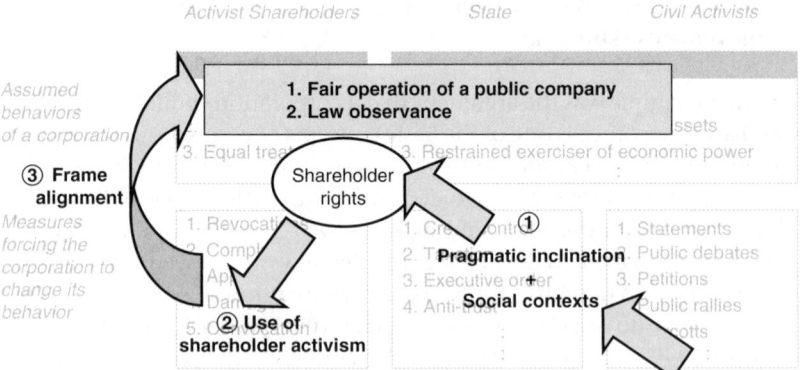

Figure 6.3   New framing from the old frames

state, exercising control over the *chaebol* through market relationships (i.e., shareholding), not through political coercion.

Figure 6.3 summarizes the discussions in this chapter on the old frames shown in Figure 6.1.

Limitations of the PSPD activism

Although shareholder activism has been powerful in attacking the *chaebol*, the PSPD members also understand that "PSPD shareholder activism is not a panacea [for the *chaebol* problem]" (PEC lawyer *C*, interview on 11 October 1999). From our observations, we can identify four challenges lying ahead.

First, with its minimalist strategy, the PSPD has avoided conflicts of interests with other interested groups. When taking action, they have never dealt with an area which might impair the interests of any groups other than the shareholders (PEC officer *E*, interview on 12 November 1999). Their response to critics was "So, have we done any damage to you or other groups [except the despotic *chongsu* and a handful of their compliant managers] with shareholder activism?" (PEC academic *D*, interview on 23 February 2001).

However, some fundamentalist groups have pointed out that the popularity of PSPD shareholder activism in dealing with corporate misdemeanors could unwittingly result in the relative neglect of the interests of groups other than shareholders. For example, Kim Sung-Gu, an economic professor at Hanshin University, argued:

> The PSPD shareholder activism is certainly a part of movements for democracy in the sense that it checks the expropriation of minority shareholders and provides a tool for democratic control of corporate management. However, in all respects, it only represents shareholder democracy, that is, the democracy of the haves [as opposed to the have-nots]. (Kim, S.-G. 1999)

Economist *I*, who was deeply involved in forming the New *Chaebol* Policy and had a less extreme view than the fundamentalists, also expressed a doubt by saying:

> The [New *Chaebol*] policy's emphasis on the shareholders was right because they had long been ignored and a balance between interested groups was required. But I think shareholder capitalism is not the ultimate solution. (Interview on 12 October 1999)

Even from within the PSPD, Cho Hee-Yeon also expressed an opinion that there still existed an ideological conflict behind PSPD shareholder activism by saying: "the PSPD shareholder activism will have to make a critical choice [between the property view and the social entity view of a corporation] [sooner or later] if it continues to use shareholder rights as a major measure" (Cho H.-Y., 2001: n.p.). He worried about the possible alienation from the social entity view if the PSPD continued to rely on shareholder activism.

Therefore, even with the minimalist approach, the PSPD did not remove the possibility of conflict completely. This conflict will remain an innate tension in Korea where a social entity view of the corporation has long prevailed.

Second, PSPD shareholder activism could not address the traditional *chaebol* problems completely. The problem of in-group transactions was the easiest to attack, "because it manifests itself very clearly" (PEC academic *D*, interview on 23 February 2001). On the other hand, the PSPD had a difficulty in addressing the issue of equity investment. "In many cases, *chaebol* companies used to argue that [equity] investment in other affiliates was purely based on business judgment. This was a grey area [difficult to find what the real motive was]" (PEC academic *D*, interview on 23 February 2001). Relying on legal activism, PSPD shareholder activism could only effectively address issues which could not be subsumed under business judgment, so that the courts could deal with them.

Furthermore, the increasing concentration of share ownership in the hands of the *chongsu* family, which had previously been identified as a key *chaebol* problem, was often thought of as "one of the desirable results that the PSPD shareholder activism brought about" (PEC academic *D*, interview on 19 January 2001). Seen from the traditional view of corporate governance, the argument goes, the *chongsu* should bear more financial risk, i.e., more shares, when he wants to exert *de facto* decision power greater than the current financial accountability.

Third, the "principles" that the PSPD shareholder activism had relied on were never fully clear. The PSPD claimed minority shareholder rights to force the *chaebol* to operate their assets fairly, but did not express who should be the beneficiaries. This is related to the first limitation. While the principle of legal observance was clear on the surface, it also remained open to debate how appropriate the existing law was.[12]

Fourth, despite relatively low mobilizing costs in some aspects, PSPD shareholder activism was still costly and time-intensive, like other cases of shareholder activism (FOE, 2000). Shareholder activism requires the ability to translate obscure demands into concrete legal arguments. It requires defending resolutions at short notice, participating in meetings with companies, and evaluating copious amounts of corporate material. It is costly if a professional such as a lawyer or an accountant is hired. It also requires a complex solicitation effort to increase votes.[13] The high costs of shareholder activism hinder many potential activists from utilizing it.

7
Resource Mobilization

This chapter examines what types of resources the PSPD needed for its shareholder activism and how it mobilized them. The first section identifies three 'internal' resources, without which the PEC[1] could not have maintained itself. They are expertise, leadership and funds. The second section investigates two 'external' resources, that is, the information of the target firms and the support of the shareholders, which the PSPD required in order to wage its shareholder activism. We can identify five different groups of shareholders to which the PSPD can turn: (1) PSPD members; (2) individual shareholders; (3) domestic institutional investors; (4) trade unions; and (5) foreign institutional investors. We will discuss the respective significance of each group within PSPD shareholder activism.[2]

Internal resources

Expertise

Shareholder activism requires input from many professionals, including lawyers, accountants and financial specialists. As of the end of 2000, the PEC comprised 22 professional executive members (Table 7.1). It has been

Table 7.1 Composition of the PEC executive members, 1997–2000

	1997	1998	1999	2000
Lawyers	4	6	8	9
Academics	2	2	4	6
Accountants	2	2	5	4
Full-time officers	1	2	3	3
Total	9	12	20	22

said that the most essential resources for PSPD shareholder activism are the PEC members and their loyalty:

> Executives of a target company once confessed to me that they were really afraid of the PEC members' loyalty. . . . When we introduced ourselves as "a group of crazy people," foreign investors were equally shocked. (PEC academic D, interview on 19 January 2001)

In fact, without the PEC members' loyalty, PSPD shareholder activism may not have been so successful. In addition to voluntary services, the members pay, like other non-executive members, a membership fee to the PEC (the PEC is financially independent of the PSPD). Even full-time officers receive only a nominal salary (0.8 to 1.2 million won per month in January 2001).[3] They meet almost every week (two to three times a week, in peak times such as before an annual general meeting) and the meeting normally lasts five hours, from seven p.m. until midnight. After the meeting they return with a considerable workload, which takes up much of their spare time. In order to attend an annual general meeting or inspect the financial statements of a particular company, they have to use their own leave. Those who are employed by a large law firm or accounting company often have to conceal their activities in the PSPD from their employers to prevent both their employers and themselves from being put at a disadvantage in business.

To what may such loyalty be attributed? Before discussing this, we should point out that the expressed motives and goals of participation in PSPD shareholder activism vary widely. Almost all members agree that they are working to reform the *chaebol*. However, the interpretation of the goals of *chaebol* reform differs from member to member. Some stick to the conventional idea of corporate governance by saying that "the aim is transparency and accountability" (PEC academic D, interview on 23 November 1999). On the other hand, others interpret the goal of reform differently:

> PSPD shareholder activism is the true practice of company law. I joined the PSPD because of intellectual curiosity and a sense of duty as a professional. We are making a society ruled by law. We are applying legalism to a corporation, the most advanced institution in the capitalist society. (PEC lawyer C, interview on 11 October 1999)

Some think that the ultimate goal is to dissolve the *chaebol*. "Personally I believe that the *chaebol* should be dissolved" (PEC lawyer B, interview on 11 February 1999). "A member used to say that he would carry on doing this [i.e., the PSPD shareholder activism] until the *chaebol* went out of business" (PEC academic *D*, interview on 19 January 2001). But others maintain a different view:

> We do not mean to bankrupt specific targets [i.e., individual *chaebol*]. We just mean to change their distorted economic behavior prevalent in our society. The *chaebol* are simply one manifestation of the most problematic distorted corporate behaviors. (PEC academic *D*, interview on 23 November 1999)

> The *chaebol* reform is to establish rational capitalism, in other words, to refine vulgar capitalism. (PEC academic *A*, interview on 21 October 2000)

How then can the PEC members act in concert despite these differences? First of all, their loyalty comes from a shared desire to contribute to society. Most members, in their thirties or twenties, saw themselves as "the generation baptized by the student movements [that sought for the democratization of the country during the 1970s and the 1980s] when in university" (PEC officer *E*, interview on 12 November 1999).[4] In fact, some of the PEC members even postponed studying and worked as union activists in order to share in the agony of labor. When asked how many of the PEC members had been involved in the student movement in university, PEC officer *E* replied:

> I think it is embarrassing to ask the executive members of the PEC about their personal history regarding the student movements. Around 80 percent of them sympathized with or participated in the movement, I would say. (Letter to the author, 23 March 2001)

Even those who had not been active participants at the time felt guilty and said that they owed something to those friends who had sacrificed themselves for the nation (PEC academic *A*, interview on 15 September 2000). For many PEC members, contribution to a better society is seen as an obligation of their generation.

Second, and related to the first reason, the PSPD provided a rare channel through which such young professionals could use their professional expertise to contribute to society:

> What could a lawyer do for the civil movements before [except defending political prisoners in court]? This [Giving them a chance to do so] is the underlying tone of the PSPD. (PEC officer *F*, interview on 1 November 1999)

For the generation affected by the student movement, being a professional on high income, such as a lawyer or an accountant, was regarded as a compromise with, or entry into, the Establishment. Although some said that they chose such jobs simply to support the family (PEC lawyer B, interview on 2 November 1999), many of them did not want to abandon their ideals. PSPD shareholder activism offered a good opportunity for these professionals to contribute to social causes without changing their careers:

> While the CCEJ was taking a scholar-centered movement, the PSPD tended to give consideration to practicing professionals. That made me comfortable, relatively speaking, with this organization [i.e., the PSPD]. (PEC lawyer B, interview on 2 November 1999)

Third, the PEC tried to accommodate its members' various beliefs as much as possible. Since decisions were made by consensus, the PEC could select its issues for action and its target firms so as to satisfy members' motivations. According to Jang Hasung, making a decision by consensus worked so well that the PEC made it a practice to set an agenda and to decide each member's role through a discussion. When an issue offered no prospect of agreement, it was tacitly agreed that members should shun raising it. For example, the ultimate goal of *chaebol* reform was not officially discussed. In so far as it catered for each member's beliefs to some extent, the PEC leaders thought, PSPD shareholder activism *per se* should not be disintegrated by such "exhausting debates" (PEC officer E, interview on 12 November 1999). The PEC adheres to this "silence strategy" against any disputable challenge from within or outside the PSPD.[5]

Fourth, for the PEC executive members, PSPD shareholder activism was a unique opportunity to develop a comprehensive view of the inside of big business. All the relevant experts met regularly to exchange their professional knowledge in respect of a real situation unfolding before their eyes. Therefore, the activity in the PEC was seen as "a lively classroom that has no match elsewhere in Korea" (PEC academic D, interview on 23 February 2001). From this viewpoint, a member might well expect that "participation in PSPD shareholder activism will make me an expert in the field of corporate governance" (PEC accountant J, interview on 26 November 1999). "With PSPD shareholder activism activities, we could enhance our understanding [of corporate governance and the *chaebol* issue] and master the technique of negotiating with management" (PEC lawyer B, interview on 2 November 1999).

For these reasons and the PSPD's successes, the PEC has grown year by year (Table 7.1). Now more professionals than can be accepted want to join the PEC, but the PEC is cautious about expanding itself for fear that the newcomers might abuse inside information for personal benefit. "We do not receive all people who hope to join us. Personal interests should be carefully scrutinized with a long-term perspective" (PEC academic D, interview on 23 February 2001).

Leadership

We cannot avoid mentioning one name when it comes to leadership. In the international context especially, Jang Hasung personifies Korean shareholder activism. This is partly because people tend to reduce a complex phenomenon to a simplified icon. But it is also true that Jang has been a key figure in consolidating resources within the organization and mobilizing those external to it. Jang contributed to PSPD shareholder activism in three ways: (1) he provided a logical justification, or frame, for tackling the *chaebol* problem with a more aggressive exercise of shareholder rights; (2) he made a timely suggestion of a strategy appropriate to the situation; and (3) he acted as an important node in mobilizing external resources. Before his joining, the PEC seemed to lack a figure who could play these roles. "In those early days, the PEC was equipped with nothing but the personnel" (PEC academic D, interview on 19 January 2001) and "the members were at pains to do something in their own way [but could not find the way for a collective endeavor]" (PEC academic D, interview on 23 February 2001). Therefore, it can be said that, as far as shareholder activism is concerned, Jang's joining was critical in putting PEC activity on its current track.

Internal consolidation (a): justification of using shareholder rights

Among the PSPD members, no one understands the logic of capital markets as well as Jang. Influenced by the anti-capitalist intellectual atmosphere in Korean progressive movements, few economists working for the PSPD tried to understand the role of the capital market in the Korean economy. In contrast, Jang studied for his Ph.D. at the Wharton School on the microstructure of the capital market, the trading system and the dissemination of market information. His academic concern is how to make real markets function as well as the theory assumes.

In this sense, we can say that the rise of PSPD shareholder activism was a process in which the Korean progressive activists embraced the logic of the capital market, which they had previously seen in a negative light. Once they decided to use shareholder rights as a measure for achieving their social ideal, they needed to justify why they had changed their position. One justification was that shareholder rights are simple tools for attaining the public cause of *chaebol* reform. Another was that shareholders are a part of the citizenry that the PSPD represented. Jang further refined these justifications by elaborating on how the players in the capital market can share interests in *chaebol* reform with the PSPD.[6] This explanation was logical enough to convince the other PEC members of the value of shareholder activism. They have come to feel more comfortable about shareholder activism than before. In other words, Jang provided a logic that turned doubtful experts into convinced contributors. Without such logic, the PEC members might have not been so loyal.

What point in Jang's logic was so impressive to other members? It was the emphasis on a principle- and reason-based movement. "He [Jang] believes that everything is going OK as long as a principle is kept" (PEC officer *F*, interview on 1 November 1999).

> In my opinion, it was a position that nobody could attack. This was because it was a position based on a principle. Because the origin [of PSPD shareholder activism] was like that, I was, I think, persuaded [to continue to participate in the PSPD shareholder activism]. . . . The other members and I have hardly been disturbed because our activities are rooted in the logic of a reasonable theory. (PEC academic *H*, interview on 10 November 1999)

Internal consolidation (b): strategic decision

Jang also made a timely suggestion for a PSPD response to fast-changing events. His ability to do this came from his experience and understanding of both the *chaebol* and capital markets. Before obtaining his Ph.D., he worked for Kumho Group, one of the top ten *chaebol* since the 1960s. Capital markets are his academic specialty. Therefore, he can be regarded as "a traitor to his class,"[7] who is much needed in shareholder activism addressing complicated business and finance matters.

> It was Professor Jang who supplied the PSPD with the logic unique to that part [i.e., shareholder activism or corporate governance in general]. It was he who introduced us to the usefulness of shareholder activism in Korean society. . . . We could hardly conceive things like the general meeting strategy. (PEC lawyer *B*, interview on 2 November 1999)

In selecting strategies, the PEC showed astonishing flexibility. While keeping to their "principles," they sometimes transcended the ideological limits of the Korean progressive movements:

> One thing with which we were seriously troubled was whether, in a proxy contest, we had to take proxies from foreign shareholders. . . .

"Ah, can this [receiving proxy votes from foreigners] be justified for a progressive organization like the PSPD? Can this be accepted?" I doubted. But it was, to my astonishment, adopted, at last. (PEC academic *H*, interview on 10 November 1999)

This flexibility based on reason was also seen as a trait of Jang (PEC academic *A*, interview on 6 February 2001). Due to this reasonable and adaptable activity, the PEC could embrace some moderate professionals who detested the dogmatic social movements of the Korean left.

It [the *chaebol* issue] had been conceived neither in terms of socialistic Capital–Labor relationship nor the vague hatred of the *chaebol*. Based on a principle, the PSPD rationally approached the [*chaebol*] issues. (PEC academic *H*, interview on 10 November 1999)

External mobilization: personal networks

Jang did not recruit PEC members personally. He thought that it was most dangerous for him to invite somebody to the PEC in person. Perhaps, this was because his introduction of new members might threaten the unity among the existing PEC members. Instead, he just solidified accepted volunteers into a coherent group as shown above.

However, in mobilizing external resources such as information, funds and shareholder supports, he acted as an important node. Jang also acknowledges his role in mobilizing resources which make the system work. "In all respects, Professor Jang retains much information. He has many contacts, including among foreigners" (PEC officer *F*, interview on 1 November 1999). For fund-raising, he sent individual handwritten letters to hundreds of possible donors and met them face-to-face.

Among the PEC members, it has been said that Jang's personal network played an important role in mobilizing external resources. It was difficult for us to confirm how much it actually contributed, but an episode illustrates how helpful his attributes could be in drawing support from academics. When I asked how he assessed PSPD shareholder activism, finance scholar *K*, who was well known for his contribution to corporate governance reform, indirectly answered by saying, "He [Jang] studied finance, too" (interview on 10 February 2000).

To conclude, Jang Hasung played a critical role in systemizing PSPD shareholder activism. However, what we should note here is not who played a key role, but what attribute made such a role possible. From the discussion above, we assume that a good knowledge of the stock market and its players are essential assets for leading shareholder activism to success.

Funds

For PSPD shareholder activism, money was not so crucial a resource. This was because a large part of the expenses were absorbed by the members' voluntary services, for which, otherwise, high costs should have been paid. In other words, the markets that shareholder activism normally relies on (i.e., legal, accounting and consulting) are all internalized in the PEC, an organization in the pursuit of a public cause.

Nevertheless, the source of the funds has been a frequently raised concern:

> When we first meet people [especially foreign investors], they, without exception, ask us who is paying the PSPD. [They also ask] "Do you disclose your financial statements as you demand of a company?" [Our answer is] "We cannot give you the list of donors, but the accounts of the PSPD are disclosed every month". (PEC academic D, interview on 19 January 2001)

A reason why the source of funds matters to the PSPD comes from an idea that the contributors may have an influence on PSPD activities. For example, the PSPD refuses government support because "if we accept that money, we are likely to be misunderstood as a pro-government organization. This can be a fatal mistake for an NGO [like the PSPD]" (PEC officer E, interview on 11 October 1999). In the same context, the PEC refuses financial support from any corporation and even from the PSPD:

> The PEC is financially independent from the PSPD. Indeed, the PEC gives 30 percent of its total income to the PSPD. This means that, even if a corporation [which may have conflict of interest with the PEC activities] donates to the PSPD, the money cannot flow into the PEC. (PEC academic D, interview on 23 February 2001)

The PEC's major source of income has been donations from individuals (Table 7.2). The donations are of two kinds: lump sums and monthly payments. As Figure 7.1 illustrates, the donations are constantly growing, which allows the PEC to stand on its own income. The primary way of mobilizing funds was through the personal networks of the PEC executive members. As PSPD shareholder activism became well known, however, independent donations started coming in.

94 Shareholder Activism

Table 7.2 Income of the PEC (won), 1998–2000

	1998		1999		2000	
Donation	62,351,771	98.0%	69,989,795	63.9%	108,158,926	92.7%
Lump-sum	60,631,911	95.3%	47,505,815	43.3%	73,170,416	62.7%
Monthly	1,719,860	2.7%	22,483,980	20.5%	34,988,510	30.0%
Others	1,241,678	2.0%	39,610,138	36.1%	8,484,986	7.3%
Total	63,593,449	100.0%	109,599,933	100.0%	116,643,912	100.0%

Source: PSPD.
Note: The finance of 1997, the first year of the PEC, was excluded from the analysis because it was negligibly small.

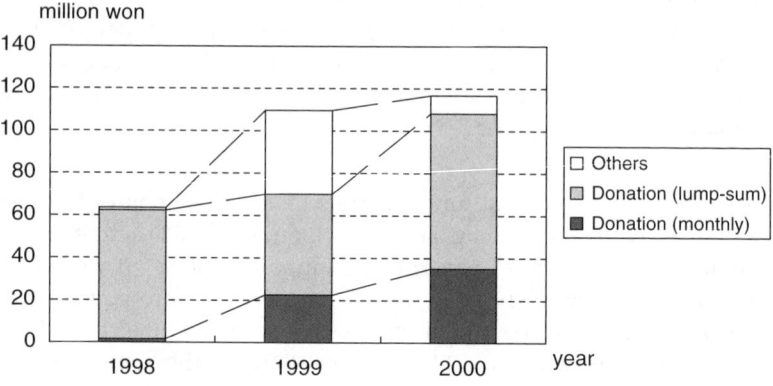

Figure 7.1 Composition of the PEC income
Source: PSPD.

Some members have suggested that PSPD shareholder activism will have to be converted into a profit-making business:

> If PSPD shareholder activism becomes independent of the PSPD and makes a profit, it can reproduce itself. (PEC officer *E*, interview on 11 October 1999)

> Some day, the PSPD shareholder activism needs to charge money to, for example, institutional investors, to meet the expenses for reinforcing professional and watching capacities. (PEC lawyer *B*, interview on 2 November 1999)

However, this suggestion has not been seriously discussed yet because of an opposing view that "it is not acceptable for an NGO like the PSPD [to accept profit-related money]" (PEC academic *D*, interview on 23 February 2001).[8] Meanwhile, the PEC sought to commercialize their activities in another way, which facilitated the spread of shareholder activism in Korea. In July 2000, a law firm named Hannuri was established. Half of its eight founding partners were executive members of the PEC (two out of six lawyers and two accountants). According to the homepage of Hannuri, the law firm has completed seven cases, and is carrying out nine more cases (hannurilaw.co.kr). Of the seven completed cases, the clients of Hannuri have won six cases. In August 2000, the PEC also launched the Corporate Governance Information Centre, renamed the Center for Good Corporate Governance (CGCG) in November 2001. The CGCG provides an information service named CGInfo, which offers company-specific information on the structures and issues of corporate governance in Korea. Currently CGInfo covers about 50 major Korean companies (www.cgcg.or.kr).

Through Hannuri and the CGCG, the PEC is commercializing the experiences accumulated from PSPD shareholder activism. This attempt allows the professionals who have participated in the PSPD shareholder activism to concentrate more on the corporate governance issue without worrying about income and other conflicts of interests. Furthermore, this is incubating more self-interested shareholder activism than the PSPD's for the purpose of institutionalizing shareholder activism in Korea:

> We [professionals who have been participating in the PSPD shareholder activism] are envisioning that this Center goes beyond the work of the PSPD and engages itself in a more in-depth systematic and professional approach to corporate governance issues in Korea. (CGCG's pamphlet, undated, n.p.)

External resources

This section investigates resources the PSPD needs to address specific problems. We will discuss two external resources. Information about the target company and its action is important to detect and analyze the problem that the PSPD is tackling. The PSPD also requires the support of shareholders in the company concerned in order to wage shareholder activism based on their analysis of the problem.

Information

By asking Jang Hasung and other PEC members how they came to perceive the problems they had raised from 1997 to 1998, we were able to identify four major sources of corporate information. They were: (1) mass media;

(2) corporate disclosure; (3) government announcements; and (4) private informants.

Two points need mentioning before further discussion. First, these sources of information are not necessarily accurate and comprehensive, since they are based on personal memory rather than contemporary records. The PSPD declined access to the internal documents which might contain this information. Nevertheless, they are still a useful way of drawing a rough picture of the information channels used by the PSPD in clarifying the existence and nature of a problem. Second, by this method, we cannot say anything about the problems to which the PSPD decided not to react. It was impossible to establish the full range of problems of which the PSPD was informed, and we could not evaluate qualitatively the relative value of each source of information in promoting a reaction.

In general, it appears that the PSPD relied on public sources of information more heavily than on private ones. In particular, the mass media was the main source of information discussed. PEC academic *D* emphasized the need to read between the lines of news reports:

> You have only to be diligent [in order to discover a corporate wrong]. . . . You can get more information [on a certain issue] from the same article, when you have a continual interest on it. For instance, in the case of Samsung's private offering of convertible bonds (CBs), nobody sensed what it meant. (Interview on 23 February 2001)

This reliance on the mass media may suggest that Korea has a relatively less developed disclosure system than other developed economies such as the United States and the United Kingdom. Despite its relative underdevelopment, however, the disclosure system was also an increasingly important source of corporate information. A series of improvements in the disclosure system reduced the PSPD's costs of gathering information tremendously (PEC academic *A*, interview on 22 February 2001). For example, the 1999 amendment of the Securities Act obliged companies listed on the Korea Stock Exchange (KSE) to produce corporate reports quarterly instead of biannually. In April 2000, the Financial Supervisory Service (FSS) opened an electronic disclosure system named "Korea Investor's Network for Disclosure System (KSE-KIND)," which contains all public notices made by listed companies as well as information on their governance structure, business areas and financial statements (kind.kse.or.kr).

Another noticeable source of information was private informants. Although it is difficult for the PSPD to disclose their identity, such informants are said to include employees, outside directors and investors in the corporations concerned. It is also said that personal networks worked to a great extent in exploiting this source of information. PEC academic *D* hinted that it was crucial for maintaining the pool of personal informants to convince the informants that the PSPD really utilized their information, and would conceal their identities (interview on 23 February 2001).

So far the PSPD has not tried to detect wrongdoing in the *chaebol* of its own accord. It is often argued that, in April 2000, the PSPD detected Hyundai Trust Investment Management misappropriating entrusted money on its own. However, this fact had been partially brought to light by the FSS eight months previously (Park, R.-J. and Choi, Y.-H., 2000). A possible reason for this lies in the economic use of limited resources. "Many problems [which the PSPD can address] were already public knowledge. There is no point in spending precious time in finding out [undisclosed] problems when you already have well-known problems at hand". (PEC officer *E*, interview on 11 October 1999)

From this discussion, it is apparent that the corporate information which underdeveloped systems of corporate governance are supposed to be lacking can be substituted to some degree by tenacious experts and their networks. And a government policy to improve the disclosure system will reduce the efforts needed by such experts.

Shareholder support

Since the PSPD started its shareholder activism without holding any shares itself, it needed the support and trust of shareholders who would let the PSPD use the legal rights based on their shareholdings. Comments on general issues do not always require this trust, but participation in a shareholders' general meeting, a proxy contest, or a legal dispute (including lawsuits and other appeals) necessarily needs shareholders' support. Here we will discuss five groups of shareholders and their respective significance for the PSPD shareholder activism.

PSPD members

Table 7.3 summarizes what kinds of shareholders supported the PSPD-led legal disputes. Shareholders' support for legal disputes is extremely difficult to obtain. This is because, once shareholders enter into the dispute, they cannot sell their shares until the dispute is settled and thus their involvement demands the greatest patience and sacrifice. This is why we have chosen legal disputes from among many possible shareholder

Table 7.3 Shareholder supports for the PEC's legal actions

	PSPD insiders	Outsiders		Total
		Individuals	Institutions	
Complaint	8	0	0	8
Revocation	4	2	0	6
Provisional disposition	2	3	1	6
Damages	1	2	0	3
Derivative Suit	0	3	0	3
Total	15	10	1	26

Sources: Various.

remedies as a basis for comparison of the degree of support from different shareholder groups.

Despite our initial understanding that the PSPD is a non-shareholding organization, Table 7.3 shows that the most supportive shareholders came from inside the PSPD. At first the PSPD did not hold any shares of the target companies, but, when necessary, it could obtain the support of shareholders from within in two ways. One was to rely on members who had accidentally purchased shares of the company concerned for their own investment purposes. The other was to buy shares of the target companies in the name of a member, using the PEC's budget. For the three years from 1998 to 2000, the PEC spent 44 million won (US$ 367,000), 30 percent of the period's total expenditures, to buy shares in its target companies (Table 7.4).

Previously, we pointed out that the PSPD internalized the markets of professional services which a shareholder would require in taking action against a corporation. Now the investment in a target company's shares also allows the PSPD to partly internalize the existence of a shareholder. This internalized shareholding enables the PSPD to respond quickly to the target company's action by minimizing transaction costs (e.g., searching for shareholders and persuading them, when needed). Although a tight budget kept the PSPD from holding enough shares to meet even the lowest requirements of important minority actions (e.g., 0.01 percent of the total issued shares for filing a derivative suit), its members could speak at a shareholders' general meeting, contest a proxy, and take some legal actions which do not require a certain level of shareholdings:

> This [the purchase of shares] is a means for giving our full-time officers or activists the status of shareholders. . . . The expenses thus

Table 7.4 PSPD shareholding of the *chaebol*, as of 28 February 2001

Member	Samsung Electronics	Samsung SDS	Hyundai Heavy Industries	Hynix (Hyundai)	Dacom (LG)	SK Telecom	Daewoo Corp.	Total
1	10	60	10	10	10	1	10	111
2	10	10	10	10	10	2	10	62
3	10	—	10	10	10	1	10	51
4	20	—	10	10	—	—	10	50
5	10	—	10	10	—	1	10	41
6	10	—	10	10	—	1	10	41
7	10	—	10	10	—	1	10	41
8	10	—	10	10	—	1	10	41
9	10	—	10	10	—	—	10	40
10	10	—	10	10	—	—	10	40
11	—	—	—	—	10	—	—	10
Total	110	70	100	100	40	8	100	528

Source: PSPD.

incurred should be seen as the cost of attaining shareholder capacity and information on the target company. (PEC academic D, interview on 23 February 2001)

In fact, the PSPD frequently used complaints, invalidations, provisional dispositions and damage suits, which are available even to a single shareholder (see Table 7.3).

This strategy of internalized shareholding was criticized for not representing other, solely financially-motivated, shareholders. In this sense, the shareholder activism organized by the PSPD could be attacked as "shareholder activism without shareholders." Many critics argued that PSPD shareholder activism did not represent the majority, never mind all, of the minority shareholders. For example, in the case of the private offering of the BWs, Samsung's refutation was that the PSPD, with only ten shares, had no right to invalidate the offering, as the rest of the shareholders expressed no discontent. The court accepted this argument, stating that, with only ten shares, the plaintiff did not have any considerable interests infringed by the action under consideration.

Therefore, despite the advantage of having its own shareholding, the PSPD requires practical support from other external shareholders for at least two reasons. One is, as shown above, to own enough shares to be able to demand the court's serious consideration. The other is to meet the minimum requirements for claiming minority shareholder rights.

We will discuss four groups of external shareholders to whom the PSPD can turn: (1) individuals; (2) domestic institutions; (3) trade unions; and (4) foreign institutions.

Individual shareholders

Individual shareholders are the most supportive of the four groups for the PSPD shareholder activism. Next to the insiders, they participated in the PSPD-led legal actions the most frequently (ten out of 26 actions in Table 7.3). Without their support, none of the three derivative suits filed by the PSPD would have been possible. However, getting support from enough individual shareholders to make a difference was not an easy task. Individual investors were so dispersed that it took the PSPD far more time and effort to gather their support than to mobilize other investors.

Table 7.5 illustrates how difficult it is to mobilize individual investors. From the 2000 annual reports of the PSPD's four target firms, we calculated the average number of shares that the different groups of shareholders held during that year. Then we compared the average holding with the 0.01 percent requirement for a derivative suit and 1.5 percent for an extraordinary general meeting, which are respectively the most relaxed and strictest conditions for a minority action, except for those actions which a shareholder with a single share can take.

The result shows that, on average, institutional investors, both domestic and foreign, can file a derivative suit independently. For individuals, in the case of Hyundai Heavy Industries, at least 23 individuals would need to cooperate to file a derivative suit. When we consider the shares held by the *chaebol* family and the managers, this picture looks even bleaker. In the worst case, 100 individual shareholders would need to cooperate to bring a derivative suit against Samsung Electronics. Moreover, when minority shareholders try to call an extraordinary general meeting, more than 2,600 individual shareholders would need to cooperate in the case of Dacom.

The result implies that, apart from the possibility of winning and recouping the expenses incurred, filing a derivative suit itself is beyond the reach of an individual investor. Even for an intermediary organization like the PSPD, it is more costly to mobilize individual shareholders than to mobilize domestic institutional or foreign investors.

Nevertheless, the PSPD generally had to take the most costly way because other potential co-operators hesitated to give the PSPD a helping hand. Domestic institutional investors and other legal persons holding *chaebol* company shares were either their affiliates or had business relationships with the *chaebol*. Foreign investors were less hesitant about

Table 7.5 Shareholder composition of the PSPD targets

	Domestic individuals	Domestic institutions	Foreigners
Samsung Electronics			
— Average shareholding	214 (178)	83,526	48,393
— Required shareholders for a derivative suit (Minimum number of shares = 17,634)	83 (100)	1	1
— Required shareholders for an EGM (Minimum number of shares = 2,645,026)	12,360 (14,860)	32	55
Hyundai Heavy Industries			
— Average shareholding	340 (264)	25,209	31,892
— Required shareholders for a derivative suit (Minimum number of shares = 7,600)	23 (29)	1	1
— Required shareholders for an EGM (Minimum number of shares = 1,140,000)	3,353 (4,319)	46	36
Dacom			
— Average shareholding	138 (138)	10,835	2,766
— Required shareholders for a derivative suit (Minimum number of shares = 2,395)	18 (18)	1	1
— Required shareholders for an EGM (Minimum number of shares = 359,145)	2,603 (2,603)	34	130
SK Telecom			
— Average shareholding	216 (215)	11,805	26,813
— Required shareholders for a derivative suit (Minimum number of shares = 8,916)	42 (42)	1	1
— Required shareholders for an EGM (Minimum number of shares = 1,337,291)	6,192 (6,249)	55	50

Sources: Each company's Annual Report of the year 2000.
Notes: 1. The figures in the parentheses are the number when the shares owned by the chaebol family and the managers are excluded.
2. "Foreigners" include individuals and institutions, but the number of shares held by foreign individuals is negligibly small.

co-operating than their domestic counterparts, but took a more cautious attitude to getting involved in a legal action than a proxy fight.

Furthermore, even if non-individual shareholders had joined PSPD shareholder activism, the PSPD might still have needed individual shareholders for other reasons. This was because the PSPD wanted its shareholder activism to appear to be supported by the whole nation, not by its specific segments (e.g., trade unions or institutional investors). In other words, individual shareholders can symbolize nation-wide, non-sectional support for the PSPD shareholder activism.

A good example of this symbolic function was the PSPD's "Ten-Share Campaign." As they initiated what was called the "citizen's action for national reform" in September 1998, the PSPD appealed to the nation to buy more than ten shares of their five target companies, that is, the core companies of the big five *chaebol*, and to entrust the shareholder rights to the PSPD.

At first, this Ten-Share Campaign gained much social attention. For example, Park Nohae, a well-known labor activist and poet, expressed a high opinion of it as follows:

> Do you know what I used to say when meeting people? . . . "Have you collected ten shares?" . . . People asked me, "What are ten shares?" Then I said, "Don't you know the PSPD shareholder activism that the PSPD is recently conducting in a revolutionary way?" (Kang, J.-M., 1998: p. 63)

In favor of the campaign, the press also highlighted the national mood for support. For example, it was reported that an architect spent 5.5 million won (US$ 4,600) to buy 50 shares, ten in each of the designated companies, not to make money but to lend his aid to the Ten-Share Campaign (Kim, T.-K., 1998). Reportedly, the participants ranged from a university graduate in his/her twenties to a senior citizen in his/her seventies, from a stall keeper to an owner of a small and medium-sized enterprise.[9]

Despite all these supports, the Ten-Share Campaign did not succeed in collecting a substantial number of shares (Table 7.6). Notwithstanding, it was successful in the sense that it demonstrated many people's concern with the PSPD shareholder activism.

Why did individual investors join the PSPD shareholder activism? The PSPD understood that they were mainly motivated by indignation. "The *chaebol*'s absurd behavior enraged them to join us" (PEC academic D, interview on 23 February 2001). From our observations, we find that such indignation came from: (1) the general negative attitude toward the *chaebol* in Korean society; (2) personal experience of the *chaebol*'s unjust conduct; and (3) failed investments in the stock market.

The general indignation was a combined result of the deep-rooted anti-*chaebol* sentiment and the constant reports of the *chaebol* wrongdoing

Table 7.6 Participants in the 10-Share Campaign, as of 8 Feb. 2000

Samsung Electronics	Hyundai Heavy Industries	LG Semiconductor	SK Telecom	Daewoo Corporation	Total*
153	213	177	42	352	817

Source: PSPD.
* The total excludes overlapping supporters.

both by the press and organizations such as the PSPD. There was a widespread belief, especially after the 1997 crisis, that the *chaebol* had ruined the nation. A slogan observed on the homepage of "Stop Samsung Campaign" (www.stopsamsung.org) reads: "A fight against the military dictatorship in the 20th century; A fight against the *chaebol* dictatorship in the 21st century." This partly expressed, though in strong terms, the prevailing antagonism vis-à-vis the *chaebol*. This public indignation made some people unconditionally entrust their shareholder rights to the PSPD in the Ten-Share Campaign.[10]

A more direct motive for joining PSPD shareholder activism often came from personal experience. Trusting his shares to the PSPD, a former Samsung employee asserted that he had been fired simply for his participation in his employer's annual general meeting (Lee, D.-H., 2000). "Too much annoyance from share investment loss" (individual shareholder L, interview on 23 December 1999) made a shareholder pay a spontaneous visit to the PSPD. Even such personal wrath was linked to the public indignation, however. In fact, it was extremely difficult to draw a boundary between a personal problem and the social problem. When individual investors sided with PSPD shareholder activism, they saw their action as based on the PSPD's central logic that shareholders could correct the *chaebol*'s unjust behavior:

> At the hand of an ordinary citizen, the behaviors of the *chaebol* companies, which drove the national economy into the [1997] crisis through mismanagement and corruption, can be amended. A citizen's exercise of rights as a minority shareholder can punish a despotic *chongsu* who illegally gives the company's money to offspring. It can prevent the mismanagement that gives arbitrary financial aid to unsound affiliates, which have pushed our economy into widespread crisis. It can make our society clean by reforming the managerial climate imbued with collusion, secret funds and bribery. (PSPD pamphlet, 9 September 1998)

On the other hand, the PSPD acknowledged that they could not completely rely upon those who were motivated mainly by personal experience:

> The PSPD's difficulty is to unite ordinary minority shareholders. They have no common belief and are mostly after a short-term speculation, so they can hardly form the foundation of a long-term and continuous movement [like the PSPD's]. (PEC officer E, interview on 2 November 1999)

> If you say that foreign funds investing in Korea are hot money pursuing capital gain through short-term arbitrage, perhaps domestic investment trust companies or individual investors would be hot, hot, hot money. (PEC academic D, 31 January 2001)

> In the case of Hyundai Securities, individual investors opposed the PSPD's position. Individual investors have no reason [to support PSPD shareholder activism, if they only care about money]. They came to us after they had found that they had no more to lose. (PSPD academic G, interview on 2 January 2001)

Therefore, we can conclude that dispersed individual shareholders render only a symbolic significance of popular backing to the PSPD shareholder activism.

Domestic institutional shareholders

Many in Korea, including the PSPD, expected domestic institutional investors, being the most interested party, to take an active role in monitoring corporate management (PEC lawyer B, interview on 2 November 1999). The PSPD thought that, despite its pioneering achievements, shareholder activism founded on individual investors could not easily be institutionalized. Without a devoted coordinator such as the PSPD, individuals could never have been mobilized. Therefore, "institutional investors should take the lead so that shareholder activism can take root as a paradigm for [corporate] reform" (PEC lawyer B, interview on 2 November 1999).

Korean financial institutions hold about 10 percent of listed companies' shares (Table 7.7). Although individuals hold the largest part of the shares (i.e., 34.7 percent), it is institutions that, on average, hold the most shares per investor. For example, an investment trust company holds, on average, 37.5 million shares. Of course, this does not necessarily mean that institutional investors are an influential minority in individual firms. This can be decided only in consideration of the degree

Table 7.7 Domestic institutional shareholdings, as of 31 Dec. 2000

	Investment Trust Companies	Banks	Insurance Companies	Securities Companies	Others	Total
Number of investors	24	23	45	56	186	310
Number of shares (mil. won)	898.9	656.1	336.4	156.8	251.5	1,400.8
Ratio to the total shares (%)	(4.5)	(3.3)	(1.7)	(0.8)	(1.2)	(10.9)
Average shareholding (mil. won)	37.5	28.5	7.5	2.8	1.4	7.4

Source: KSE (2001a).

of dispersion of their investment. Nevertheless, according to the existing theory of shareholder activism, high average shareholdings means high incentives and low costs of corporate monitoring.

In practice, however, Korean funds, the type of institutions which have taken the lead in shareholder activism in other economies like the United States, are not active investors in the local stock market. Of the 75 funds which operated in Korea as of the end of 2000, only three pension funds (i.e., National Pension Fund, Government Employees Pension Fund, Teachers Pension Fund) invested directly in shares, and only on a small scale. It was said that this passivity was due to three reasons (MOFE 2000). First, the Framework Act on Fund Management prohibits, in principle, stock investments by a public fund. Second, funds which could invest in shares have regulated stock investment internally because they consider such investment too risky. Third, the fund managers tend to avoid stock investment for fear of reprimand if they lose on the investment.

Nor were other institutions proactive. From the PSPD's perspective, with institutional investors' cooperation, PSPD shareholder activism could have been much easier. As illustrated in Table 7.5, a single institutional investor can bring a derivative suit against the PSPD shareholder activism's target company, which could have saved the PSPD the trouble of gathering scattered individual investors.

For this reason, the PSPD tried to persuade domestic institutional investors into PSPD shareholder activism by pointing out that it was not merely their discretion but their duty to correct faulty corporate management:

> Your company has not only the right but also the duty to reform faulty corporate management. Especially, your company, as an institutional

Table 7.8 Institutional shareholdings (%), 1986–1999

	Banks	Investment trust companies	Securities firms	Insurance companies
1986	7.04	0.76	6.72	4.98
1987	5.61	0.77	2.63	4.41
1988	6.52	0.53	3.14	4.02
1989	3.15	2.67	5.07	2.60
1990	7.34	8.15	4.74	5.48
1991	8.92	7.68	4.92	5.54
1992	8.75	7.50	5.19	5.89
1993	10.72	6.17	4.72	5.78
1994	10.47	6.88	3.60	5.39
1995	11.17	6.26	2.86	5.65
1996	10.55	5.77	2.23	6.46
1997	9.42	2.66	2.11	6.34
1998	3.58	1.99	1.30	3.62
1999	3.50	4.79	0.84	1.79

Sources: KSE (various years). Jusik (Stock).

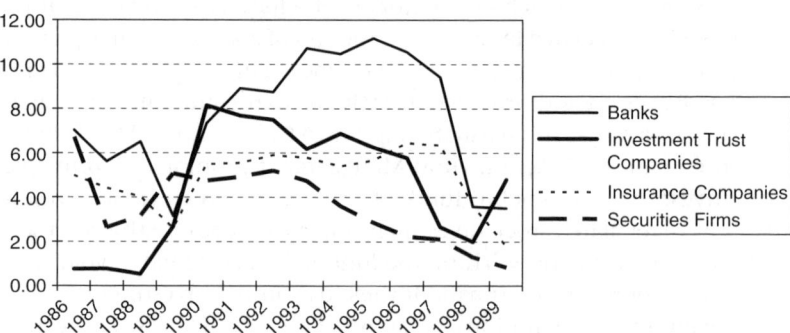

Figure 7.2 Institutional shareholdings (%), 1986–1999
Sources: KSE (various years). Jusik (stock).

investor, is obliged to protect the interests of investors who trusted the money to your company in good faith. . . . Therefore, your company's intervention in the derivative suit [concerned] will not only further the interests of your company and your customers but also create a precedent that re-establishes the status and role of institutional investors in this country. (PSPD's letter to institutional investors, 7 August 1998)

However, the responses from domestic institutional investors were at best half-hearted. "Foreign institutions visited us of their own accord

Table 7.9 Institutions controlled by non-financial companies, as of 31 July 1999

	Investment trust companies	Banks	Life insurance companies	Securities companies	Merchant banks
Institutions controlled by non-financial corporations	11	7	14	16	6
Total number of institutions	24	18	29	30	11

Source: Heo and Suh (1999).

[when they heard of the PSPD shareholder activism]. But we visited domestic institutions only to get a cold reply" (PEC academic *D*, interview on 23 February 2001).

Why were domestic institutional investors so passive? One reason was a perceived conflict of interests. Roughly speaking, in Korea, non-financial corporations have controlling shares in half of the domestic institutional investors (Table 7.9), so institutional investors controlled by a non-financial corporation tend to avoid exercising voting rights in other non-financial corporations for fear of a retaliatory vote (Heo and Suh, 1999). Furthermore, even some of the institutions not controlled by a non-financial corporation can hardly exercise their voting right against the management, because they need to maintain business relations with the corporation. For example, a bank may have business, such as corporate accounts or foreign exchange dealings, with a corporation whose shares it owns. Of course, different conflicts of interests may exist in different types of institutional investors. The single phrase "institutional investor", therefore, may obscure such differences. Notwithstanding, we just note here that institutional investors commonly experience the problem of conflicts of interest. PSPD members also believed that conflicts of interest were the main obstacle to institutional investors' activism (PEC officer *E*, interview on 11 October 1999; PEC lawyer *B*, interview on 2 November 1999).

A second reason for the passivity of domestic institutional investors was the remnants of previous regulations. Before 1998, institutional investors did not need to bother themselves with voting, because there were restrictions on institutional investors' voting through the Monopoly Act and the Ministry of Finance and Economy (MOFE) regulations. Since the 1986 amendment of the Monopoly Act, a financial institution affiliated to a *chaebol* could not exercise its voting right in other affiliates. This regulation aimed to prevent the *chaebol* from expanding or consolidating its group using money deposited by customers with its affiliated financial institutions. In 1995, MOFE regulations stipulated that banks and investment trust companies should follow shadow voting[11] for all shares purchased with trust property. This was to keep these institutions from exercising their voting right beyond the limits of their fiduciary duty (i.e., multiplying the client's property). In that year, for example, when Dongbu Group tried to acquire an agrochemical company, Hannong Co., Ltd., institutional investors' proxies were virtually all in favor of the acquisition (Chung, G.-J., 1995). This was because it was a custom at that time for institutional investors to issue proxies at the request of the company management. As a consequence, the institutions unwittingly endorsed the acquisition. To avoid this problem, by introducing shadow voting, the government neutralized institutional voting rights based on trust property.

The PSPD saw that the attitude of institutional investors was changing gradually in favor of its shareholder activism. In fact, since the government lifted the MOFE restrictions in 1998, institutional investors' voting has been increasing (Table 7.10). However, despite this change, institutional investors still remain conservative. In the case of the 2001 annual general meetings, only one voted against the management's proposal (Table 7.11). The partial objections in 2001 were only made to the minority

Table 7.10 Institutional investors' voting in the AGMs of all listed firms

	14.3.2000	14.3.2001	Change
Investment Trust Management Companies	58	214	156
Investment Companies	19	56	37
Banks	56	44	−12
Total	133	314	181

Source: KSE (2001b).

Table 7.11 Positions of institutional investors

	14.3.2000	14.3.2001	Change
Not determined	8	21	13
Objection	6	1	−5
Partial approval	0	38	38
Approval	119	254	135
Total	133	314	181

Source: KSE (2001b).

shareholders' proposals in Samsung Electronics, so we can conclude that institutional investors were still supportive of the management.

The PSPD also saw that newly established funds, presumably with less vested interests, showed a more positive attitude to shareholder activism:

> Fund managers' interests are gradually coinciding with PSPD shareholder activism. . . . A realization that reforming the management is of benefit to them is spreading. (PEC officer *E*, interview on 11 October 1999)

> New small-sized funds such as Mirae Asset Securities and Midas Asset Management tend to keep in step with us. (PEC academic *D*, interview on 23 February 2001)

Nevertheless, even cooperating with those new funds was not so easy. Kim Kihwan, a director in charge of asset management in Midas, once said that the PSPD's exposure of the misappropriation of Hyundai Investment Trust Management affected the stock market negatively, at least in the short term (Kim, K., 2000). On the very day of the 2001 annual general meeting of Samsung Electronics, Mirae reversed its previous public notice to support the PSPD-proposed candidate for internal director, Junn Sung-Chull, a lawyer and Dean of the Graduate School of Business Administration, Sejong University. Including Mirae, 19 institutions amended their original notice of an unconditional approval of the appointment of all the directors proposed to a partial approval with an objection to the PSPD-proposed candidate. Mirae explained that the earlier announcement had been a simple clerical mistake (Park, B.-K., 2001). Among 48 public notices[12] to the KSE, only one institutional investor, Seoul Investment Trust Management and two funds that it managed, supported the PSPD.

However, this picture does not show that the PSPD totally failed to obtain cooperation from domestic institutional investors. For example, a shareholder proposal organized by the PSPD in relation to Samsung Electronics needed one percent support of the total issued shares, and in this case the PSPD secured the support of 184,311 shares (1.19 percent of the total shares) from 66 domestic and foreign individuals and institutions (PSPD, 2001b). Furthermore, at the annual general meeting of Samsung Electronics, 14,221,582 shares (16.07 percent of the attended shares with a voting right) supported the PSPD proposal and, among others, domestic public pension funds such as the National Pension Corporation, the Korea Local Administration Officials' Mutual Fund, and the Government Employees Pension Corporation supported it for the first time (PSPD, 2001c).

Table 7.12 Institutions' response to a PSPD proposal in Samsung Electronics

	Support	Change from support to objection	Objection
Number of institutions	3	19	26
Number of shares	3,100	959,595	6,563,290
Ratio to total shares	(0.0018%)	(0.5442%)	(3.7221%)

Source: KSE-KIND (kind.kse.or.kr).

From this discussion, we cannot predict clearly the future path that domestic institutions will take. It is certain that those institutions' attitude toward active monitoring has been changing. But we will need more time and study to see where they are going.

Trade unions

As of the end of 2000, the ESOAs, which were established in 702 listed companies, owned 264,104 shares of the companies. In other words, ESOAs have 376 shares per company. In terms of the average shareholding, an ESOA has little more than the individuals in these companies. However, an alliance with an ESOA, whose management is closely related to the trade union's policy, has some advantages for the PSPD.

First of all, it means that PSPD shareholder activism can accommodate the leftist tradition of the Korean social movements, which, in turn, mitigates the criticism that PSPD shareholder activism is supporting capitalism. Labor's participation in management has long been a concern in Korean social movements (and even in policy circles). When it formed the Committee on Concentration of Economic Power, the predecessor of the PEC, the PSPD adopted it as one of its options for countering the concentration of economic power (PSPD, 1996).

Second, even with the same amount of shares as an individual, an ESOA has more bargaining power vis-à-vis the companies, because it is backed up by an organized, influential trade union.

Third, an ESOA also enables PSPD shareholder activism to target an unlisted company. The ESOAs in unlisted companies have recently been growing fast, while those in listed companies are almost saturated (Figure 7.3). This means that allying with an ESOA will considerably enlarge the scope of PSPD shareholder activism.

At the early stage of its shareholder activism, the PSPD tried to invite trade unions to join the movement. At the 1997 annual general meeting

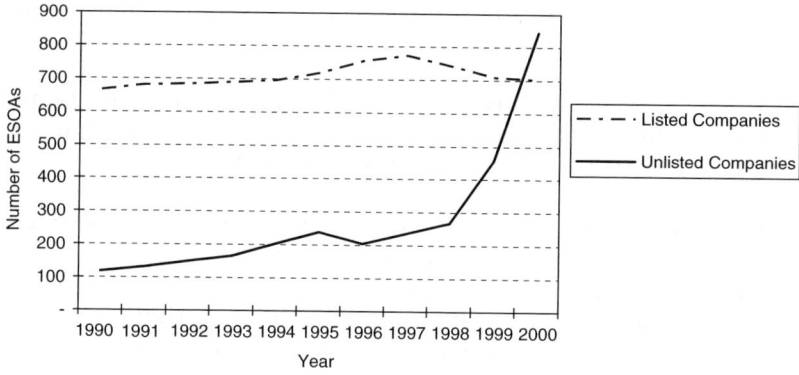

Figure 7.3 Growth of ESOAs, 1990–2000
Source: Korea Securities Finance Corporation.

of the KFB, for example, a PSPD representative blamed the management for having brought the employees' dedication to naught:

> As I see it, the employees of the KFB . . . are working really hard. However, [the management] ruined the result [of such hard work] in a single case of Hanbo. The whole staff took pains with the work, but . . . did the management work for the KFB and shareholders? (KFB, 1997: pp. 24–5)

Nevertheless, co-operation with trade unions has not been simple. The only significant exception was when seven members of the Kia ESOA joined in a suit claiming damages against Chungwoon Accounting, which was Kia's external auditor, and its seven accountants. In this PSPD-coordinated suit, the ESOA members argued that they had suffered from a loss in the value of shares of their employer, Kia Motors, due to the accounting company's inaccurate auditing. But this co-operation was made only in the members' private capacity.

Why did the PSPD and the trade unions co-operate so little, despite their shared opinion that the *chaebol* needed reform? As for the PSPD, the trade union was not seen as a "trustworthy partner in PSPD shareholder activism which requires a long-term perspective and patience" (PEC academic *D*, interview on 23 February 2001). In previous cases such as the KFB and Hyundai Heavy Industries, the PSPD found that the ESOA quickly compromised with the management when favorable conditions were offered to them. From this, the PSPD concluded that the ultimate goal of ESOAs was not to improve corporate governance. According to the PSPD, the trade union could see no further than its nose:

> The trade union itself is a self-interested group. But many people have an illusion that the trade union represents the public interest. (PEC academic D, interview on 23 February 2001)

> The trade union pays attention only to wage negotiations. They are more concerned with getting a bigger slice of the existing pie than making the pie bigger [through improved corporate governance]. . . . They insist on participation in management. But this is used only as leverage in wage negotiations. This made us cautious in allying ourselves with the trade union. (PEC academic D, interview on 23 November 1999)

For these reasons, the PSPD finally decided that the PSPD shareholder activism should not ally with the ESOAs representing self-interest (PEC lawyer C, interview on 11 October 1999).

From the standpoint of the trade union, participating in PSPD shareholder activism also caused problems. The union acting as a shareholder means that it shares some interests with the dominant shareholders and the management. Apart from the ideological dilemma it poses, this challenges the conventional view of the role of the union. By acting as shareholders, the trade union is pressed to decide whether utilizing employee stocks is a new tactic [of the traditional labor movement] or a new role [as shareholders] (Schwab and Thomas, 1998).[13] Here, we can observe another type of "decomposition of labor."[14] In fact, the PSPD urged the trade unions to take the status of shareholder as a new role rather than a new tactic:

> You [workers] are capitalists, too. . . . The ESOA [and thus the trade union] should be concerned with making labor earn capital gain. . . . In SK Telecom, many employees have made fortunes of a hundred, a thousand million [won]. The price of the employees' stocks, which were obtained at five thousand won, has now gone up to 2 million won. (PEC academic D, interview on 23 November 1999)

However, if the trade unions are to take a new role, they would have to abandon not only the past course of action but also many of the personnel accustomed to it. In fact, the radical Korean Confederation of Trade Unions (KCTU), which is comprised of 19 industrial federations and 1,226 individual unions, has been one of the groups which have been most suspicious of PSPD shareholder activism. The KCTU only refrains from criticizing it publicly because of its many other cooperative relations with the PSPD (PEC academic A, interview on 3 April 2001).

It is acknowledged by the PSPD that "of course, we have to keep a good relationship with the trade unions because they are important interested parties [of a corporation]" (PEC academic D, interview on 23 February 2001). When the government formed a Committee on Corporate Governance to come up with a best practice code of corporate governance, the PSPD seceded from the committee on account that "the committee has no member who represents employees, one of the directly interested parties to the corporate management" (PSPD's letter to the MOFE, 23 March 1999).

Nevertheless, some PSPD members blamed the trade unions for non-cooperation with PSPD shareholder activism.

> The trade union and the institutional investors should take on the work beyond PSPD shareholder activism's reach. But they did not. . . . The PSPD is only playing a role within its limited scope. (PEC lawyer B, interview on 2 November 1999)

> We do not have to worry about the relationship with the trade union because we don't work for the labor movement. . . . The lack of cooperation is not our fault but the trade union's. (PEC academic D, interview on 23 February 2001)

However, we should also note that some took a different view that the estrangement with the trade union was not their responsibility but the shared responsibility of the both sides:

> [Such estrangement] was due to the absence of a channel through which both sides could cooperate with trust. In the PSPD, no one has kept the channels of communication constantly open with labor. And to do so, one should contribute significantly to the labor movement [but the PSPD did not]. Even those who participated in the labor movement in the past no longer maintain such a channel. (PEC academic A, interview on 3 April 2001)

To sum up, the trade unions and ESOAs experience a structural difficulty in collaborating with the PSPD in shareholder activism. The same is true the other way round. Despite many advantages, we cannot foresee a dramatic development in the relationship between the two in the near future.

Foreign institutional shareholders

As of the end of 2000, 11,748 foreign investors held 13.9 percent of the total shares of listed companies in Korea. 99.7 percent of the foreign investors were institutional investors. Investment companies and banks, the two largest categories of foreign investors, had 78.4 percent of the foreigner-held shares.

It is not certain to what extent foreign investors have supported PSPD shareholder activism. Unlike the case of domestic individuals and institutions, the PSPD said that had no information about foreign investors' support for its shareholder activism.

Despite the lack of available information, foreign investors do seem to have been potentially the most potent allies of the PSPD shareholder activism. Although PSPD shareholder activism with foreign support has not been successful enough to outmaneuver management, it would be a constant threat to the management that foreign investors with considerable shareholdings might collaborate with the PSPD at any time. In fact, such a threat has been realized. "Samsung was shocked at the outcome of the 1999 annual general meeting. Foreign shareholders supported our proposal [to amend the articles of association] with 15 percent of the voted shares" (PEC academic D, interview on 19 January 2001). However, it is not known exactly how supportive foreign investors have been in proxy fights.

What is clear is that the support of foreign investors has been of limited scope. For example, foreign institutions were cautious in participating in lawsuits. It was not until November 2000 that foreign institutions such as the Korea Fund (US) and Emerging Market Investors Fund (Canada) first joined a lawsuit (*Yonhap News*, 2000). Since the suit was a provisional disposition to suspend the directors of Samsung Electronics from their duties, it may have appeared less burdensome than other lawsuits such as derivative suits.

In the previous discussion about domestic financial institutions, it was said that, unlike their domestic counterparts, foreign institutions voluntarily visited the PSPD to find out about PSPD shareholder activism. Why were foreign investors more active than their domestic counterparts in this respect? A PSPD member argues that it is because foreign fund managers shared their fate with the Korean economy:

> Korea and the fund managers of the foreign financial institutions are all in the same boat. Asia has become one of the most important parts of the so-called emerging market. Foreign institutions cannot simply sell their Asian shares and move into another region. . . . If Korea

collapses, about 100 fund managers specializing in the Asian region might lose their job. (PEC academic *D*, interview on 19 January 2001)

When it comes to shared fate, it is perhaps more plausible that domestic institutions might be more desperate than foreigners. The PSPD understood, however, that domestic institutions did not see things in that light. Furthermore, it was pointed out that, even if they did, they could not take any action due to the conflict of interest.

Support from foreign investors was relatively readily available, but never free from complication. Cooperating with foreign investors is one of the most sensitive issues for PSPD shareholder activism. For a recent example, in a contribution to a local newspaper, the *Chosun Ilbo*, Bahk Jaewan,[15] a public administration professor of Sungkyunkwan University, criticized the PSPD's overseas road shows[16] as creating "a situation in which, in a fight over the control of our corporation, domestic dominant and minority shareholders are begging a favor from foreign capital without reaching a point of mutual beneficial agreement" (Bahk, 2001).

Others pointed out that, even if the PSPD acted with honorable intentions, foreign investors might take advantage. "In the interests of specific shareholders [indicating foreign investors], the PSPD intervenes in the affairs that they do not need to" (executive *M* of a target firm, interview on 3 November 1999). "As was the case with Hyundai Heavy Industries, it was often argued that we [the PSPD] intentionally targeted companies that had many foreign investors" (PEC academic *D*, interview on 19 January 2001).

Furthermore, the PSPD itself was watchful of the alliance:

> The PSPD made it an important principle of PSPD shareholder activism not to cooperate with short-term investors. We have stuck to this principle when contacting foreign investors. (PEC academic *D*, interview on 31 March 2001)

On top of the criticisms from outside the PSPD, insiders also expressed anxieties about the alliance. In discord with the alliance on this point, one lawyer transferred from the PEC to another PSPD body. Some worried about the possible loss of popular support if PSPD shareholder activism failed to produce a remarkable success with foreigners' support:

> I'm worried about the PSPD shareholder activism's estrangement from the general public. . . . If it fails despite the alliance with foreign investors, the PSPD shareholder activism might lose its domestic footing, especially the trade union's [implicit] support [including refraining

from criticizing the PSPD shareholder activism in public]. (PSPD academic G, interview on 2 January 2001)

Others were concerned about whether they were breaking a new path mainly for the sake of foreign investors: "I was always wondering whether we can indeed match them [if we happen to get into conflict with the currently collaborating foreign institutions]?" (PEC academic A, interview on 22 February 2001). Encountering foreign investors reminded some PSPD members of the tale of the Trojan Horse.

How did the PSPD respond to such criticisms? First, some said that foreign investors were a last resort:

> The trouble was that [individual] minority shareholders were, by nature, not to be organized. [Domestic] institutional investors were either affiliated to the *chaebol* or heavily indebted, and thus virtually owned by the state [which owns or controls many banks]. In this situation, we had to join hands with foreign institutional investors. (PSPD academic G, interview on 2 January 2001)

> So, there may be a body of criticisms [regarding our alliance with foreign investors]. But we are determined to put up with it [because we think there is no alternative]. (PEC academic D, interview on 23 November 1999)

Second, some maintained that there was no reason to prioritize the selection of investors supporting their movement according to nationality:

> It is hard to find a difference between domestic and foreign institutional investors. Those who argue the difference tell an obscure story, when asked for a real example. [For example, it is said that] our institutions invest in the longer term; they [foreigners] just try to make money. But institutional investors are all the same in trying to make money. (PEC academic D, interview on 23 February 2001)

The PSPD believed that it would be natural for any participant in PSPD shareholder activism to try to gain materially from it. "Without such an incentive, who would join the PSPD shareholder activism?" (PEC academic D, 23 November 1999). However, an investor who supports PSPD shareholder activism might exploit the PSPD only as a way to improve their short-term bargaining position. For example, in August 1999, SK Group acquired 9.5 percent of SK Telecom shares from Tiger Management, a New York-based fund. At an extraordinary general meeting due four days later, a plan for a rights issue proposed by the management was to proceed to a vote. The PSPD and Tiger Management had been in opposition to the plan. The SK Group's purchase of Tiger-held shares, however, made the group hold 36.5 percent of SK Telecom shares and have the plan approved successfully. The PSPD criticized the decision of Tiger Management:

> The PSPD expects Tiger Fund to exercise its voting rights at this coming shareholders' general meeting, as originally manifested. Should Tiger Fund conclude the transaction [i.e., transfer of shares] on condition of voting for the management in this EGM, it will be a typical greenmail. For this, both Tiger Fund and SK Group cannot avoid criticism and legal responsibility. (PSPD's statement, 23 August 1999)

Third, the PSPD emphasized that they were independent of the foreign investors. For example, responding to a news report that identified the PSPD's claim with that of the foreign investors, the PSPD refuted:

> It was known recently that SK Telecom and foreign shareholders such as Tiger Fund reached an agreement regarding transparency improvement and shareholder rights protection. On this fact, some of the press reported as if the PSPD had agreed with SK Telecom. . . . [But] this agreement has nothing to do with the PSPD [which has pursued its own agreement with SK Telecom]. (PSPD's statement, 21 March 1998)

The PSPD emphasized that they took the initiative in raising issues themselves and did not follow the demands of specific shareholders. The PSPD raised issues only in consideration of the public interest, and it would not discriminate between supportive investors in so far as they shared a "long-term" goal with the PSPD. "We choose an issue to be raised, and they [any type of investors] decide whether they will follow us or not" (PEC academic D, interview on 19 January 2001). Jang Hasung pointed out that "we have requested support from domestic and foreign shareholders alike, and have never solicited a specific foreign short-term investor" (private letter to Bahk responding to his contribution, 31 January 2001).

In sum, compared with other available supporting groups, such as PSPD members and individual shareholders, foreign institutions are one of the most powerful shareholders that can assist the PSPD shareholder

Table 7.13 Comparing shareholder groups

	Opportunities	Challenges
PSPD members	• Prompt action	• Lack of representativeness and significance
Individuals	• Symbol of nation-wide support	• High mobilizing costs • Divergent interests (Pursuit of private gains) • Instability
Domestic institutions	• Large shareholdings • Changing positive attitude toward corporate governance issues	• Conflict of interest with target firms
Trade unions	• Embracing the past left-wing tradition • Greater bargaining power • Accessibility to some unlisted companies	• Pursuit of private gains • Conflict of interest with existing activists
Foreign institutions	• Large shareholdings • Relatively positive attitude toward corporate governance issues	• Criticisms within and without the PSPD

activism. However, to keep the relationship with their foreign partners, the PSPD will have to cope with worries raised from within and without the PSPD. The main concern is that the foreign institutions would make use of the PSPD, its target corporations, and the Korean economy as a whole, in their greed for money.

To conclude the discussion of shareholder support, Table 7.13 summarizes the advantages and disadvantages of the PSPD's collaborating with the five different groups of shareholders.

8
Conclusion

Based on the previous three chapters, this chapter will draw some conclusions on the rise of shareholder activism in Korea. As Chapter 1 elaborates, there are three interconnected but separate levels of 'emergence' which a researcher will have to investigate: (1) how a potential activist group which has not previously used shareholder activism gets to grips with it; (2) what makes it continue, or even boost, its shareholder activism; and (3) how shareholder activism increases steadily on an aggregate level. The first section will answer the three questions based on the findings previously made. The second section will discuss implications for scholars, policymakers and managers with regard to shareholder activism and corporate governance in general.

Findings on three emergences

First use

The study of PSPD activism finds that the cognitive linkage between an already given problem (i.e., the *chaebol* problem) and a new ameliorative action (i.e., shareholder activism) is more crucial than the very existence of the problem itself to explain the initial use of shareholder activism. This point gives rise to more specific questions: (1) how shareholder activism entered into the alternative set of the potential activist, PSPD; and (2) why the activist chose it from among many remedies.

With regard to the first question, we have argued that socio-political contexts provided the PSPD with a clue to utilizing shareholder activism. These contexts include the domestic debates on corporate governance reform and resulting government policy. The policy debates produced a new prognostic frame suggesting that claiming minority shareholder rights might check the arbitrariness of controlling shareholders like the *chaebol chongsu*, one of the main concerns of Korean civil organizations including the PSPD. Even before it was implemented, the government announcement to give minority shareholders more power reinforced the framing process in the sense that the government authorized the new frame and assured the public of its legitimacy.[1]

With regard to the second question as to the selection of shareholder activism, we found no definite evidence that the PSPD fully appreciated the effects that might be caused by their activism when first deciding to take up shareholder activism. On the contrary, our understanding is that the PSPD did not understand the effectiveness of shareholder activism until they made use of it. Thus seen, the first emergence of PSPD shareholder activism is quite close to the explanation offered by the contingent decision-making model of the garbage can (Cohen, March and Olsen, 1972), which highlights organizational decision as a timely combination of situation, problem, actor and alternative.

However, this does not necessarily lead to a conclusion that we can say nothing about the first emergence of PSPD shareholder activism. We have argued that the pragmatic attitude of the PSPD functioned as a guide throughout the process of their noticing and selecting shareholder activism. Having realized that the traditional tools of civil movements have few teeth in addressing the *chaebol* problem, the PSPD steadily and pragmatically sought a way of making the most of legal power of enforcement. What we are emphasizing here is that the actor's pragmatic disposition and the favorable social contexts between them threw a new element of shareholder activism into the garbage can and rendered a greater cohesive power to the PSPD than to other potential activists who also had the same problem and socio-political contexts (e.g., the CCEJ).

This explanation of the emergence of shareholder activism as closely related to prognostic framing seems to hold in other cases, too. To illustrate, let us take an example of the first social reform campaign in the United States which sought to mobilize shareholders (Talner, 1983). In September 1966, a Rochester, NY, ghetto organization named Freedom, Integration, God, Honor–Today (FIGHT) demanded that the city's largest employer, Eastman Kodak, provide blacks with employment opportunities. Three months later, John B. Mulder, an assistant vice president at Kodak, and Rev. Franklin Delano Roosevelt Florence, FIGHT's president, signed an agreement. However, Kodak's top management repudiated the company's participation in anything that hinted at compliance with FIGHT's demands.

In this situation, FIGHT needed to force their demands on Kodak, but they found conventional mediums of influence such as demonstrations or economic boycotts ineffective. In his book *Rules for Radicals*, Saul Alinsky, a well-known American activist who had been invited to lead FIGHT, recalled the birth of a new tactic of proxy fight as follows:

> As the lines were drawn for battle it became clear that the usual strategy of demonstrations and confrontations would be unavailing. . . . We then began looking for appropriate tactics. An economic boycott was rejected because of Kodak's overwhelming domination of the film-negative market. . . . Other wild ideas were tossed about. . . . The proxy idea first came up as a way to gain entrance to the annual stockholders' meeting for harassment and publicity. . . (Alinsky, 1971: pp. 170–2)

Furthermore, Alinsky endeavours to persuade fellow activists that rationality does not work much in creating a new tactic as follows:

> [T]actics are not the product of careful cold reason. . . . [T]hey do not follow a table of organization or plan of attack. Accident, unpredictable reactions to your own actions, necessity, and improvisation dictate the direction and nature of tactics. (Alinsky, 1971: p. 165)

At first glance, our explanation looks similar to the previous theories that understand the emergence of shareholder activism basically as a result of choice among monitoring mechanisms. However, in at least three points, our argument is different from that of the existing studies.

First, previous theories delimit the actors of shareholder activism and their motive, albeit implicitly. They assume that shareholders resort to activism for financial interest. By contrast, our emphasis on cognitive linkages in shareholder activism does not necessarily presume any actor or motive. On the contrary, our explanation underlines the indeterminacy of actor and aim of shareholder activism. According to our framework, shareholder activism can occur even when non-shareholders who face various problems other than stock returns recognize the adequacy of shareholder rights as a remedy to their own problems.

Second, partly related to the first point, previous theories assume that shareholder activism always exists in the alternative set of the actor and that the actor is fully aware of it. On the other hand, our study highlights that, when explaining the emergence of shareholder activism, we should generally investigate the process of incorporating shareholder activism into the existing alternative set and of selecting it out of the extended alternative set. This is important even for a traditional type of shareholder activism in which shareholders pursue their own financial interests because, for many shareholders, activism has not been a conventional way of dealing with low stock returns.

Third, also related to the first point, the factors in favor of shareholder activism introduced by existing theories have very limited applicability. The story is mostly about institutional investors. Our study suggests that these factors do not generally encourage other types of shareholder activism. Furthermore, we argue that factors affecting the emerging process of shareholder activism are too various and case-specific to generalize. Among various external factors, the impact of government policy is the only factor that existing studies and our own have in common. However, we point out in the following section that even government policy does not have a decisive impact on the emergence of shareholder activism. Therefore, generalization should be sought in the inherent characteristics of shareholder rights, which really is a common element of all types of shareholder activism, instead of a variety of external factors. These characteristics of shareholder rights will be summarized below.

Regular ongoing use

How could the PSPD shareholder activism transform itself from an unconvincing one-off trial into a regular instrument? The answer lies in both sides of the cost-effectiveness of PSPD shareholder activism.

Shareholder activism as an effective remedy

Shareholder rights are an effective medium of influence on the corporation, because of two unique characteristics: the rights to residual claims and to residual control.

The PSPD discovered that, being a residual claimant, a shareholder can argue even non-financial issues more extensively and more legitimately than other stakeholders such as employees and social activists. In many cases, shareholders can link a seemingly unethical or unfair decision of a corporation (e.g., pollution) with their investment return (e.g., loss of sales due to a boycott by environment-conscious consumers). For a similar example from the case the Medical Committee's antiwar campaign against Dow Chemical, Dr Quentin Young argued that the Medical Committee was motivated primarily by moral concerns for the preservation of human life but also by concern for the financial consequences to the firm from negative publicity generated by protests against

Dow (Talner, 1983). This is a persuasive argument in mobilizing the shareholders, attacking corporate policy, and resorting to the courts.

Furthermore, the shareholders are endowed with residual control rights over a corporation such as a right to participate in general shareholder meetings, to which other stakeholders are not entitled. Some of this access can be gained by holding only one share. In 1969, for another example, Charles Pillsbury purchased one share of Honeywell stock and then asked the company to provide him with a list of its shareholders so that he could share his concerns about Honeywell's production of war material with fellow owners (Talner, 1983). In this sense, shareholder rights can also be an economic way of gaining access to the company.

Based on this effectiveness and a favorable socio-political context, the PSPD won several consecutive victories after the first trial at the KFB. These successes reinforced the PSPD's incentive to continue using minority shareholder rights. Popular responses also encouraged the PSPD to enlarge the scope of its shareholder activism to the big five chaebol.

Efficient management

Since it is costly to maintain continuous shareholder activism and its mobilizing structure, it is crucial to reduce costs as much as possible. The PSPD case suggested a few ways of reducing costs.

First, the PSPD started with less costly activities such as attending shareholder general meetings because, at least at the initial stage, there were few resources to mobilize and the prospect of success was relatively unclear. This also applies to Saul Alinsky's FIGHT case in which they also started by attending an annual general meeting, which requires a relatively small number of shareholders and experts, compared with other activist action such as proxy fights or derivative suits.

Second, existing studies of shareholder activism do not deal specifically with how to mobilize resources, but they implicitly assume that these exist outside of the actor of shareholder activism and are therefore costly. However, the PSPD showed that some essential resources such as expertise and shareholders can be internalized within the organization, which greatly reduced mobilizing costs.

Third, by a masterful, albeit imperfect, framing that accommodated the minimum essence of the new and old views of a corporation, the PSPD managed to acquire support from company law specialists and institutional investors who sympathized with the new view as well as from social activists who supported the old. This suggests that the costs of mobilizing resources can be changed not only by government policy but also by cultural manipulation.

Thus seen, under a given set of conditions, an entrepreneurial organizer can reduce the costs of shareholder activism significantly by: (1) choosing a target action deliberately; (2) internalizing some essential resources within the mobilizing structure; and (3) reinterpreting the given situation from the viewpoint of essential resource providers.

Society-wide spread

It is too early to decide whether PSPD activism will lead to a general spread of shareholder activism in Korean society. Nonetheless, we can see two aspects of PSPD activism which may induce society to accommodate shareholder activism more than before.

Producing a new script

The use of shareholder activism ceases when the user achieves his/her goal. We presume that this is what happened with most of the shareholder action before the PSPD's. The shareholder activism prior to the PSPD's was short-lived and thought of as an exceptional incident rather than common practice. For this reason, many people even believe that there was no shareholder activism before the PSPD's activity.

Contrarily, whenever it has succeeded in fighting an issue, the PSPD has shifted its concern to another *chaebol* issue in the same company or to an issue in another company which can be tackled with shareholder activism (see Table 5.4). This continuous issue raising is important for the institutionalization of shareholder activism. Barley and Tolbert's (1997) explanation of institutionalization is a useful concept here. According to them, institutional change occurs when a new script different from the previous ones is formed and maintained. Here scripts mean observable, recurrent activities and patterns of interaction characteristic of a particular setting. If we find differences between recent and past scripts, we could say that the institution has changed. For an institutional change, we need an actor which forms a new script and continuously acts, or forces other actors to act, according to the new script.[2]

From this perspective, we can say that throughout their activities, the PSPD have produced a 'script' to the effect that the *chaebol* shall experience shareholder activism whenever they attempt to engage in activities such as ownership concentration, diversification and in-group support. At the same time, they have produced a script to the effect that shareholders whose wealth has been appropriated by corporate insiders have a way of putting pressure on management through the various tools of shareholder activism.

Organizational spin-offs

Related to the issue of continuity, one thing that we should note here is the reproduction of a key actor. This includes the voluntary imitation by other actors, but an interesting point from the PSPD case is the diversification of the original activist group once it becomes aware of the potential of shareholder activism. Through the establishment of the law firm Hannuri and the CGCG, the PSPD sought to institutionalize its shareholder activism so that it could be operated on a commercial basis.

Social movement theorists have identified two dynamic processes through which movement entrepreneurs have been produced: (1) cultivation within an organization; and (2) cadre diversification between organizations. Seldom do individuals join a movement organization *per se*, at least initially. Rather, it is far more common for individuals to agree to participate in some activity or campaign by devoting some measure of time, energy, or money (Lofland and Jamison, 1984; McAdam, 1984; Snow, Zurcher and Ekland-Olson, 1980). Through their participation some members are cultivated into more enthusiastic entrepreneurs.[3]

Once cultivated, hard-core activists can move into and open other fields of social movement. Among social movement scholars, this "cadre diversification" was thought to be critical in launching a wide array of social movements (Jenkins, 1983b). In other words, the movement entrepreneurs are typically generated by the "fractionalization of previous movements." The dynamic processes of mobilization, cultivation and cadre diversification are illustrated in Figure 8.1.

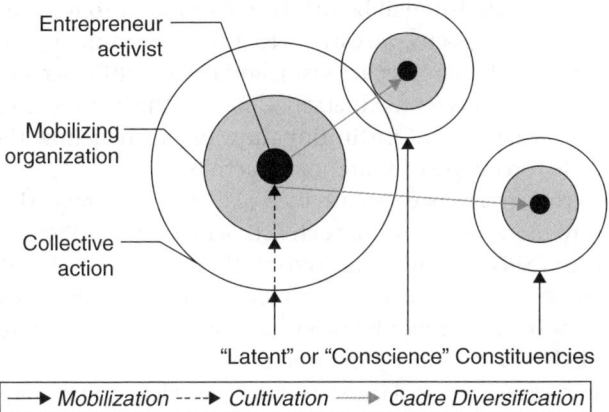

Figure 8.1 Dynamics of collective action organization

From this, in order to understand the institutionalization of shareholder activism, we need to pay more attention to the rise of the key actors who continuously raise issues and to the transmitting mechanism of shareholder activism to other actors. Viewed from the important role of a change agent in institutionalization, efforts by many governments to foster an actor triggering institutional changes in corporate governance are thought to be adequate. For example, the Malaysian Institute of Corporate Governance (www.micg.net) was incorporated under the Companies Act of 1965 in March 1998 as a public company. Similar examples in the Asian region include the Indonesian Institute for Corporate Directorship (www.iicd.or.id), the Chinese Center of Corporate Governance and the Center for Corporate Responsibility (Philippines, www.rvr.aim.edu.ph).

Implications

Policymakers

Many believe that corporate governance reforms which promote shareholder monitoring positively affect the emergence of shareholder activism. From our study, we can say that government policy is important in the sense that it can encourage the potential activist to include shareholder activism in his/her choice set and can reduce the costs of shareholder activism.

Corporate governance reform influences the emergence of shareholder activism through at least three channels, two of which we can find in the PSPD case.

The strongest and most assured way of triggering and institutionalizing shareholder activism will be for the government to force it by legislation. When this happens, we can say that the government policy causes the emergence of shareholder activism, and there is little need for further study about the reasons for its emergence. Rather, the focus of study should be on the informal side of institutionalization, such as how the society adjusts to the forced use of shareholder activism.

Another role that government can play to encourage shareholder activism is to reduce the costs of such activism, such as solicitation costs. In the case of PSPD shareholder activism, they could not file a derivative suit, which costs more but has a greater impact than the early actions such as attending a shareholder meeting, until the shareholding requirements for a derivative suit were lowered.

Lastly, an important role of the state, which previous studies have missed, is that it can hint, to a potential activist, at a new frame which links shareholder activism to a given problem and justifies the use of shareholder activism. We have mentioned this point with regard to the impact of the socio-political context on the PSPD's noticing shareholder activism. From the PSPD case study, we can say that in influencing the emergence of shareholder activism, this role of the government precedes the role of reducing monitoring costs. If a potential actor does not include shareholder activism in his/her choice set of ameliorative actions, reduced monitoring costs will be irrelevant.

Nevertheless, it should be noted that it is not a decisive factor in making shareholder activism occur unless it removes the potential actor's freedom of choice by forcing shareholder activism. The final action by the potential activist is more critical to the emergence of shareholder activism than government action. This leads to the second implication for the adequacy of the current policy model.

As shown in the Introduction, among policymakers, it has been understood that there exists a virtuous cycle between corporate governance reform and shareholder activism (Figure 0.1). The policymakers' understanding of shareholder activism as described here is based on the return maximization assumption of shareholder behavior and the shareholder model of a firm. Let's see how these assumptions work in designing corporate governance reform.

A reason for the importance of corporate governance based on the shareholder model is that it enhances individual countries' long-term economic performance (Wright, 1999). A basic assumption of this belief is that a shareholder is a beneficiary of residual returns and a rational economic agent maximizing returns. Since shareholders' efforts to increase their own residual returns will increase the value of the firm with the amount of investment unchanged, efficiency, which is measured by the ratio of output to input, will also increase. Shareholders' self-interested behavior to increase their own income will force managers to choose management strategies to maximize firm value, and eventually maximize the total value of the firm in which they have invested (Alchian and Demsetz, 1972).

To present the general understanding of shareholder activism depicted in Figure 0.1 more clearly, Figure 8.2 adds the return maximization assumption of shareholder behavior and the shareholder model regarding the nature of the firm necessary to make this virtuous cycle logical.

However, the emergence in Korea of shareholder activism that does not seem to follow the shareholder model challenges the premise on which the current interest in shareholder activism has been based. We have argued that the emergence of shareholder activism may be a combined result of the actor's pragmatic disposition, the coercive power of

128 *Shareholder Activism*

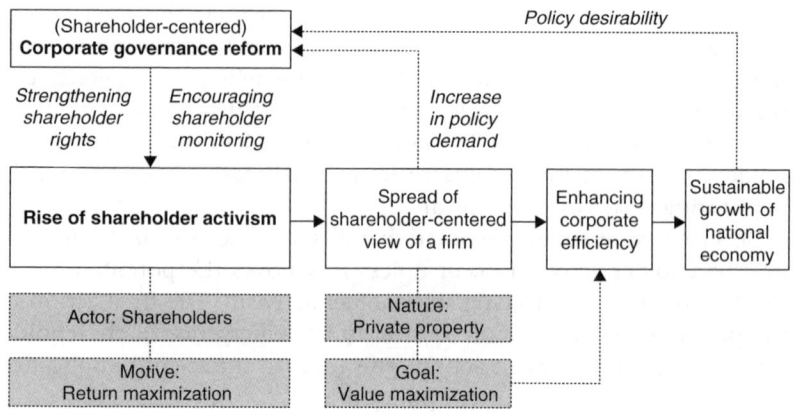

Figure 8.2 Assumptions underlying corporate governance reforms

shareholder rights and favorable social contexts. One of the most important inferences drawn from this argument is that shareholder activism can be combined with either a private property view or a social entity view of the corporation. According to our framework, shareholder activism may occur even when non-shareholders who face various problems other than stock returns recognize the adequacy of shareholder rights as a remedy to their own problems.

This point can be illustrated as follows. There are two cogwheels: (1) shareholder activism based on the shareholder model; and (2) one based on a stakeholder model. They are engaging each other, and the point of contact, that is, a common element of both shareholder activisms, is the characteristics of shareholder rights as an effective influence on a corporation. Let's suppose that we are oiling Wheel I in order to make the wheel (i.e., shareholder activism based on the shareholder model) rotate more smoothly. But, since the two wheels are engaging each other, the oiling also affects the other wheel's rotation. Which wheel will rotate faster will be determined by the size of each wheel. But strangely these cogwheels can vary in size, and we cannot predict which wheel will spin faster. The relative size of the two cogwheels depends on the framing, that is, who will take notice of the power of shareholder rights, and from what perspective.

Can the government separate these two wheels artificially? Institutionalization includes both a formal part such as regulatory changes, which the government can control almost completely and a informal

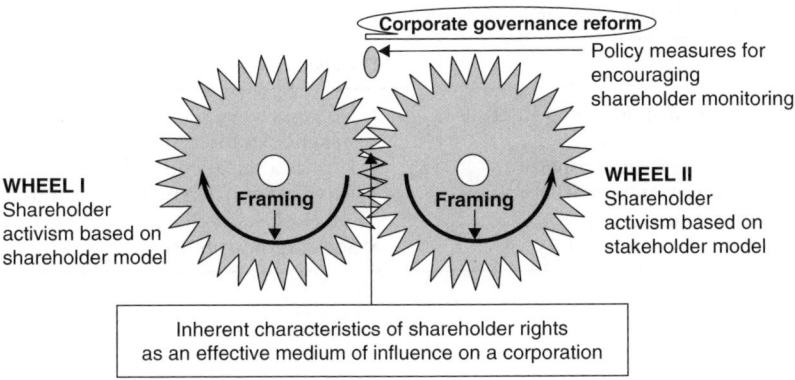

Figure 8.3 Shareholder activism as spinning cogwheels

part more or less out of the government's control. It is difficult for the government to manipulate shareholder behavior in order to suppress the emergence of types of shareholder activism which the government did not expect when designing corporate governance reform. Buying shares gives the shareholder a right to residual control and to residual claims. However, this does not oblige the shareholder to maximize investment returns. Even if the shareholder pursues return maximization, it has been argued that there are various ways of pursuing it.

Furthermore, informal institutions can affect their formal counterparts. As discussed in Chapter 1, for example, the Medical Committee for Human Rights who protested against the use of napalm in the Vietnam War obtained a historical decision of the US Court of Appeals for the District of Columbia Circuit which allowed the use of shareholder proposals to confront management on business matters with social impact (Talner, 1983).

Therefore, we can conclude that the government cannot separate these two wheels. It is certain that government policy is one of the powerful tools to change people's behavior. Institutional change is frequently analyzed as a result of supply and demand for policy (Alston, 1996; Lin and Nugent, 1995). However, government action does not determine the whole direction of institutional change.[4] If the group targeted by a policy does not act as predicted by the policy, then policymakers should investigate what this unpredicted behavior means to the original policy goal and how they should deal with it (Hogwood and Gunn, 1984).

Table 8.1 Two models of corporate governance

Shareholder model	Stakeholder model
• Primacy of shareholder interest	• No predetermined primacy among stakeholder interests
• Firm as a private property	• Firm as a social entity
• Maximization of market value of the firm	• Balanced enhancement of various stakeholders' welfare
• Financial accountability	• Social responsibility

Scholars

In the corporate governance literature, it is said that there are two different views of a corporation: the shareholder model and the stakeholder model[5] (Mayer, 1996; Shleifer and Vishny, 1997; OECD, 1998b). According to the shareholder model, or private property view, the objective of the firm is to maximize shareholder wealth. This model views the corporation as the private property of shareholders and its market value as a major performance standard. On the other hand, the stakeholder model, or social entity view, sees the corporation as responsible to all stakeholders in the firm, a wider constituency than shareholders. According to this view, the corporation is not strictly private and should be a socially responsible institution managed in the public interest. Accordingly, performance is judged by the overall advancement of the general welfare of the various constituencies. Some distinct characteristics of these two models are compared in Table 8.1.

From the discussion of PSPD shareholder activism, we can see that these two views interacted to cause one of the most successful shareholder activisms in developing countries. In Figure 8.4, we illustrate the emergence and institutionalization of PSPD shareholder activism, a simplified version of Figure 6.3. Throughout the process these two models, which previous scholars have taken to be different and irreconcilable, are closely intertwined. Therefore, we will have to reconsider the argument that the two models are distinct.

In this sense, two recent developments are observable. First, actors in shareholder activism have diversified to other stakeholder groups. In 2005, for example, 44 percent of corporate governance proposals in the US were made by trade unions (Georgeson Shareholders, 2005). Religious organizations account for 6 percent and public pensions, the main object of previous studies, only 4 percent. Second, activist concerns are blending. It is usually understood that shareholder activism has addressed two

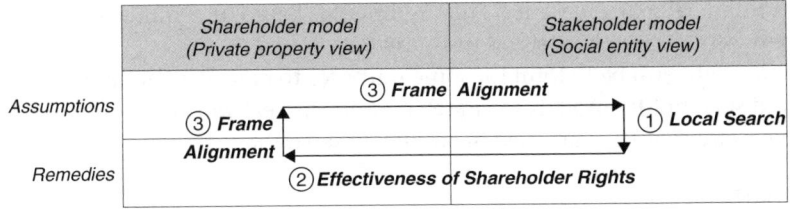

Figure 8.4 Circular relation between the two models

distinct issues – financially-oriented corporate governance issues and politically-motivated social issues – and these two types of shareholder activism should be studied separately for they do not share a common element in terms of motives, objectives and goals. However, recent developments witness that social activists have become much interested in conventional corporate governance issues and shareholders are much concerned about social issues. Shareholder activism is now evolving into a means of influence exploited by wider stakeholders (Cespa and Cestone, 2002; O'Rourke, 2003; Doh and Guay, 2006).

Our argument is supported further by recent discussion on ethical investment. Current debate has developed in two directions. One direction includes a movement from the stakeholder model to the shareholder model (e.g., Simon, Powers and Gunnemann, 1972; EIRIS, 1993; Sparkes, 1995). The argument goes: "Are you conscious of corporate wrongdoing such as child labor? Then buy some shares of the corporation concerned. If you become an owner (i.e., shareholder) of the corporation, then you can have a legitimate say in the corporation's unethical behaviors." Obviously, this argument is based on the lack of any powerful influence within the traditional alternative set (① in Figure 8.4), and on the unique characteristics of shareholder rights, discussed above (② in Figure 8.4).

The other direction moves from the shareholder side to the stakeholder side. This argument highlights the fact that stakeholder-sensitive management will improve not only the social but also the financial performance of the corporation (e.g., Johnson and Greening, 1999; Weaver, Trevino and Cochran, 1999; Roman, Hayibor and Agle, 1999; Harrison and Freeman, 1999). A typical argument goes: "Are you worrying about low returns in your stock investment? A reason may be that the company has low ethical standards. If you want to increase your investment returns, you will have to be concerned with corporate citizenship as well as financial management." This argument is based on a frame alignment between the two models (③ in Figure 8.4).

It might still be helpful for some purposes to consider the shareholder and stakeholder models separately, but in the real world we will have to be aware that they are never completely separable.

Managers

What changes can be brought to corporate management by changes in corporate environment such as strengthened shareholder rights?

Recent corporate responses to corporate governance reform have centered on investor relations. Investor relations are a company activity which provides information about the company's business and financial performance to existing and potential shareholders. Is it sufficient for managers to prepare only for financial shareholder activism?

In lieu of the possibility of the simultaneous rotation of the two wheels, managers cannot safely disregard any issues that a shareholder raises. They cannot ignore them for the simple reason that they are not financial. In other words, as financially motivated shareholder activism puts pressure on managers, so does politically motivated activism. Furthermore, as shown in the PSPD case, in some social contexts, politically motivated activism might put a greater pressure on a corporation and its managers than financially motivated activism. Therefore, as far as managers are forced to listen to the demand of shareholder activists, whether motivated by a non-financial or financial cause, there is no point, from the manager's point of view, in excluding non-financial activism from consideration *a priori*.

In order to respond to the demands of various types of shareholder activism, managers must understand what exactly the activists pursue and under what conditions they campaign against a corporation. This book suggests that, in coping with shareholder activism with various demands, the business may need to take specific case-by-case approach. In other words, "stakeholder analysis" may be required rather than investor relations or overall public relations in the age of shareholder activism proliferation. According to Freeman and Reed (1983):

> The propositions of stakeholder analysis advocate a thorough understanding of a firm's stakeholders (in the wide sense) and recognize that there are times when stakeholders must participate in the decision-making process. The strategic tools and techniques of stakeholder analysis yield a method for determining the timing and degree of such participation. At the absolute minimum this implies that boards

of directors must be aware of the impact of their decisions on key stakeholder groups. As stakeholders have begun to exercise more political [sic] power and as marketplace decisions become politicized, the need for awareness to grow into responsiveness has become apparent. Thus, the analytical model can be used by boards to map carefully the power and stake of each group. (pp. 95–6)

In fact, managers frequently have to determine case-by-case whose interests should have priority. To put it in another way, more often than not other stakeholders' interests are also allocated *ex post facto* and they will possibly compete with shareholders' share. No matter how strongly the proponents of the shareholder model may argue that managers are agents of a single principal, i.e., shareholders, the reality makes them agents of plural principals (Bowie and Freeman, 1992).

Notes

Introduction: Shareholder Activism and Corporate Governance Reform

1 The term 'corporate governance' has been used in various ways (Cochran and Wartick, 1988). Here we will start our discussion by adopting one of the most prevalent definitions of corporate governance, that is, "relationship amongst shareholders, boards of directors and managers" (Business Sector Advisory Group on Corporate Governance, 1998: p. 7. See also Monks and Minow, 1995.). This definition will be reviewed in Chapter 8 with regard to the academic implications.
2 Chapter 1 will discuss the concept of shareholder activism in a greater detail.
3 Securities Commission Act, §57.
4 This study focuses on the early stage of PSPD activism (1997–2000) and draws on interview and archival data sources.

1 Defining the Object of Study

1 The first two sections of this chapter are mostly based on Rho (2006).
2 One thing to note in relation with this trend is that the new terms for social issue activism also contain Hirschman's (1970) exit option through divestment and negative screening. If we agree with the previous discussion that the voice option is a distinguishing feature of shareholder activism, then the new terms go beyond the boundary of shareholder activism in this discussion. Figure 1.1 appearing later will make this point clear. (See the differences between shareholder monitoring and shareholder activism in broader terms.)
3 Here Black's (1990) expression of "to communicate a desire for change (p. 522, fn.3)" can be regarded as voice.
4 For this reason, Black's definition of shareholder activism should be read as 'monitoring and communications' rather than 'monitoring or communications' as originally suggested.
5 Although voice alone is viewed as shareholder activism in narrower terms, monitoring is a prerequisite for the voice option. This point will be elaborated on in the section of 'Who does what? – On shareholder proactivity'.
6 There are two types of lawsuits shareholders can bring to enforce managers' fiduciary duty. One is a derivative suit brought by shareholders on the corporation's behalf; the other is a direct suit brought by shareholders in their own right. Again, according to the scope of parties bound by the results of the action, the latter can be divided into two: an individual (or personal) action and a class (or representative) action.
7 Here we will use the two terms of 'emergence' and 'rise' interchangeably. Some scholars have used one term more frequently than the other (for 'rise' Davis

and Thompson, 1994; Bethel and Gillan, 2002; Song and Szewczyk, 2003; for 'emergence' Smith, 1996; Marens, 2002), but their meanings remain within the same scope of the discussion in this section.

2 Explaining Activism (1)

1 Most of this paragraph is drawn from MacKinlay (1997) and Weston, Chung and Siu (1998). For more detailed discussion about the procedure of an event study, see both.

5 Political Opportunity

1 Korean business conglomerate groups such as Hyundai and Samsung are generally referred to as the '*chaebol*'. A *chaebol* can be defined as a business group consisting of companies controlled by family members in many diversified business areas (Steers, Shin and Ungson, 1989). Sometimes, the *chaebol* represents the dominant family itself. A '*chongsu*' is a representative figure of the dominant family of a *chaebol*. Usually a *chongsu* is titled as chairman of the group. For example, Lee Kun Hee is the *chongsu*, or chairman, of the Samsung Group.
2 Chung Kwang Sun has frequently been involved in Korean government policy in the financial sector. Recently he has been a member of the Securities and Futures Commission in the Financial Supervisory Commission (FSC), a government agency. Chung has also been active in the academic discussion on corporate governance. In 1990, he co-authored a textbook of finance-based corporate governance theory (Weston, Chung, and Hoag, 1990), the second edition of which was published in 1998 (Weston, Chung, and Siu, 1998). In October 1994, a few months before the *Segehwa* committee, Chung had written a report *Corporate Competitiveness and Corporate Governance* commissioned by the Korea Institute of Finance (KIF), a research center established by the Korea Federation of Banks.
3 On 21 October 1994, Seongsu Bridge, then the third most congested of the 15 bridges in Seoul, collapsed. This accident claimed 32 lives including 9 schoolgirls on their way to school. As soon as questions were raised as to who was responsible, Dong Ah Engineering and Construction, the constructor of the bridge, announced that it would donate a replacement to the country. Reflecting the national sentiment, the OSS described this as an attempt to relieve the company's chairman (and controlling shareholder) Choi Won-suk from legal and moral responsibilities at the cost of minority shareholders' wealth.
4 A cumulative voting is a method of voting for corporate directors where each shareholder can multiply the number of shares owned by the number of directorships being voted on. The shareholder can then cast the entire total for only one director (or any other distribution as the shareholder pleases). This creates a strong possibility that minority shareholders can elect their representative to the directorship.
5 On 3 August 1972, the Korean government wrote off, at a stroke, all private loans of less than 300 thousand won in value and granted up to a year's grace

to debts less than 3 million won in order to ease the burdensome liabilities of Korean companies. This is called the '8.3 Measure'.
6 In 1997, on the abolition of the Capital Market Furtherance Act, the provisions for ESOAs were integrated into the Securities Act. See Figure 7.3 for the recent 10 years' growth of the ESOAs.
7 In the Monopoly Act, a more formal term "the large-scale business group" was introduced instead of the colloquial term of 'the *chaebol*.' And for the sake of administrative accuracy, the Monopoly Act requires that the FTC annually designate the business group and its affiliates. Therefore, the large-scale business group is an accurate expression when we mention the object of the Monopoly Act. Notwithstanding, we will use the term *chaebol* for terminological simplicity. The *chaebol* in our study (such as Samsung, Hyundai, and SK) have always been on the FTC list of large-scale business groups.
8 In the face of increasingly large mass demonstrations calling for direct presidential election, the government finally accepted the nation's ardent wish on 29 June 1987. That period was commonly called the "Spring of Democratization".
9 There existed a fourth group when the PSPD was founded. It was the human rights activist group. Most of the group members had joined in the *Sarangbang* (meaning "a Korean lounge in a traditional private house") Group for Human Rights led by Suh June-Sik since 1992. The *Sarangbang* Group went back to its own way very soon, and did not have any direct connection with the rise of PSPD shareholder activism.
10 We indicate the identity of the interviewee in the order of his/her occupation and alphabet showing personal identity (e.g., individual shareholder L). As for the PSPD members, we add the information about whether the interviewee is affiliated to the PEC or not (e.g., PEC lawyer C or PSPD academic G). A main reason for this is to distinguish the members engaged in real action (i.e., key agents) from those who are not (i.e., broader contexts).
11 The Participatory Economy Committee (PEC) is a subsidiary body of the PSPD in charge of the PSPD's shareholder activism. In most cases, these two names can be used interchangeably. To avoid reader's confusion, we will use the PSPD as a generic term for the collective agent of the Korean shareholder activism under study because it is better known to the outside world than the PEC. However, the views held by these two groups are not always consistent. Therefore, we will mention the PEC instead of the PSPD only when the action or interpretation under discussion does not necessarily apply to that of the PSPD. Especially, the discussion about resources mobilization in Chapter 7 will focus on the PEC not the PSPD. This is because it is the PEC which has mobilized shareholder activism.
12 In an interview with the author, Jang Hasung, the then Chairman of the PEC, said that the PEC executive members each had their own specialties (e.g., finance, law, and so on) and that Kim Ki-Won was an expert in conceptualizing the *chaebol* problem as a whole.

6 Framing Process

1 This distinction can easily be found in other economies. For example, William Allen argued that two "schizophrenic" conceptions of the corporation

co-existed in American society (Monks and Minow, 1995). Also, these two conceptions can be referred to as the shareholder model and the stakeholder model of a corporation, respectively.
2 For earlier examples of each case, see Rho (2002).
3 *Dong-A Ilbo* is the newspaper with the largest circulation in Korea (Editor and Publisher, 2000).
4 The CCEJ also associated shareholder rights with the abuse of economic power. However, as usual, the CCEJ only demanded that the government grant minority shareholders more power. A fundamental difference between the CCEJ framing and the PSPD framing is that the shareholders stay within the PSPD movement, but not in the CCEJ's. Our interpretation is that this is mainly due to the PSPD's movement tending to involve a legally interested party.
5 The PSPD disclosed that 12 shareholders had trusted the PSPD with their shareholder rights (PSPD, 1997).
6 It is believed that drawing public attention to its activities is important for it creates a favorable political opportunity for other interested parties such as employees and other shareholders to ponder the problem that the activists raised and to rethink what their corporation should be (FOE, 2000).
7 Certainly the major reason for the expansion was the apprehension that the big five would survive the government's policy to suppress group management (PSPD, 1998). Notwithstanding, if the PSPD members had doubted the effectiveness of shareholder activism, such expansion could have not been that prompt.
8 To borrow a term developed in social movement theory, the PSPD used a "frame bridging" strategy. From observations of various social movements, Snow et al. (1986) propose four types of frame alignment processes: (1) frame bridging; (2) frame amplification; (3) frame extension; and (4) frame transformation. Among them, frame bridging is to link two or more ideologically congruent but structurally unconnected frames regarding a particular issue or problem.
9 Influenced by the traditional notion that working with shareholders is basically representing capitalist interests, some PSPD members were suspicious about the compatibility between shareholder causes and those of the PSPD. "In the leftist tradition [which influenced the PSPD], something [capitalist] like shareholders or the board of directors had never been a consideration" (PEC academic A, interview on 6 February 2001). In other words, shareholder interests were not thought to be compatible with progressive movements like the PSPD's.
10 We can see the similarity of this view with the government's view described in Chapter 5 regarding the expected role of the *chaebol* as a 'prudential trustee of national assets'.
11 The PSPD's minimalist approach can also be found in its selection of a target firm and collecting information about the firm. The PSPD shareholder activism concentrated on a small number of core firms of the big *chaebol*. They also focused on the analysis of revealed events instead of finding new hidden problems.
12 It was pointed out, for example, that in other economies, such as the United Kingdom, company law should be more accommodating to the economic reality of a business group.

138 *Notes*

> The central problem raised by the group business is: How can the group be allowed to operate as a group while at the same time ensuring full protection to minority shareholders in (and creditors of) the subsidiary company or companies? The law has failed to answer this very difficult question, and the economic reality is ignored in favour of the legal reality, namely that each and every company within the group is a separate legal entity, and that therefore the directors of each company owe an overriding duty to that company to act honestly in the interests of that company irrespective of the interests of other companies in the group or of the 'group enterprise' (of which there is no legal definition). (Xuereb, 1989: p. 6)

13 It should be noted that, due to the voluntary services of its members, PSPD shareholder activism cost much less than other shareholder activism. Therefore, the PSPD did not have to worry much about the costs. For them, the heaviest cost was that of failure, which they tried to avoid by starting with less disputable problems. Chapter 7 will discuss this in detail.

7 Resource Mobilization

1 When we discuss internal resources, we usually indicate the PEC instead of the PSPD. This is because the PEC leads the PSPD shareholder activism, although, to the outside world, the PSPD is better known as the actor of shareholder activism than the PEC.
2 One thing that we should mention here is that the analysis in this chapter was made mainly from the PSPD's view. Since the mobilization is an interactive process between the mobilizer and the mobilized, the motivation of resource providers should also be studied. However, the study of resource providers could be such a large task in itself that it could require a separate research project. For this reason, this chapter will describe the motives of respective resource providers only briefly, within the limits of the observations made.
3 The standard cost of living for a four-member family is 2.9 million won per month (PSPD, 2001a).
4 This does not mean that older members are not inclined toward social reform. Korea has a long tradition of student movements, which is one of the major streams of progressive movements. This simply explains that the younger generation who are in a majority on the PEC (19 out of 22 members as of the end of 2000) share an inclination toward social reform.
5 This attitude is closely related to the PSPD's minimalist strategy. We can say that the PEC keeps silent outside of the scope established by the minimalist approach. See Chapter 6 for more about the minimalist approach.
6 His contribution in this frame alignment is more evident in the diagnostic frame than in the prognostic frame. See Chapter 6 for some results of this frame alignment.
7 This is the title of a biography of Robert A. G. Monks, a well-known American shareholder activist, written by Rosenberg (1999).
8 The increased percentage of other revenues in 1999 was rather incidental. In that year the PEC took over a training program for outside directors, which

the Institute for Business Research and Education, Korea University, the original organizer, could not manage for various reasons. This was temporary and such a training program was not held again by the PEC. So far, the PEC has refrained from increasing revenues through profit-making business.

9 Given their wide range, different supporters wanted different things. An unemployed person cut his living expenses "to prevent the *chongsu*'s arbitrariness" while another supporter bought and entrusted to the PSPD his shares "just to contribute to a clean and stable society" (Lee, J., 1999).

10 Although the anti-*chaebol* sentiment of the nation has been a great burden for the *chaebol*, no thorough study has been made of it. A few studies, cited in Kang, Choi and Chang (1991) and Cho D.-S. (1997), have surveyed public attitudes toward the *chaebol*, but how the nation has come to have such a negative attitude has not yet been investigated. This is a topic beyond the scope of this book. Here, we just note that the sentiment has defined the environment in which the *chaebol* operate. A huge placard hung outside the FKI building saying "Let's love the firm; Let's revive the economy" was observed during the fieldwork, which well illustrates how desperate the *chaebol* feel about reversing the sentiment.

11 Shadow voting means that institutional shareholders proportion their votes to other shareholders' so that they cannot affect others' decision. For example, when other shareholders vote on an item at the ratio of seven for and three against, institutional investors' votes should be distributed at the same ratio.

12 The KSE's *Regulation on Disclosure of Exercising Voting Rights to Listed Corporations by Securities Investment Trust Companies*, formulated December 1998, stipulates that a securities investment trust company, securities investment company, or trust company shall disclose its position by five days prior to the date of the shareholder meeting, when it intends to exercise its voting rights at a shareholder meeting of a listed corporation.

13 Schwab and Thomas (1998) suggested four reasons why the US unions were taking a new role as shareholders. First, employees are also residual claimants. Second, they have insider information. Third, they have fewer conflicts of interest than institutional investors. Fourth, the younger generation of the union is more interested in capital gains than in stable job conditions. However, the first three reasons exist at all times, so it still needs to be explained why the US unions decided to take a new role to monitor the management at a specific point in time. Furthermore, the third reason, fewer conflicts of interest, should be reconsidered because taking a role as a capital provider seriously challenges the existence and strategy of a traditional trade union as explained in this study with regard to the decomposition of labor.

14 Originally, "decomposition of labor" refers to the process of differentiation within the working class, such that it is no longer a homogeneous group, but is instead stratified internally by skill level (Dahrendorf, 1959). On the other hand, our discussion about a new type of decomposition of labor entails internal stratification according to shareholdings.

15 Bahk, a Harvard graduate, has participated in the CCEJ. In 2000, he took office as Vice Chairman of the Economic Justice Research Institute, a research arm of the CCEJ.

16 In 1998, the PSPD started a road show to explain their position and to secure support from foreign investors.

8 Conclusion

1 In the same vein, it is also expected that the worldwide expansion of corporate governance debates and of shareholder activism will draw global attention to shareholder activism. However, our assumption is that this global expansion is likely to be transmitted, amplified, and modified by local actors to produce a country-specific impact rather than to exert a global blanket influence. In our case, Chung Kwang Sun's *Segehwa* report and its social impact support this assumption. See Chapter 5.
2 Institutional change is a continuous process of making initial scripts and acting on the basis of such scripts. In fact, this is what most social movement organizations do to change the established system. Within the established system, the means of institutional change is similar. For example, in order to form a script that a seat belt should be worn at all times when driving, the police launch various campaigns such as education and ticketing.
3 Strictly speaking, cultivation is a part of the resource mobilization process. But, by and large, the term "cultivation" applies only to mobilization within an organization, while mobilization includes activities inviting sympathizers to participate in the social movement.
4 There have been some efforts to pay attention to the view of those who are affected by the government action. Sociology of law, for example, has established a strong tradition of pluralistic conceptions of law. In contrast to "juridical monism" which understands that the law comes into existence only by state action, "juridical pluralism" views state law as only one form of law and is not necessarily to be seen in sociological terms as dominant (Cotterrell, 1995). "Law may be seen as including unofficial as well as official and intuitive as well as positive forms" (ibid.: p. 30). Also in policy evaluation, there has been an attempt to listen directly to those who are affected by the policy (Salmen, 1987; Stone, 1992).
5 The word "stakeholder," coined in an internal memorandum at the Stanford Research Institute in 1963, refers to those groups without whose support the organization would cease to exist (Freeman and Reed, 1983). The list of stakeholders include: (1) contractual partners (e.g., shareholders, creditors, employees, suppliers, and customers); and (2) other social constituents (e.g., members of the community in which the firm is located, environmental interests, local and national governments, and society at large) (OECD, 1998b).

References

ACGA (Asian Corporate Governance Association) (2005). Emerging institutional shareholder activism in Asia. Presentation to Faculty of Law, Hong Kong University, 23 Nov. [Internet] Available from: <http://www.acga-asia.org/public/files/JamieAllen_HKU_Nov05.pdf> [Accessed on 1 March 2006].

Ackoff, R.L. (1990) The role of business in a democratic society. In: Collins, E.G.C. and Devanna, M.A., (Eds) *The Portable MBA*, pp. 335–60. New York: John Wiley & Sons.

Adams, J.S. (1965). Inequity in social exchange. In: Berkowitz, L. (ed.) *Advances in Experiential Social Psychology*, pp. 267–300. New York: Academic Press.

Admati, A.R., Pfleiderer, P. and Zechner, J. (1994) Large shareholder activism, risk sharing, and financial market equilibrium. *Journal of Political Economy*, 102 (6), pp. 1097–1130.

Alchian, A.A. and Demsetz, H. (1972) Production, information costs, and economic organization. *The American Economic Review*, 62 (5), pp. 777–95.

Alinsky, S.D. (1971) *Rules for Radicals: A Practical Primer for Realistic Radicals*, New York: Random House.

Allison, G.T. (1971). *Essence of Decision Explaining the Cuban Missile Crisis*, Boston: Little, Brown.

Alston, L.J. (1996) Empirical works in institutional economics: An overview. In: Alston, L.J., Eggertsson, T. and North, D.C., (Eds) *Empirical Studies in Institutional Change*, pp. 25–30. Cambridge: Cambridge University Press.

Alvesson, M. (1998) The business concept as a symbol. *International Studies of Management and Organization*, 28 (3), pp. 86–108.

Amsden, A.H. (1989) *Asia's Next Giant: South Korea and Late Industrialization*, New York: Oxford University Press.

Anheier, H. (2003) Movement development and organizational networks: The role of 'single members' in the German Nazi Party, 1925–30. In: Diani, M. and dMcAdam, D., (Eds) *Social Movements and Networks: Relational Approaches to Collective Action*, pp. 49–76. Oxford: Oxford University Press.

Bahk, J. (2001) Juju Chonghoe wa 'Oese' Yeongip (AGM and inviting 'foreign power'). *Chosun Ilbo*, 1 February, p. 7.

Barley, S.R. and Tolbert, P.S. (1997) Institutionalization and structuration: Studying the links between action and institution. *Organization Studies*, 18 (1), pp. 93–117.

Beck, J.D. and Bhagat, S. (1998). Shareholder litigation: Share price movements, news releases, and settlement amounts. *Managerial and Decision Economics*, 18, pp. 563–86.

Bethell, J.E. and Gillan, S.L. (2002). The impact of the institutional and regulatory environment on shareholder voting. *Financial Management*, 31 (4), pp. 29–54.

Bizjak, J.M. and Marquette, C.J. (1998). Are shareholder proposals all bark and no bite? Evidence from shareholder resolutions to rescind poison pills. *Journal of Financial and Quantitative Analysis*, 33 (4), pp. 499–521.

Black, B.S. (1990) Shareholder passivity reexamined. *Michigan Law Review*, 89 (3), pp. 520–608.

Black, B.S. (1998) Shareholder activism and corporate governance in the United States. In: Newman, P.K., (Ed.) *The New Palgrave Dictionary of Economics and the Law*, pp. 459–65. Basingstoke: Macmillan – now Palgrave Macmillan.

Black, B.S. (1999) Creating strong stock markets by protecting outside shareholders. Paper presented in the OECD Conference on Corporate Governance in Asia: A Comparative Perspective, Seoul, 3–5 March 1999.

Black, B.S. and Coffee Jr., J.C. (1994) Hail Britannia? Institutional investor behavior under limited regulation. *Michigan Law Review*, 92, pp. 1997–2087.

BOK (Bank of Korea) (1993) *Urinaraui Geumyung Jedo* (Financial System of Korea). Seoul: BOK.

Boros, E.J. (1995) *Minority Shareholders' Remedies*, Oxford: Clarendon.

Bowie, N.E. and Freeman, R.E., (Eds) (1992) *Ethics and Agency Theory: An Introduction*, New York: Oxford University Press.

Brockett, C.D. (1991). The structure of political opportunities and peasant mobilization in Central America. *Comparative Politics*, pp. 253–74.

Brown, S.J. and Warner, J.B. (1980) Measuring security price performance. *Journal of Financial Economics*, 8, pp. 205–58.

Business Sector Advisory Group on Corporate Governance (1998) *Corporate Governance: Improving Competitiveness and Access to Capital in Global Markets*. Paris: OECD.

Carleton, W.T., Nelson, J.M. and Weisbach, M.S. (1998) The influence of institutions on corporate governance through private negotiations: Evidence from TIAA–CREF. *Journal of Finance*, 53 (4), pp. 1335–62.

Central European (1999) Knives are out in corporate Hungary. 9 (6), p. 11.

Cespa, G. and Cestone, G. (2002) Stakeholder activism, managerial entrenchment, and the congruence of interests between shareholders and stakeholders. Working Paper, Universitat Pompeu Fabra.

Chan, L.K.C. and Lakonishok, J. (1993) Institutional trades and intraday stock price behavior. *Journal of Financial Economics*, 33, pp. 173–200.

Chan, L.K.C. and Lakonishok, J. (1995) The behavior of stock prices around institutional trades. *Journal of Finance*, 50 (4), pp. 1147–74.

Chakrabarti, M. (2004). Labor and corporate governance: Initial lessons from shareholder activism. *WorkingUSA*, 8 (1), pp. 45–69.

Charkham, J. (1994) *Keeping Good Company: A Study of Corporate Governance in Five Countries*, Oxford: Clarendon Press.

Chidambaran, N.K. and Woidtke, T. (1999). The role of negotiations in corporate governance: Evidence from withdrawn shareholder-initiated proposals. Working Paper, New York University.

Cho, D.-S. (1997) *Hankuk Chaebol* (Korean Chaebol). Seoul: Maeil Economic News.

Cho, H.-Y. (1999) Chamyeoyendae O Nyeonui Seongchalgwa Jeonmang (Reflection on the PSPD's five years and its prospect). A paper presented to the Symposium in commemoration of the founding of the PSPD, 4 September 1999, Seoul.

Cho, H.-Y. (2001) Soaekjuju undong gwa Cho Hee-Yeon (PSPD shareholder activism and Cho Hee-Yeon). 10 May. [Internet] Available from: <http://socialmovements.skhu.ac.kr/> [Accessed on 17 May 2001].

Choi, W.-Y. and Cho, S.H. (2003). Shareholder activism in Korea: An analysis of PSPD's activities. *Pacific-Basin Finance Journal*, 11, pp. 349–64.

Chung, G.-J. (1995) Kigwan Uigyeolgwon Juchong Season Gwansimsaro (Institutional votes, concerns in the AGM season). *Korea Economic Daily*, 7 March, p. 18.

Claessens, S., Djankov, S., Fan, J. and Lang, L.H.P. (1999) Expropriation of minority shareholders: Evidence from East Asia. Policy Research Working Paper No. 2088, Washington, DC: World Bank, Financial Sector Practice Department.
Cochran, P.L. and Wartick, S.L. (1988) Corporate governance: A review of the literature. In: Tricker, R.I., (Ed.) *International Corporate Governance: Text, Readings, and Cases*, pp. 8–18. New York: Prentice Hall.
Cohen, M.D., March, J.G. and Olsen, J.P. (1972) A garbage can model of organizational choice. *Administrative Science Quarterly*, 17, pp. 1–25.
Cotterrell, R. (1995) *Law's Community: Legal Theory in Sociological Perspective*, Oxford: Clarendon.
Cyert, R.M. and March, J.G. (1963) *A Behavioral Theory of the Firm*, Englewood Cliffs, NJ: Prentice-Hall.
Dahrendorf, R. (1959) *Class and Class Conflict in Industrial Society*, Stanford, CA: Stanford University Press.
Daily, C.M., Johnson, J.L., Ellstrand, A.E. and Dalton, D.R. (1996). Institutional investor activism: Follow the leaders? Working Paper, Purdue University.
Davis, G.F. and Kim, E.H. (forthcoming) Business ties and proxy voting by mutual funds. *Journal of Financial Economics*.
Davis, G.F. and Thompson, T.A. (1994) A social-movement perspective on corporate-control. *Administrative Science Quarterly*, 39 (1), pp. 141–73.
Del Guercio, D. and Hawkins, J. (1999). The motivation and impact of pension fund activism. *Journal of Financial Economics*, 52 (3), pp. 293–340.
Doh, J.P. and Guay, T.R. (2006) Corporate social responsibility, public policy, and NGO activism in Europe and the United States: An institutional-stakeholder perspective. *Journal of Management Studies*, 43 (1), pp. 47–73.
Dong-A Ilbo (1994) Kieop Jibae Gujo Gaepyeon Piryo (Need for corporate governance reform). 21 October, p. 10.
Donnelly Jr., J.H., Gibson, J.L. and Ivancevich, J.M. (1995) *Fundamentals of Management*, 9th edn. Chicago: Irwin.
Easterbrook, F.H. (1984) Two agency-cost explanations of dividends. *American Economic Review*, 74 (4), pp. 650–9.
Editor and Publisher (2000) Top Newspapers by 1999 Circulation. [Internet] Available from: <http://www.mediainfo.com/ephome/research/researchhtm/world100.htm> [Accessed on 8 March 2001].
EIRIS (Ethical Investment Research Service) (1993) *Attitudes to Ethical Investment*, London: EIRIS.
Eisinger, P.K. (1973) The conditions of protest behavior in American cities. *American Political Science Review*, 67 (1), pp. 11–28.
EIU (Economist Intelligence Unit) (2001) M&A, OK. 26 July. [Internet] Available from <http://biz.yahoo.com/ifc/kr/news/72601-1.html> [Accessed on 8 September 2001].
English II, P.C., Smythe, T.I. and McNeil, C.R. (2004). The 'CalPERS effect' revisited. *Journal of Corporate Finance*, 10 (1), pp. 157–74.
EPB (Economic Planning Board) (1993) *Singyeongje Ogaenyeon Gyehoek: Gongeong Gyeongjaeng Jilseoui Jungchakgwa Kieop Gyeongyeong Hyeoksin Bubun* (5 Year Plan for New Economy: Establishing Fair Competition Practices and Innovating Corporate Management). Seoul: EPB.
Fabozzi, F.J., Modigliani, F. and Ferri, M.G. (1994) *Foundations of Financial Markets and Institutions*, Englewood Cliffs, NJ: Prentice Hall.

Fama, E.F. and Jensen, M.C. (1983) Separation of ownership and control. *Journal of Law and Economics*, 26, pp. 301–25.
Fama, E.F., Jensen, M.C. and Roll, R. (1969) The adjustment of stock prices to new information. *International Economic Review*, 10, pp. 1–21.
Flynn, J. (1998) Bosses under fire: European CEOs are scrambling to meet demands from shareholders. *Business Week*, 30 November, p. 22.
FOE (Friends of the Earth) (2000). The potential & limitation of shareholder activism. [Internet] Available from: <www.foe.org/international/shareholder/potential.html> [Accessed on 2 August, 2000].
Forbes (2001) Pack of watchdogs: Off with their perks! 14 May. [Internet] Available from: <http://www.forbes.com/legacy/global/2001/0514/024tab1_table.shtml> [Accessed on 8 September 2001].
Freeman, R.E. and Reed, D.L. (1983) Stockholders and stakeholders: A new perspective on corporate governance. *California Management Review*, 25 (3), pp. 88–106.
FTC (Fair Trade Commission) (1994) "*Gyeongjeryeok Jipjung Gwanryeon Gongjeong Georae Bobui Gaejeong Baegyeong* (Background of the Amendment of the Monopoly Regulation and Fair Trade Act Concerning the Concentration of Economic Power)." Press Release, 8 August. Seoul: FTC.
FTC (Fair Trade Commission) (1999) 99*nyeon Daegyumo Kieop Jipdan Jusik Soyu Hyeonhwang* (1999 State of Share Ownership in the Large-Scaled Business Groups). Seoul: FTC.
FTC (Fair Trade Commission) (2000) *Daegyumo Kieop Jipdan Sosok Geumyung Boheomsaui Uigyeolgwon Haengsa Jehan Wibanhangwie Daehan Geon* (Announcement of contraventions of Article 11 of the Monopoly Regulation and Fair Trade Act). Press Release, 27 July. Seoul: FTC.
Galbraith, J.K. (1984) *The Anatomy of Power*, London: Hamish Hamilton.
Gamson, W.A. and Meyer, D.S. (1996) Framing political opportunity. In: McAdam, D., McCarthy, J.D. and Zald, M.N., (Eds) *Comparative Perspective on Social Movements*, pp. 275–90. Cambridge: Cambridge University Press.
Georgeson Shareholder (2005). *Annual Corporate Governance Review 2005*, New York: Georgeson Shareholder.
Gerhards, J. and Rucht, D. (1992) Mesomobilization: Organizing and framing in two protest campaigns in West Germany. *American Journal of Sociology*, 98 (3), pp. 555–96.
Gillan, S.L., Kensinger, J.W. and Martin, J.D. (2000) Value creation and corporate diversification: The case of Sears, Roebuck and Co. *Journal of Financial Economics*, 55, pp. 103–37.
Gillan, S.L. and Starks, L.T. (1996). Relationship investing and shareholder activism by institutional investors: The wealth effects of corporate governance related proposals. Working Paper, University of Texas.
Gillan, S.L. and Starks, L.T. (1998) A survey of shareholder activism: Motivation and empirical evidence. *Contemporary Finance Digest*, 2 (3), pp. 10–34.
Gillan, S.L. and Starks, L.T. (2000) Corporate governance proposals and shareholder activism: The role of institutional investors. *Journal of Financial Economics*, 57 (2), pp. 275–305.
Goffman, E. (1974) *Frame Analysis: An Essay on the Organization of Experience*, Cambridge, MA: Harvard University Press.
Graves, S.B., Waddock, S. and Rehbein, K. (2001). Fad and fashion in shareholder activism: The landscape of shareholder resolutions, 1988–1998. *Business and Society Review*, 106 (4), pp. 293–314.

Grundfest, J.A. and Perino, M.A. (1996). The Pentium Papers: A case study of collective institutional investor activism in litigation. *Arizona Law Review*, 38 (2), pp. 559–626.
Gusfield, J.R. (1968) The study of social movements. In: *Encyclopedia of the Social Sciences*, pp. 445–52. New York: Macmillan.
Gusfield, J.R., (Ed.) (1970) *Protest, Reform, and Revolt: A Reader in Social Movements*. New York: John Wiley & Sons.
Hankyoreh (1992) *Baik Ki-Wan Daeseon Hubo Juyo Gongyak* (Major election pledges of a Presidential candidate, Baik Ki-Wan). 20 November, p. 6.
Harrison, J.S. and Freeman, R.E. (1999) Stakeholders, social responsibility, and performance: Empirical evidence and theoretical perspectives. *Academy of Management Journal*, 42 (5), pp. 479–85.
Hawthorne, F. (1993) What the SEC rules do for activism. *Institutional Investor*, 27 (4): pp. 47–51.
Hernández-López, E. (2003). Bag wars and bank wars, the Gucci and Banque National de Paris hostile bids: European corporate culture responds to active shareholders. *Fordham Journal of Corporate & Financial Law*, 9 (1), pp. 127–90.
Heo, J.-S. and Suh, J.-U. (1999) Kieop Jibae Gujo Gaeseoneul wihan Kikwan Tujagaui Yeokal (Role of institutional investors in corporate governance improvement). *Josa Tonggye Wolbo*, September, pp. 1–30.
Hirsch, P.M. (1986) From ambushes to golden parachutes: Corporate takeovers as an instance of cultural framing and institutional integration. *American Journal of Sociology*, 91 (4), pp. 800–37.
Hirschman, A.O. (1970) *Exit, Voice, and Loyalty: Responses to Decline in Firms, Organizations, and States*, Cambridge, MA: Harvard University Press.
Hogwood, B.W. and Gunn, L.A. (1984) *Policy Analysis for the Real World*, Oxford: Oxford University Press.
Holthausen, R., Leftwich, R. and Mayers, D. (1987) The effect of large block transactions on security prices: A cross-sectional analysis. *Journal of Financial Economics*, 19 (2), pp. 237–68.
Holthausen, R., Leftwich, R. and Mayers, D. (1990) Large-block transactions, the speed of response, and temporary and permanent stock-price effects. *Journal of Financial Economics*, 26, pp. 71–95.
Homans, G.C. (1951) *The Human Group*, London: Routledge & Kegan Paul.
Homans, G.C. (1961) *Social Behavior: Its Elementary Forms*, New York: Harcourt, Brace & World.
Huson, M. (1997). Does governance matter? Evidence from CalPERS interventions. Working Paper, University of Alberta.
ICCR (Interfaith Center on Corporate Responsibility) (2005). Companies, resolutions and states: 2004–2005 season. [Internet] Available from: <http://www.iccr.org/shareholder/proxy_book05/05statuschart.php> [Accessed on 1 March 2006].
IMF staff (1998) The Asian crisis: Causes and cures. *Finance & Development*, 35 (2), pp. 18–21.
Iskander, M., Meyerman, G., Gray, D.F. and Hagan, S. (1999) Corporate restructuring and governance in East Asia. *Finance & Development*, 36 (1): pp. 42–5.
Jayasankaran, S. (2000) Revolt of the small investors. *Far Eastern Economic Review*, 2 November, pp. 60–1.
Jenkins, J.C. (1983a) Resource mobilization theory and the study of social movements. *Annual Review of Sociology*, 9, pp. 527–53.

Jenkins, J.C. (1983b) The transformation of a constituency into a movement: Farm-worker organizing in California. In: Freeman, J., (Ed.) *Social Movements of the Sixties and Seventies*, pp. 52–70. New York: Longman.
Jenkins, J.C. and Perrow, C. (1977) Insurgency of the powerless: Farm worker movements (1946–1972). *American Sociological Review*, 42 (2), pp. 249–68.
Johnson, M.F. and Shackell, M.B. (1997). Shareholder proposals on executive compensation. Working Paper, University of Michigan, Ann Arbor.
Johnson, R.A. and Greening, D.W. (1999) The effects of corporate governance and institutional ownership types on corporate social performance. *Academy of Management Journal*, 42 (5), pp. 564–76.
Johnson, S., La Porta, R., Lopez-de-Silanes, F. and Shleifer, A. (2000) Tunneling. *American Economic Review*, 90 (2), pp. 22–7.
Johnston, H. and Klandermans, B. (1995) The cultural analysis of social movements. In: Johnston, H. and Klandermans, B., (Eds) *Social Movements and Culture*, pp. 3–24. Minneapolis, MN: University of Minnesota Press.
Kang, C.-G., Choi, J.-P. and Chang, J.-S. (1991) *Chaebol: Seongjangui Juyeokinga, Tamyogui Hwasininga?* (Chaebol: A Leading Player for Growth or An Avaricious Incarnate?), Seoul: Bibong Publishing.
Kang, J.-M. (1998) *Inmulgwa Sasang* (People and Thoughts). Seoul: Gaemagowon.
Karpoff, J.M. (1998) The impact of shareholder activism on target companies: A survey of empirical findings. Working paper, University of Washington.
Karpoff, J.M., Malatesta, P.H. and Walkling, R.A. (1996) Corporate governance and shareholder initiatives: Empirical evidence. *Journal of Financial Economics*, 42, pp. 365–95.
Kaufman, G. (1991) Problem solving and creativity. In: Henry, J., (Ed.) *Creative Management*, pp. 103–34. New York: Sage.
KDI (Korea Development Institute) (1995) *Hankuk Gyeongje Bansegi: Jeongchaek Jaryojip* (Half A Century of Korean Economy: A Collection of Policy Documents). Seoul: KDI.
Keim, D.B. and Madhavan, A. (1996) The upstairs market for large-block transactions: Analysis and measurement of price effects. *Review of Financial Studies*, 9 (1), pp. 1–36.
KFB (Korea First Bank) (1997) *Je 117 Ki Juju Chonghoe Sokkirok* (Stenographic Record of the 117th General Meeting), Seoul: KFB.
Kim, H. (1995) *Kieop Jibae Gujo Keun Pajang Yego* (Big change in corporate governance foreseeable). *Korea Economic Daily*, 17 June, p. 4.
Kim, K.-W. (1999) Chaebol Gaehyeogeul Dulleossan Jaengjeom (Issues in dispute concerning Chaebol reform). A paper presented in a joint conference of the Korea Social and Economic Studies Association and Korea Social Science Institute, 20 November, Seoul.
Kim, K. (2000) Money plaza. *Naeway Economics*, 26 April.
Kim, S.-G. (1999) Gwadaepojangdoen Soaekjujuundong (Over-evaluated MSRC). *Hankyoreh 21*, 29 April. [Internet] Available from: <http://www.hani.co.kr/h21/data/L990419/1p5s4j01.html> [Accessed on 17 July 2001].
Kim, T.-K. (1998) Chaebol Gamsi Jageun Son Dongcham Botmul (Individual minority shareholders flooding into chaebol monitoring activities). *Hankyoreh*, 26 October, p. 26.
Kim, Y.-B. (1995) Roh Tae Woo shock. *Joong-Ang Ilbo*, 3 November, p. 5.

Kim, J. and Kim, J. (2001). Shareholder activism in Korea: A review of how PSPD has used legal measures to strengthen Korean corporate governance. *Journal of Korean Law,* 1 (1), pp. 51–76.
Kleindorfer, P.R., Kunreuther, H.C. and Schoemaker, P.J.H. (1993) *Decision Sciences: An Integrative Perspective*, Cambridge, UK: Cambridge University Press.
Korean Government (1993) *Singyeongje Ogaenyeon Gyehoek: 1993–1997* (5 Year Plan for New Economy: 1993–1997). Seoul: EPB.
Kraus, A. and Stoll, H.R. (1972) Price impacts of block trading on the New York Stock Exchange. *Journal of Finance,* 27 (3), pp. 569–88.
Kriesi, H. (1989) New social movements and the new class in the Netherlands. *American Journal of Sociology,* 94 (5), pp. 1078–1116.
Kriesi, H., Koopmans, R., Duyvendak, J.W. and Giugni, M.G. (1992) New social movements and political opportunities in Western Europe. *European Journal of Political Research,* 22, pp. 219–44.
KSE (Korea Stock Exchange) (2001a) *Jusik* (Stock), April. Seoul: KSE.
KSE (Korea Stock Exchange) (2001b) Gigwan Tujaga Uigyeolgwon Haengsa Gongsi (Disclosure of exercising voting rights by institutional investors). Press Release. 15 March. Seoul: KSE.
Lannoo, K. (1999) A European perspective on corporate governance. *Journal of Common Market Studies,* 37 (2), pp. 269–94.
Lee, C.S. (1997) Rock the house: Hanbo Steel's collapse rattles Korea Inc. *Far Eastern Economic Review,* 13 February, p. 53.
Lee, D.-H. (2000) Jujuchonghoe Chamseokhandago Jingyehan Samsung Jeonja (Samsung Electronics reprimanding the participants in the AGM). 21 August [Internet] Available from: <http://pspd.or.kr/cgi-bin/cug//read.cgi?board=sam_free&y_number=7> [Accessed on 20 July 2001].
Lee, G.-S. (1992) Jeongchaek Yeongu Jojikwaro Hwallo Mosaek (Finding a way out with organised policy studies). *Hankyoreh,* 24 January, p. 9.
Lee, J. (1999) Chamyeoyeondae Sibju Gatgi Yeolgi (Frenzy participation in the PSPD's Ten-Share Campaign). *Dong-A Ilbo,* 1 February, p. 8.
Lee, K.U. and Lee, S.-S. (1985) *Kieop Gyeolhapgwa Gyeongjeryeok Jipjung* (Corporate Integration and Concentration of Economic Power), Seoul: KDI.
Lee, K.U. and Lee, J.-H. (1990) *Kieop Jipdangwa Gyeongjeryeok Jipjung* (Business Group and Concentration of Economic Power), Seoul: KDI.
Lee, S.-H. (1999) Chaebol Gaehyeogwa Simin Undong (Chaebol Reform and Civil Movements). In: Kim, D.-H. and Kim, K., (Eds) *Hankuk Chaebol Gaehyeok Ron* (On Korean Chaebol Reform), pp. 405–23. Seoul: Nanam Publishing.
Lin, J.Y. and Nugent, J.B. (1995) Institutions and economic development. In: Behrman, J. and Srinivasan, T.N., (Eds) *Handbook of Development Economics*, pp. 2301–70. Amsterdam: Elsevier Science B.V.
Lofland, J. and Jamison, M. (1984) Social movement locals: Modal member structure. *Sociological Analysis: A Journal in the Sociology of Religion,* 45, pp. 115–29.
MacKinlay, A.C. (1997) Event Studies in Economics and Finance. *Journal of Economic Literature,* 35 (1), pp. 13–39.
Maeil Business Newspaper (1999) *Gukmin Sahoejuui Jeongseo Ganghada* (Nation shows strong socialist sentiment), 25 March, p. 1.
Malkiel, B.G. and Radisich, A. (2001) The growth of index funds and the pricing of equity securities. *Journal of Portfolio Management,* 27 (2), pp. 9–21.

Manne, H.G. (1965) Mergers and the market for corporate control. *Journal of Political Economy*, 73 (2), pp. 110–20.

Marens, R.S. (2002). Inventing corporate governance: The mid-century emergence of shareholder activism. *Journal of Business and Management*, 8 (4), pp. 365–89.

Marens, R.S. (2004) Waiting for the North to rise: Revisiting Barber and Rifkin after a generation of union financial activism in the US. *Journal of Business Ethics*, 52 (1), pp. 109–23.

Marshall, G., (Ed.) (1994) *The Concise Oxford Dictionary of Sociology*, Oxford: Oxford University Press.

Mayer, C. (1996) Corporate governance, competition and performance. *OECD Economic Studies*, 27, pp. 7–34.

McAdam, D. (1982) *Political Process and the Development of Black Insurgency 1930–1970*, Chicago: University of Chicago Press.

McAdam, D. (1984) Structural versus attitudinal factors in movement recruitment. Paper presented at the meetings of the American Sociological Association, San Antonio.

McAdam, D. (1996) Conceptual origins, current problems, future directions. In: McAdam, D., McCarthy, J.D. and Zald, M.N., (Eds) *Comparative Perspective on Social Movements*, pp. 23–40. Cambridge: Cambridge University Press.

McAdam, D. (1999) *Political Process and the Development of Black Insurgency*, 2nd edn. Chicago: University of Chicago Press.

McAdam, D., McCarthy, J.D. and Zald, M.N. (1996a) Opportunities, mobilizing structures, and framing processes – toward a synthetic, comparative perspective on social movements. In: McAdam, D., McCarthy, J.D. and Zald, M.N., (Eds) *Comparative Perspective on Social Movements*, pp. 1–20. Cambridge: Cambridge University Press.

McAdam, D., McCarthy, J.D. and Zald, M.N., (Eds) (1996b) *Comparative Perspective on Social Movements*. Cambridge: Cambridge University Press.

McAdam, D., Tarrow, S. and Tilly, C. (1997) Toward an integrated perspective on social movements and revolution. In: Linchbach, M.I. and Zuckerman, A.S., (Eds) *Comparative Politics: Rationality, Culture and Structure*, pp. 142–73. Cambridge: Cambridge University Press.

McAdam, D., Tarrow, S. and Tilly, C. (2001) *Dynamics of Contention*, Cambridge: Cambridge University Press.

McCarthy, J.D. and Zald, M.N. (1973) *The Trends of Social Movements in America: Professionalization and Resource Mobilization*, Morristown, NJ: General Learning Press.

McCarthy, J.D. and Zald, M.N. (1977) Resource mobilization and social movements: A partial theory. *American Journal of Sociology*, 82, pp. 1212–41.

McCombs, M.E. and Shaw, D.L. (1972). 'The agenda-setting function of mass media.' *Public Opinion Quarterly*, 36(Summer), pp. 176–87.

Meyer, D.S. and Staggenborg, S. (1996) Movements, countermovements, and the structure of political opportunity. *American Journal of Sociology*, 101 (6), pp. 1628–60.

Milgrom, P. and Roberts, J. (1992) *Economics, Organization and Management*, Englewood Cliffs, NJ: Prentice-Hall.

Milhaupt, C.J. (2004) Nonprofit organizations as investor protection: Economic theory, and evidence from East Asia. *Yale Journal of International Law*, 29, pp. 169–207.

MOFE (Ministry of Finance and Economy) (2000) Yeonkikeum Jusik Tuja Jeyakyoin Haesobangan (Ways to remove restraints on share investment of funds). Press Release. 14 October. Seoul: MOFE.
MOFE (Ministry of Finance and Economy) and KDI (Korea Development Institute) (1997) *Yeollin Sijang Gyeongjero Gagiuihan Gukka Gwaje* (Policy Agenda toward Open Market Economy). Seoul: KDI.
Monks, R.A.G., Miller, A. and Cook, J. (2004). Shareholder activism on environmental issues: A study of proposals at large US corporations (2000–2003). *Natural Resources Forum*, 28 (4), 317–30.
Monks, R.A.G. and Minow, N. (1991) *Power and Accountability*, New York: Harper Business.
Monks, R.A.G. and Minow, N. (1995) *Corporate Governance*, Cambridge, MA: Blackwell.
MOTIE (Ministry of Trade, Industry, and Energy) (1997) *Kieop Jibae Gujoui Gukjejeok Nonui Donghyang mit Hyanghu Daeeung Banghyang* (International Trend in Corporate Governance Discussions and Korea's Future Policy Direction). Seoul: MOTIE.
Murphy, K.J. and Van Nuys, K.E. (1994) State pension funds and shareholder activism. Working Paper, Harvard Business School.
Nesbitt, S.L. (1994). Long-term rewards from shareholder activism: A study of the 'CalPERS effect'. *Journal of Applied Corporate Finance*, 6 (4), pp. 75–80.
Norburn, D., Boyd, B.K., Fox, M. and Muth, M. (2000) International corporate governance reform. *European Business Journal*, 12 (3), pp. 116–33.
O, W. (1996) *Hankukhyeong Gyeongje Geonseol: Engineering Approach* (Constructing Korean-Style Economy: Engineering Approach). Vol. 1. Seoul: Kia Institute of Economic Research.
Oberschall, A. (1978) Theories of social conflict. *Annual Review of Sociology*, 4, pp. 291–315.
OECD (Organization for Economic Co-operation and Development) (1998a) *OECD Economic Surveys: Korea*, Paris: OECD.
OECD (Organization for Economic Co-operation and Development) (1998b) *Corporate Governance and Corporate Performance*, Paris: OECD.
OECD (Organization for Economic Co-operation and Development) (1999) *OECD Principles of Corporate Governance*, SG/CG(99)5, Paris: OECD.
Olson Jr., M. (1965) *The Logic of Collective Action: Public Goods and the Theory of Groups*, Cambridge, MA: Harvard University Press.
Olson Jr., M. (1991) Collective action. In: Eatwell, J., Milgate, M. and Newman, P., (Eds) *The New Palgrave Dictionary of Economics*, pp. 474–7. London: Macmillan.
Opler, T.C. and Sokobin, J. (1995) Does coordinated institutional shareholder activism work? An analysis of the Council of Institutional Investors. Working Paper, Ohio State University and Southern Methodist University.
Opp, K.-D. (1988) Grievances and Participation in Social Movements. *American Sociological Review*, 53 (6), pp. 853–64.
O'Rourke, A. (2003) A new politics of engagement: Shareholder activism for corporate social responsibility. *Business Strategy and the Environment*, 12 (4), pp. 227–39.
Oxford Analytica (2000) Business and socially responsible investment. [Internet] Available from: <www.oxan.com/iblf/sri.html> [Accessed on 14 April, 2000].
Park, B.-K. (2001) Maloman Uigyeolgwon Haengsa (Voting rights as a lip service). *Maeil Economic News*, 9 March, p. 1.

Park, J.-B. (1996) *Sosu Jujudeul Imsi Juchong Heoga Sincheong* (Minority shareholders applied for the court permission to convene an extraordinary shareholder meeting). *Korea Economic Daily*, 7 November, p. 26.

Park, R.-J. and Choi, Y.-H. (2000) Chamyeoyeondae Buy Korea Fund Suikryul Jojak (PSPD said Buy Korea Fund manipulated the yield rates). *Dong-A Ilbo*, 25 April, p. 33.

Parkinson, J.E. (1993) *Corporate Power and Responsibility: Issues in the Theory of Company Law*, Oxford: Clarendon.

PIRC (Pensions & Investment Research Consultants) (1996). *Controversies Affecting Shell in Nigeria*. Report to Clients, March. London: PIRC.

PIRC (Pensions & Investment Research Consultants) (1998). *Environmental and Corporate Responsibility at Shell: The Shareholder Role in Promoting Change*. November. London: PIRC.

Pistor, K. (2000) *Patterns of Legal Change: Shareholder and Creditor Rights in Transition Economies*. European Bank for Reconstruction and Development Working Paper 49, London: European Bank for Reconstruction and Development.

Plender, J. (2000) Weeding out corruption. *Financial Times*, 25 April. [Internet] Available from: www.globalarchive.ft.com [Accessed on 13 October, 2000].

Pound, J. (1992a) Raiders, targets, and politics: The history and future of American corporate control. *Journal of Applied Corporate Finance*, 5, pp. 6–18.

Pound, J. (1992b) Beyond takeovers: Politics comes to corporate control. *Harvard Business Review*, 70 (2), pp. 83–93.

Prevost, A.K. and Rao, R.P. (2000). Of what value are shareholder proposals sponsored by public pension funds? *Journal of Business*, 73 (2), pp. 177–204.

PSPD (People's Solidarity for Participatory Democracy) (1995) *Chamyeoyeondae Je Il Cha Jungki Chonghoe* (Report to the First General Meeting). 23 March. Seoul: PSPD.

PSPD (People's Solidarity for Participatory Democracy) (1996) *Chamyeoyeondae Je I Cha Jungki Chonghoe* (Report to the Second General Meeting). 13 March. Seoul: PSPD.

PSPD (People's Solidarity for Participatory Democracy) (1997) Simindeuri Jeonheyonjik Eunhaeng Gamdogwonjangmit Eunhaengjang Gobal (Citizens made a complaint against former and current bank presidents). Press Release. 31 January. Seoul: PSPD.

PSPD (People's Solidarity for Participatory Democracy) (1998) Jeongbuneun Gangdonopeun Kieop Gujo Jojeongeul Chujinhaeya (The government must drive a thorough structural adjustment in the corporate sector). Statement. 25 May. Seoul: PSPD.

PSPD (People's Solidarity for Participatory Democracy) (2001a) Gansa Geubyeowa Pyojun Saengyebi (Salary of PSPD officers and standard costs of living). [Internet] Available from: <http://www.peoplepower21.org/mirror/5-6.html> [Accessed on 20 July 2001].

PSPD (People's Solidarity for Participatory Democracy) (2001b) Samsung Jeonja Juju Chongheo Isa Sunimui Keon Jean (Proposal regarding the election of directors at the AGM of Samsung Electronics). Press Release, 1 February. Seoul: PSPD.

PSPD (People's Solidarity for Participatory Democracy) (2001c) Samsung Jeonja Juju Chongheo Bodo Jaryo (Press Release about the AGM of Samsung Electronics). Press Release, 8 March. Seoul: PSPD.

Rho, H.-K. (2002) Changing institutions in Korea: Corporate governance reform through shareholder activism. PhD thesis, University of Cambridge.
Rho, H.-K. (2004). From civil society organization to shareholder activist: The case of the Korean PSPD. Working Paper, Brunel University.
Rho, H.-K. (2006) On defining shareholder activism: Exploring the terrain for research. *Corporate Ownership & Control*, 4 (3). (In press).
Roe, M.J. (1994) *Strong Managers, Weak Owners: The Political Roots of American Corporate Finance*, Princeton, NJ: Princeton University Press.
Rogers, M.F. (1974) Instrumental and infra-resources: The bases of power. *American Journal of Sociology*, 79 (6), pp. 1418–33.
Roman, R.M., Hayibor, S. and Agle, B.R. (1999) The relationship between social and financial performance. *Business and Society*, 38 (1), pp. 109–25.
Romano, R. (1991). The shareholder suit: Litigation without foundation? *Journal of Law, Economics, and Organization*, 7 (1), pp. 55–87.
Romano, R. (1993). Public pension fund activism in corporate governance reconsidered. *Columbia Law Review*, 93 (4), pp. 795–853.
Romano, R. (2001) Less is more: Making shareholder activism a valuable mechanism of corporate governance. *Yale Journal on Regulation*, 18, pp. 1–78.
Rosenberg, H. (1999) *Traitor to His Class: Robert A.G. Monks and the Battle to Change Corporate America*, New York: John Wiley & Sons.
Rowley, T.J. and Moldoveanu, M. (2003). When will stakeholder groups act? An interest- and identity-based model of stakeholder group mobilization. *Academy of Management Review*, 28(2), pp. 204–19.
Rozeff, M. (1982) Growth, beta and agency costs as determinants of dividend pay-out ratios. *Journal of Financial Research* 5, pp. 249–59.
Rucht, D. (1996) The impact of national contexts on social movement structures: A cross-movement and cross-national comparison (Part II: Mobilizing Structures). In: McAdam, D., McCarthy, J.D. and Zald, M.N., (Eds) *Comparative Perspective on Social Movements*, pp. 185–204. Cambridge: Cambridge University Press.
Russell, B.A.W. (1938) *Power: A New Social Analysis*, London: George Allen & Unwin.
Ryan, L.V. and Schneider, M. (2003) Institutional investor power and heterogeneity: Implications for agency and stakeholder theories. *Business and Society*, 42 (4), pp. 398–429.
Salmen, L.F. (1987) *Listen to the People: Participant-Observer Evaluation of Development Projects*, New York: Oxford University Press.
Schwab, S.J. and Thomas, R.S. (1998) Realigning corporate governance: Shareholder activism by labor unions. *Michigan Law Review*, 96 (4), pp. 1018–94.
Schwartz, D.E. (1971) The public-interest proxy contest: Reflections on Campaign GM. *Michigan Law Review*, 69 (3), pp. 419–538.
Schwartz, D.E. (1983) Shareholder democracy: A reality or chimera? *California Management Review*, 25 (3), pp. 53–67.
Sethi, S.P. (1977) *Up against the Corporate Wall: Modern Corporations and Social Issues of the Seventies*, 3rd edn. Englewood Cliffs, NJ: Prentice-Hall.
Sethi, S.P. (1982) *Up against the Corporate Wall: Modern Corporations and Social Issues of the Eighties*, 4th edn. Englewood Cliffs, NJ: Prentice-Hall.
Sherer, P.M. (1999) Raising Their Voices. *Wall Street Journal* Interactive edn., 26 April. [Internet] Available from: <interactive.wsj.com/public/current/articles/SB92462716875786 0048.htm> [Accessed on 2 August, 2000].

Shleifer, A. and Vishny, R.W. (1986) Large shareholders and corporate control. *Journal of Political Economy*, 94 (3), pp. 461–88.
Shleifer, A. and Vishny, R.W. (1997) A survey of corporate governance. *Journal of Finance*, 22 (2), pp. 737–83.
Sias, R.W. and Starks, L.T., (1998) Institutional investors in equity markets. Working paper, Washington State University.
Simon, H.A. (1997) *Administrative Behavior: A Study of Decision-making Processes in Administrative Organizations*, 4th edn. New York: Free Press.
Simon, J.G., Powers, C.W. and Gunnemann, J.P. (1972) *The Ethical Investor: Universities and Corporate Responsibility*, New Haven: Yale University Press.
Smith, M.P. (1996) Shareholder activism by institutional investors: Evidence from CalPERS. *Journal of Finance*, 51 (1), pp. 227–52.
Smith, R. (1984) California official moves to organize pension funds to combat greenmail. *Wall Street Journal*, 26 July, 1. [Internet] Available from: <http://proquest.umi.com/pqdweb?did=27109772&sid=1&Fmt=3&clientId=29708&RQT=309&VName=PQD> [Accessed on 7 September, 2005].
Snow, D.A. and Benford, R.D. (1988) Ideology, frame resonance and participant mobilization. In: Klandermans, B., Kriesi, H. and Tarrow, S., (Eds) *International Social Movement Research*, pp. 197–218. Greenwich, CT.: JAI.
Snow, D.A., Rochford Jr., E.B., Worden, S.K. and Benford, R.D. (1986) Frame alignment processes, micromobilization, and movement participation. *American Sociological Review*, 51 (4), pp. 464–81.
Snow, D.A., Zurcher Jr., L.A. and Ekland-Olson, S. (1980) Social networks and social movements; A microstructural approach to differential recruitment. *American Sociological Review*, 45 (5), pp. 787–801.
Song, W.-L. and Szewczyk, S.H. (2003) Does Coordinated Institutional Investor Activism Reverse the Fortunes of Underperforming Firms? *Journal of Financial and Quantitative Analysis*, 38 (2), pp. 317–36.
Sparkes, R. (1995) *The Ethical Investor: How to Make Money Work for Society and the Environment as well as for Yourself*, London: Harper Collins.
Steers, R.M., Shin, Y.K. and Ungson, G.R. (1989) *The Chaebol: Korea's New Industrial Might*, New York: Harper & Row.
Stone, A.H.W. (1992) *Listening to Firms: How to Use Firm-Level Surveys to Assess Constraints on Private Sector Development*. Policy Research Working Papers No. 923, Washington DC: World Bank.
Strati, A. (1998) Organizational symbolism as a social construction: A perspective from the sociology of knowledge. *Human Relations*, 51 (11), pp. 1379–402.
Strickland, D., Wiles, K.W. and Zenner, M. (1996) A requiem for the USA: Is small shareholder monitoring effective? *Journal of Financial Economics*, 40, pp. 319–38.
Suh, S.-B. (1997) Simin Danche Chamyeohan Eunhaeng Juchong (Civil activists participating a bank AGM). *Hankook Ilbo*, 8 March, p. 21.
Suh, Y.-A. (1997) Igineun Simin Undong Ggum (Winning civil movements, My dream). *Weekly Dong-A*, 2 October, p. 102.
Talner, L. (1983) *The Origins of Shareholder Activism*, Washington DC: IRRC.
Tarrow, S. (1983) Struggling to reform: Social movements and policy change during cycles of protest. Western Societies Program Occasional Paper No. 15, Ithaca, NY: New York Center for International Studies.
Tarrow, S. (1989) *Democracy and Disorder: Protest and Politics in Italy 1965–1975*, Oxford: Oxford University Press.

Tarrow, S. (1994) *Power in Movement: Social Movements, Collective Action and Mass Politics in the Modern State*, Cambridge: Cambridge University Press.
Teoh, S.H., Welch, I. and Wazzan, C.P. (1999). The effect of socially activist investment policies on the financial markets: Evidence from the South African boycott. *Journal of Business*. 72 (1), pp. 35–89.
Thompson, T.A. and Davis, G.F. (1997) The politics of corporate control and the future of shareholder activism in the United States. *Corporate Governance: An International Review*, 5 (3), pp. 152–9.
TIAA-CREF (Teachers Insurance and Annuity Association-College Retirement Equities Fund) (2000) TIAA-CREF Policy Statement on Corporate Governance. [Internet] Available from: <http://www.tiaa-cref.org/libra/governance/index.html#policy> [Accessed on 22 May, 2001].
Tilly, C. (1978) *From Mobilization to Revolution*, New York: Random House.
Trost, C. (1984) Corporate activism by pension managers is urged by labor agency's Robert Monks. *Wall Street Journal*, 21 June. [Internet] Available from: <http://proquest.umi.com/pqdweb?did=27083042&sid=1&Fmt=3&clientId=29708&RQT=309&VName=PQD> [Accessed on 7 September, 2005].
Useem, M., Bowman, E.H., Myatt, J. and Irvine, C.W. (1993) US institutional investors look at corporate governance in the 1990s. *European Management Journal*, 11(2), pp. 175–89.
Vogel, D. (1978) *Lobbying the Corporation: Citizen Challenges to Business Authority*, New York: Basic Books.
Vogel, D. (1983) Trends in shareholder activism: 1970–1982. *California Management Review*, 25 (3), pp. 68–87.
von Neumann, J. and Morgenstern, O. (1953) *The Theory of Games and Economic Behavior*, 3rd edn. Princeton, NJ: Princeton University Press.
Wahal, S. (1996) Pension fund activism and firm performance. *Journal of Financial and Quantitative Analysis*, 31 (1), pp. 1–23.
Weaver, G.R., Trevino, L.K. and Cochran, P.L. (1999) Integrated and decoupled corporate social performance: Management commitments, external pressures, and corporate ethics practices. *Academy of Management Journal*, 42 (5), pp. 539–52.
Weston, J.F., Chung, K.S. and Hoag, S.B. (1990) *Mergers, Restructuring and Corporate Control*, Englewood Cliffs, NJ: Prentice Hall.
Weston, J.F., Chung, K.S. and Siu, J.A. (1998) *Takeovers, Restructuring, and Corporate Governance*, 2nd edn. Upper Saddle River, NJ: Prentice Hall.
Williamson, O.E. (1985) *The Economic Institutions of Capitalism: Firms, Markets, and Relational Contracting*, New York: Free Press.
Wilson, J. (1973) *Introduction to Social Movement*, New York: Prentice-Hall.
Worlfram, S. (2005). Definition. *The Oxford Companion to Philosophy*. Oxford: Oxford University Press. [Internet] Available from: <http://www.oxfordreference.com/views/ENTRY.html?subview=Main&entry=t116.e581> [Accessed on 1 March 2006].
Woo, J.-E. (1991) *Race to the Swift: State and Finance in Korean Industrialization*, New York: Columbia University Press.
World Bank (1999) *Corporate Governance: A Framework for Implementation – Overview*. Washington, DC: World Bank.
World Bank (2000) *Malaysia: Social and Structural Review Update*, Washington, DC: World Bank.

Wright, R. (1999) Corporate Governance goes global: Riding the rising tide. *Impact* (Summer): Washington, DC: International Finance Corporation.

Xuereb, P.G. (1989) *The Rights of Shareholders*, Oxford: BSP Professional Books.

Yim, H.-K. (1998) Sangsa Beopjeui Byeoncheon (Changes in the laws on commercial matters). *Beopje Yeongu*, 15, pp. 12–33.

Yim, K.-J. (1995) *Sangjangsa Jeungyeo Chulja, Jusik Maegak, Bandeusi Juchong Gyeorui Geocyeoya* (Listed Companies need approval of general meeting, in gift, investment, share sale). *Maeil Business Newspaper*, 23 January, p. 20.

Yonhap News (2000) Oegugin Juju deung, Samsung Jeonja Isa Sangdae Kacheobun Sincheong (Foreign investors applied the court for a provisional disposition against directors of Samsung Electronics). 23 November.

Yoo, S.M. (1992) Urinara Kieop Jipdanui Soyu Gyeongyeong Gujowa Jeongchaek Daeeung (Ownership and management structure of Korean business groups and relevant policy agenda) *Hankuk Gaebal Yeongu*, 14 (1), pp. 3–33.

Yoo, S.M. (1997) *Evolution of Government-Business Interface in Korea: Progress to Date and Reform Agenda Ahead*. KDI Working Paper No. 9711, Seoul: KDI.

Zajac, E.J. and Westphal, J.D. (1995) Accounting for the explanations of CEO compensation: Substance and symbolism. *Administrative Science Quarterly*, 40 (2), pp. 283–308.

Zald, M.N. (1996) Culture, ideology, and strategic framing. In: McAdam, D., McCarthy, J.D. and Zald, M.N., (Eds) *Comparative Perspective on Social Movements*, pp. 261–74. Cambridge: Cambridge University Press.

Zald, M.N. and McCarthy, J.D. (1987) *Social Movements in an Organizational Society: Collected Essays*, New Brunswick, NJ: Transaction.

Index

1997 Asian crisis, xvii, xxi
  cause of, xxi
  and corporate governance, xxi
8.3 Measure, 50, 57, **135–6**
ABI (Association of British Insurers), 9, 43
abnormal return, 18, 21, 22, 24
  average (AR), 19
  control-firm-adjusted, 21
  cumulative (CAR), 19, 23–4
  industry-adjusted, 21, 22
  market-adjusted, 19, 21, 22
ACGA (Asian Corporate Governance Association), 8
AFL-CIO (American Federation of Labor and Congress of Industrial Organizations), 16
agency theory, 17, **18**, 25, *see also* return maximization
  firm as a nexus of contracts, 18
  of plural principals, 133
  principal–agent contract, 18
agenda-setting, 14
AGM, *see* annual general meeting
Alinsky, Saul, 76, 121, 123
Allen, Jamie, 8
Allied Policy Group, 62
American Federation of Labor and Congress of Industrial Organizations, *see* AFL-CIO
annual general meeting, 13, 75, 77, 79, 103, 108, 110, 114, 121, 123
Anti-Corruption Act, 73
anti-takeover measure, 29–30, 41
  poison pill, 29
ASA (Australian Shareholders Association), 9
Apartheid, 3
APEC (Asia Pacific Economic Co-operation), 47
AR, *see under* abnormal return

Asia Pacific Economic Co-operation, *see* APEC
Asian Corporate Governance Association, *see* ACGA
Asia Week, xx
  Asia's best Advocates of Shareholder's Rights, xx
Association of British Insurers, *see* ABI
Association of Minority and Smaller Investors in India, 9
Association for Sustainable and Responsible Investment in Asia, *see* ASrIA
ASrIA (Association for Sustainable and Responsible Investment in Asia), 9
AST Research, 64
Australian Shareholders Association, *see* ASA
average abnormal return, *see under* abnormal return

Bahk, Jaewan, 115
Board Analysts, 10
bond with warrants, 78, 99
Bon-Moo Koo, *see* Koo, Bon-Moo
business judgment, 84
Business Sector Advisory Group on Corporate Governance, *see under* OECD
Business Week, xx
  Asian Stars, xx
BW, *see* bond with warrants
Byung-Chull Lee, *see* Lee, Byung-Chull

Cadbury, Adrian, xx
Cadbury Report, 31
cadre diversification, 125
California Public Employee Retirement System, *see* CalPERS
California State Teachers Retirement System, *see* Calstrs

155

CalPERS (California Public Employee Retirement System), 3, 22, 32
Calstrs (California State Teachers Retirement System), 32
Campaign GM, 70
Capital Market Furtherance Act, 50, 57, 136
CAR, *see under* abnormal return
causal explanation, 19–20, 24
CB, *see* convertible bond
CCEJ (Citizens' Coalition for Economic Justice), **59–62**, 63, 68, 75, 76, 81, 89, 120, 137, 139
Center for Corporate Responsibility, 126
Center for Good Corporate Governance, *see* CGCG
Center for Research in Security Prices, *see* CRSP
CGCG (Center for Good Corporate Governance), 95, 125
CGInfo, 95
chaebol
 antagonism against, 102–3, 139
 definition of, 135
 expected role of, **56–8**
 national support for, 56
 policy of the Korean government, **49–56**
 problem, 49, 59, 63, 75, 78–84, 119, 124, 136, *see also* ownership concentration, ownership succession, diversification, intra-group support
 reform, 87–8, 89–91
Cha-Kyung Koo, *see* Koo, Cha-Kyung
Chey, Jong-Hyun, 53
Chey, Jong-Kun, 53
Chey, Tae Won, 53
Chinese Center of Corporate Governance, 126
Cho, Hee-Yeon, 62, 81, 84
Choi, Won-suk, 71, 135
chongsu, 50, 51, 56, 58, 70–1, 73, 79, 81, 83–4, 103, 120, 139
 definition of, 135
Chosun Ilbo, 115
Chung Hee Park, *see* Park, Chung Hee
Chung, Ju Yung, 53, 70
Chung, Kwang Sun, 48, 71, 135, 140
Chung, Mong Heon, 53
Chung, Mong Koo, 53
Chung, Se Young, 53
Chung, Tae Soo, 72
Chungwoon Accounting, 111
CII (Council of Institutional Investors), 9, 43
Citizens' Coalition for Economic Justice, *see* CCEJ
collective action theory, **27**, 37
 'by-product' theory, 37
 free-rider problem, 27, 30
 selective incentive, 37
Colorado Public Employee Retirement System, *see* Colpera
Colpera (Colorado Public Employee Retirement System), 32
Commercial Act, 79, 82
Committee on Concentration of Economic Power, *see under* PSPD
Committee on Corporate Governance, 113
Constitutional Court, 66
convertible bond, 64, 96
CoreRatings, 10
corporate citizenship, 131
corporate governance
 activism, 7
 and national prosperity, 56
 definition of, 134
 in Korea, xxi
 market-based model of, 30
 politics-based model of, 30, *see also* shareholder activism
 private property view of, **67–9**, 84, 128, 130, *see also* shareholder model
 reform, xvii–xviii, **126–9**
 reform in Korea, 47–9, *see also* New *Chaebol* Policy
 shareholder model, 82, 127–32, 136–7, *see also* private property view
 social entity view of, 57, **67–9**, 84, 128, 130, *see also* stakeholder model
 stakeholder model, 128–32, 136–7

Corporate Governance Information Center, 95, *see also* Center for Good Corporate Governance
Corporate Governance Quotient, 10
corporate social responsibility, 81, 130
  law observance as, 81, 84
Council of Institutional Investors, *see* CII
Court of Appeals for the District of Columbia Circuit, 6, 9, 129
CRISIL Ltd, 10
cross equity investment, *see under* intra-group support
cross shareholding, *see* cross equity investment
CRSP (Center for Research in Security Prices), 21
cultivation, 125, 140
cumulative voting, 49, 135

Daewoo Group, 80
  Daewoo Corporation, 99, 103
decomposition of labor, 112, 139
definition
  elements of, 4: *genus*, 4; *differentia*, 4
Deminor Rating, 10
Department of Labor, 31
Deutsche Bank, xviii
Deutsche Schutzvereinigung für Westpapierbesitz, *see* DSW
diversification, **52–4**, 124
  specialization policy, 53
divestment, 134
Dong Ah Engineering and Construction, 48, 70–1, 135
Dong-A Ilbo, 137
Dongbu Group, 108
Doosan Group, 61
Dow Chemical, 6, 8, 122–3
DSW (Deutsche Schutzvereinigung für Westpapierbesitz), xviii

Eastman Kodak, 76, 120–1
Economic Justice Research Institute, 139
economic power, **54**, 56, 57–8, *see also* intra-group support
  concentration of, 54, 58, 63, 82
  types of concentration, 54: general, 54; industrial, 54; market, 54
economies of scale, 30
economies of scope, 30
EGM, *see* extraordinary general meeting
EIRIS (Ethical Investment Research and Information Service), 9
emergence of shareholder activism
  explanations of, xx
  levels of, **14–16**, **119–26**
  meaning of, **14–16**, 134–5
Emerging Market Investors Fund, 114
Employee Retirement Income Security Act, *see* ERISA
employee stock ownership association, *see* ESOA
equity theory, **17**, 24
ERISA (Employee Retirement Income Security Act), 31
ESOA (employee stock ownership association), 50, 57, 110–13, 136
ethical investment, 7–8, 131, *see also* socially responsible investment
Ethical Investment Research and Information Service, *see* EIRIS
European Sustainable and Responsible Investment Forum, *see* Eurosif
Eurosif (European Sustainable and Responsible Investment Forum), 9
event study, **18–19**, 20
  comparable group, **21**, 25
  estimation window, 19, 24–5
  event period, *see* event window
  event window, 19
exit option, **4**, **26–7**, 28, 134
expected utility theory, **27–8**
extraordinary general meeting, 49, 68, 100–1, 116

Fair Trade Commission, *see* FTC
Federation of Korean Industries, *see* FKI
FIGHT (Freedom, Integration, God, Honor-Today), 120–1, 123
Financial Supervisory Commission, *see* FSC
Financial Supervisory Service, *see* FSS
Financial Times, xx

Five-Year Economic Development Plan, 50
FKI (Federation of Korean Industries), 48, 139
Florence, Franklin Delano Roosevelt, 120
Florida State Board of Administration, *see* FSBA
fractionalization, *see* cadre diversification
Framework Act on Fund Management, 105
framing process, xxii, 37, **40–1**, 43, 120, 123, 126, 128
　compatibility problem, 80–1, 84, 137
　elements of successful, 40–1: diagnostic, 40, 67, 80; motivational, 40–1, 67; prognostic, 40, 67, 80, 119
　frame alignment, 40, 80, 82, 90–1, 131, 138: frame amplification, 137; frame bridging, 137; frame extension, 137; frame transformation, 137
　minimalist strategy, 80–4, 137, 138
　interpretation of 'public company', 81
Freedom, Integration, God, Honor-Today, *see* FIGHT
FSBA (Florida State Board of Administration), 32
FSC (Financial Supervisory Commission), 135
FSS (Financial Supervisory Service), 96–7
FTC (Fair Trade Commission), 55, 82, 136

gadflies, 41, 66
garbage can model, *see under* human action
gate-keeping, 14
Georgeson Shareholder, 7
Government Employees Pension Corporation, 109
Government Employees Pension Fund, 105
GovernanceMetics International, 10
greenmail, 117

Hanbo Group, 61, 72–4, 79, 111
　Hanbo Iron and Steel, 72, 74
Hankook Explosive Group, 61
Hannong Co., 108
Hanuri, 95, 125
Hasung Jang, *see* Jang, Hasung
Hee-Yeon Cho, *see* Cho, Hee-Yeon
Hermes Lens Asset Management, xviii
Hoechst, xix
Honeywell, 123
human action
　bounded rationality, 34
　corrective action, 25
　exit-voice choice, 4, 10–11, 25, **26–7**, *see also* exit option, voice option
　garbage can model, 74, 120
　motivation: content theory, 17; process theory, 17
　political model of group decision-making, 35
　rational unitary actor model, xx, **34–5**
　satisficing, 34
　simple model of, 10–11
Hyundai Group, 53, 70–1, 77, 80, 135, 136
Hynix, 99, *see also* Hyundai Electronics
Hyundai Electronics, 65, *see also* Hynix
Hyundai Heavy Industries, 65, 99–101, 103, 111, 115
Hyundai Merchant Marine, 65
Hyundai Securities, 65, 104
Hyundai Trust Investment Management, 97, 109
Kia Motors, 65, 111

ICCR (Interfaith Center on Corporate Responsibility), 7, 9, 15–16
ICGN (International Corporate Governance Network), xx
　Annual Awards, xx
ICRA Ltd, 10

indexing investment, 28–9, 30, 31–33, 41
  equity turnover as a measurement, 32
Indonesian Institute for Corporate Directorship, 126
in-group transaction, *see* preferential transaction
Inheritance Tax and Gift Tax Act, 51
In-Hwoi Koo, *see* Koo, In-Hwoi
Institute for Business Research and Education, 139
institutional change, 124, 129, 140
  change agent, 126
  formal, 128–9
  informal, 126, 128–9
  script, **124**
Institutional Shareholder Services, *see* ISS
Interfaith Center on Corporate Responsibility, *see* ICCR
internal ownership, *see under* ownership concentration
International Bank for Reconstruction and Development, *see* World Bank
International Corporate Governance Network, *see* ICGN
intra-group support, **54–6**, 124, *see also* economic power
  cross equity investment, **54–5**, 84
  mutual loan guarantee, **55**
  preferential transaction, **55–6**, 84
investor relations, 132
Investor Responsibility Research Center, *see* IRRC
Investors Rights Association of America, *see* IRAA
IRAA (Investors Rights Association of America), 15–16
IRRC (Investor Responsibility Research Center), 9
ISS (Institutional Shareholder Services), 9

Jaewan Bahk, *see* Bahk, Jaewan
Jae-Yong Lee, *see* Lee, Jae-Yong
Jang, Hasung, xx, 81, 89, 90–2, 95, 117, 136
jawboning, *see* private negotiation

Jong-Hyun Chey, *see* Chey, Jong-Hyun
Jong-Kun Chey, *see* Chey, Jong-Kun
June-Sik Suh, *see* Suh, June-Sik
Junn, Sung-Chull, 109
juridical monism, 140
juridical pluralism, 140
Ju Yung Chung, *see* Chung, Ju Yung

KCCI (Korea Chamber of Commerce and Industry), 48
KCTU (Korean Confederation of Trade Union), 112
KDI (Korea Development Institute), 54, 72
KFB (Korea First Bank), xxi, 72, 74–9, 111, 123
KIF (Korea Institute of Finance), 135
Kim, Kihwan, 109
Kim, Ki-Sik, 63
Kim, Ki-Won, 63, 71, 136
Kim, Sung-Gu, 83
Kim, Young Sam, 47
Kihwan Kim, *see* Kim, Kihwan
Ki-Sik Kim, *see* Kim, Ki-Sik
Ki-Wan Paik, *see* Paik, Ki-Wan
Ki-Won Kim, *see* Kim, Ki-Won
Koo, Bon-Moo, 53
Koo, Cha-Kyung, 53
Koo, In-Hwoi, 53
Korea Chamber of Commerce and Industry, *see* KCCI
Korea Development Institute, *see* KDI
Korea Federation of Banks, 135
Korea First Bank, *see* KFB
Korea Fund, 114
Korea Institute of Finance, *see* KIF
Korea Investor's Network for Disclosure System, *see* KSE-KIND
Korea Local Administration Officials' Mutual Fund, 109
Korea Stock Exchange, *see* KSE
Korean Confederation of Trade Union, *see* KCTU
KSE (Korea Stock Exchange), 96, 109, 139
KSE-KIND (Korea Investor's Network for Disclosure System), 96
Kumho Group, 91
Kun Hee Lee, *see* Lee, Kun Hee

Kwang Sun Chung, *see* Chung, Kwang Sun
Kyu Uck Lee, *see* Lee, Kyu Uck

LAPFF (Local Authority Pension Fund Forum), 13
large-scale business group, 136, *see also chaebol*
large shareholding, 29–31, 33–4, 41
Lawyers for a Democratic Society, *see* Minbyun
League of Members of Society for Participatory Democracy, 63
Lee, Byung-Chull, 53
Lee, Jae-Yong, 53, 64–5
Lee, Kun Hee, 48, 53, 135
Lee, Kyu Uck, 54, 58, 59
Lee, Seung-Hee, 63
LG Group, 53, 65, 80
  Dacom, 65, 99–101
  LG Semiconductor, 65, 103
litigation, 12
  class action, 134
  derivative suit, 12, 49, 79, 100–1, 105–6, 114, 123, 126
  direct suit, 134
  individual action, 134
Local Authority Pension Fund Forum, *see* LAPFF
Local Government Pension Scheme, 13
Lukomnik, John, 33

Malaysian Institute of Corporate Governance, 126
market for corporate infiltration, 78
market portfolio, 28
market-to-book ratio, 20, 23–4
mediating group, 9–10, 13–14, 42–3
  as an agenda-setter, 13–14
  as a gate-keeper, 13–14
Medical Committee for Human Rights, 6, 8–9, 122, 129
Metro, xix
Midas Asset Management, 109
Millstein, Ira, xx
Minbyun (Lawyers for a Democratic Society), 62
Ministry of Finance and Economy, *see* MOFE

minority shareholder rights, 72, 75, 79, 81, 84, 123
  legal requirement for, 49
Mirae Asset Securities, 109
Mirror Group, xviii
MOFE (Ministry of Finance and Economy), 107–8
Mong Heon Chung, *see* Chung, Mong Heon, 53
Mong Koo Chung, *see* Chung, Mong Koo
monitoring
  concepts, broader and narrower, 11
  cost, 30, 126
  shareholder activism and, 11
Monks, Robert A.G., 138
Monopoly Act, *see* Monopoly Regulation and Fair Trade Act
Monopoly Regulation and Fair Trade Act, 51, 54–5, 60–1, 66, 67–8, 79, 81, 107, 136
Montgomery, David, xviii
Moody's, 9
Mulder, John B, 120
mutual loan guarantee, *see under* intra-group support

Nader, Ralph, 70
NAPF (National Association of Pension Funds), 9, 43
National Association of Pension Funds, *see* NAPF
National Pension Corporation, 109
National Pension Fund, 105
negative screening, 134
net cash flow, 18
New *Chaebol* Policy, 47, 49, 71–2, 83
New York State Common Retirement System, *see* NYSCR
Nohae Park, *see* Park, Nohae
normal return, 18, 19
NYSCR (New York State Common Retirement System), 32

OECD (Organization for Economic Co-operation and Development), xvii, 56
  Business Sector Advisory Group on Corporate Governance, 56
  Principles of Corporate Governance, 68

Office of Securities Supervision, *see* OSS
Open Compliance Ethics Group, 10
operating income, 21, 23–4
Organization for Economic Co-operation and Development, *see* OECD
OSS (Office of Securities Supervision), 48, 71, 135
ownership concentration, 50–1, 84, 124
  internal ownership, **51–2**
ownership succession, **51–3**

Paik, Ki-Wan, 59
Park, Chung Hee, 56, 67
Park, Nohae, 102
Park, Won-Soon, 62
Participatory Economy Committee, *see* PEC
PEC (Participatory Economy Committee), *see under* PSPD
Pensions and Investment Research Consultants Ltd., *see* PIRC
People's Solidarity for Participatory Democracy, *see* PSPD
Phillips and Drew Fund Management, xviii
Pilsbury, Charles, 123
PIRC (Pensions and Investment Research Consultants Ltd.), xx, 9, 13
Plender, John, xx
political model of group decision-making, *see under* human action
political opportunity, xxii, 37, **38–9**, 41–2, 137, *see also* regulatory change
  structure of, 38–9: formal vs. informal, 38–9
portfolio theory, 28
preferential transaction, *see under* intra-group support
private negotiation, 12
probability regression, **22–4**
proxy fight, 12, 91–2, 101, 114, 121, 123
PSPD (People's Solidarity for Participatory Democracy), xxi, 49, 58, **62–6**
  Committee on Concentration of Economic Power, 63, 68, 110
  founding groups of, 62–3, 136
  Justice Watch, 70
  legal pragmatism of, **62–6**, 70, **73–5**, 120
  National Assembly Watch, 70
  PEC (Participatory Economy Committee), 63, 77, 82, 110, 136, 138: human resource of, 86–90; financial resource of, 93–5
  Public Interest Litigation Center, 70
PSPD activism
  information sources for, **95–7**
  political opportunity for: formal, **47–58**; informal, **58–66**
  principles of, 81, 84, 91–2, 115
  resources of: external, 86, **95–118**; internal, **86–95**
  shareholder support for, **97–118**: domestic institutional shareholder, 104–10; foreign institutional shareholder, 114–17; individual shareholder, 100–4; PSPD member, 97–100; trade union, 110–13
Public Citizen, 70, 76
  Congress Watch, 70
  Global Trade Watch, 70
  Litigation Group, 70
Public Corporation Inducement Act, 50

rational unitary actor model, *see under* human action
regulatory change, 32, 41–2, *see* institutional change, political opportunity
residual claim, 18, 122, 127, 129, 139
residual control, 123, 129
residual return, *see* abnormal return
residual risk, 18
resource mobilization, xxii, 37, **38–40**, 42–3, 125, 140
  classification of resources, 39
  cost, 84–5
  internalization: of professional service, **86–90**, 98, 123, 138; of shareholder support, 98–100

resource mobilization – *continued*
  level of, 39–40: macro-mobilization, 39; meso-mobilization, 39–40; micro-mobilization, 39–40
return maximization, 22, 25, 69, 127–8, 129, *see also* agency theory
  criticism on, 25
return on assets, 21, 23
return on equity, 21, 23
return on sales, 23, 24
Rhee, Syngman, 67
Roh, Tae Woo, 48, 70–1, 73
Royal Dutch Shell, 13
  Brent Spar, 13
  operation in Nigeria, 13

Samsung Group, 48, 53, 61, 77, 80, 96, 114, 135, 136
  Cheil Communications, 65
  Joong-Ang Ilbo, 64
  Lee Chun Electric, 64
  Samsung Corporation, 65
  Samsung Electro-Mechanics, 64
  Samsung Electronics, 64, 99–101, 103, 109–10, 114
  Samsung Fine Chemicals, 65
  Samsung General Chemicals, 64
  Samsung Life Insurance, 65
  Samsung Motors, 64–5
  Samsung SDI, 64
  Samsung SDS, 65, 78, 99
S&P 500 (Standard & Poor's 500 Common Stock Index), 28, 32
Sarangbang Group for Human Rights, 136
Schacht, Kurt, 33
SEC (Securities and Exchange Commission), 6, 8, 31, 41
Securities Act, *see* Securities and Exchange Act
Securities and Exchange Act, 47, 49, 50, 82, 96, 136
Securities and Exchange Commission, *see* SEC
Securities and Futures Commission, 135
Securities Commission Act, xviii
Segehwa, **47–8**, 76, 135, 140
Seongsu Bridge, 58, 70–1, 135

Seoul Investment Trust Management, 109
Seung-Hee Lee, *see* Lee, Seung-Hee
Se Young Chung, *see* Chung, Se Young
shadow voting, 108, 139
shareholder activism
  company-specific vs. general issue, 33
  concepts, broader and narrower, 11
  and corporate governance reform, xvii–xviii, 127–8
  definition of, 3–14: normative vs. descriptive, 8–9; operational, 12
  dichotomy of, 7
  dimensions of, 3, **5–14**: action, 10–14; actor, 9–10, 41; target, 5–9
  as an effective tool of influence, **75–8, 121–3**, 128
  growth of, xviii–xix
  institutionalization of, **124–6**, 130
  interactive model of, 13
  issues of, 6–7
  Korean, xx–xxii, *see also* PSPD activism
  and monitoring, 11
  policy desirability of, xvii–xviii
  pull factors of, 28, **30–1**
  push factors of, **28–30**
  rise of, *see under* emergence of shareholder activism
  study of, xix–xx, 17–43
  two cogwheel model of, 128–9
shareholder capitalism, 83
shareholder democracy, 83
shareholder proactivity, 9, 12–14
shareholder proposal, *see* shareholder resolution
shareholder resolution, xviii–xix, 6–7, 12, 14–16
shareholder rights movement, xx, 6
Sheet Metal Workers' International Association, *see* SMWIA
SIC (Standard Industrial Classification), 21, 33
Siemens, xix
SK Group, 53, 61, 64–5, 80, 116–17, 136
  Daehan Telecom, 64

SK Engineering and Construction, 64
SK Securities, 64
SK Telecom, 64–5, 99–101, 103, 112, 116–17
SMWIA (Sheet Metal Workers' International Association), 16
social movement theory, xx, xxii, 35, **36–41**
  framing, *see under* framing process
  grievance theory, 36
  movement entrepreneur, **37**, 41
  political opportunity, *see under* political opportunity
  political process theory, 36
  resource mobilization, *see under* resource mobilization
  resource mobilization theory, 36
  symbolic theory, 36
socially responsible investment, 7, *see also* ethical investment
specialization policy, *see under* diversification
Spring of Democratization, 59, 136
stakeholder, 140
stakeholder analysis, 132–3
Standard & Poor's, 9
Standard & Poor's 500 Common Stock Index, *see* S&P 500
Standard Industrial Classification, *see* SIC
Stanford Research Institute, 140
State of Wisconsin Investment Board, *see* SWIB
Stop Samsung Campaign, 103
Suh, June-Sik, 136
Sunkyung Group, *see* SK Group
Sung-Chull Junn, *see* Junn, Sung-Chull
Sung-Gu Kim, *see* Kim, Sung-Gu
SWIB (State of Wisconsin Investment Board), 32–3
Syngman Rhee, *see* Rhee, Syngman

Tae Soo Chung, *see* Chung, Tae Soo
Tae Won Chey, *see* Chey, Tae Won
Tae Woo Roh, *see* Roh, Tae Woo
targeting, 12

Teachers Insurance and Annuity Association: College Retirement Equities Fund, *see* TIAA-CREF
Teachers Pension Fund, 105
Ten-Share Campaign, 102–3
TIAA-CREF (Teachers Insurance and Annuity Association: College Retirement Equities Fund), 32–4
Tiger Management, 116–7
'traitor to his class', 91
tunneling, 79

UBCJA (United Brotherhood of Carpenters and Joiners of America), 16
UKSA (United Kingdom Shareholders Association), 9
United Brotherhood of Carpenters and Joiners of America, *see* UBCJA
United Kingdom Shareholders Association, *see* UKSA
United Shareholders Association, *see* USA
univariate comparison, **22–3**
USA (United Shareholders Association), 9, 22, 23, 42–3

value maximization, *see* return maximization
voice option, **4**, 6, **26–8**, 134
  method of, 12, *see also* litigation, private negotiation, proxy fight, shareholder resolution, targeting
  monitoring and, 10–11, 134
  takeover and, 4, 26–8

Wall Street Rule, 29
Wilshire Associate, 9
Won-Soon Park, *see* Park, Won-Soon
Won-suk Choi, *see* Choi, Won-suk
World Bank, xvii–xviii

Young, Quentin, 122
Young Sam Kim, *see* Kim, Young Sam

Zenith, 65